FRANCE

Studies in Modern European History

Frank J. Coppa
General Editor

Vol. 37

PETER LANG
New York • Washington, D.C./Baltimore • Boston • Bern
Frankfurt am Main • Berlin • Brussels • Vienna • Oxford

Guy R. Mermier

FRANCE

Past and Present

PETER LANG
New York • Washington, D.C./Baltimore • Boston • Bern
Frankfurt am Main • Berlin • Brussels • Vienna • Oxford

Library of Congress Cataloging-in-Publication Data

Mermier, Guy R.
France: past and present / Guy R. Mermier.
p. cm. — (Studies in modern European history; vol. 37)
Includes bibliographical references and index.
1. France—Civilization. I. Title. II. Series.
DC33 .M447   944—dc21   99-051813
ISBN 0-8204-4455-3
ISSN 0893-6897

Die Deutsche Bibliothek-CIP-Einheitsaufnahme

Mermier, Guy R.:
France: past and present / Guy R. Mermier.
—New York; Washington, D.C./Baltimore; Boston; Bern;
Frankfurt am Main; Berlin; Brussels; Vienna; Oxford: Lang.
(Studies in modern European history; Vol. 37)
ISBN 0-8204-4455-3

Cover design by Lisa Dillon

The paper in this book meets the guidelines for permanence and durability
of the Committee on Production Guidelines for Book Longevity
of the Council of Library Resources.

© 2000 Peter Lang Publishing, Inc., New York

Printed in the United States of America

To Jeff

With Grateful Thanks for His Invaluable Help

And

To Our Friend L.L. Always with Us

Table of Contents

Preface

Facing the Challenges of the Third Millennium

There is no denying, generalities are frequently wrong, but they some-times contain interesting elements of truth, and so it might be useful at the beginning of a book on France and its people to present some of the traditional clichés and stereotypes attached both to the country and its population.[1] Some of these beliefs are either ancient or recent, and are frequently due to unfortunate experiences people had while visiting Paris or the *Hexagone,*[2] as France is often called because of its six-sided shape.

You may hear that the French are difficult, selfish and morose (they rarely smile), that they never agree with anyone, and even worse they seem to argue constantly even with their friends. In addition the French are accused of being arrogant, impolite and pompous. Many believe that they drink too much and eat too much fat (*foie gras* [pâté]) for instance, and *cassoulet* (a dish stew of beans, pork and goose fat, a Languedoc specialty). People find French women elegant and sexy, but they also think that they are too dominated by food, fashion and sex. You'll also hear that the French hate work: after all they take six weeks of paid vaca-tions and they strike constantly to earn more for less work. People also wonder when the French actually work, considering that they sit for hours in cafés. People are also appalled by some of the French eating habits: they eat funny (some say disgusting) things like rabbit, frog legs and blood sausage.[3] Finally, some people think that the French are unpleasant snobs who dislike everything that is not French. We could continue. . . .

But not all Frenchmen are like this, in fact only a very few would fit the above descriptions. The French happen to be, on the whole, a very intel-ligent, proud and tolerant people. They have their own views, naturally, but because they do not fit the expectations of foreigners, they are not bad. France has a long tradition of culture with great names like Molière,

Racine, Corneille, La Fontaine, just to mention some great names of the seventeenth century Classical era. France is also admired for its language, clear, pure and musical. And French is not only spoken in France, but in Belgium, Switzerland and many other lands, such as areas of Africa, Senegal, Madagascar, the Maghreb (North Africa), La Réunion, Martinique, Guadeloupe, St. Barth and many islands of the Pacific Ocean.

France's artistic treasures abound: museums, monuments, statues, bridges, many dating to the Roman colonization, not mentioning some famous prehistoric archaeological sites like Lascaux and Les Eyzies in central France. In addition, France is a beautiful country with an incredible variety of landscapes. It is a constant surprise, considering that the country is roughly the size of Texas. France's originality is everywhere and most obvious in the multiplicity of its faces. Geographically and ethnically, France is a quilt, sometimes controversial, always fascinating.

Some of the negative perceptions of France, it is true, can be explained by the attitude of some of its citizens. Général de Gaulle, for example, always felt that France had a privileged mission to fulfill in Europe and the world, and therefore he appeared haughty, snobbish and xenophobic. When President Chirac was elected, he wanted also to be a major guide of Europe into the Third Millennium. Such political visions, sincere as they may be, led people to think that all Frenchmen thought that they were the center of the universe, but this is far from the truth. The French people include over sixty one million individuals; therefore it would be a mistake to suggest that they are all alike. In fact, France and the French are constantly changing and adapting to the passing of time, as stated by Michel Faure, in an article "The Way We Were" of *France* magazine (summer 1995, p. 17): "Yeah, we've changed since the beginning of the '80s". . . "No question about it, the average Frenchman has definitely changed. You may still picture him as short, sporting a beret and an arrogant mustache, reeking of garlic, armed with a baguette and carrying a few liters of table wine tucked into his wicker basket. That Frenchman is passé, extinct, gone the way of the dodo bird and the dinosaur". . . "La *Vieille France*, la '*Douce France*' that Charles Trenet sang about in the '50s is fading fast."

Yes, at the eve of the Third Millennium there is a New France, still strong in its ancient and solid roots, a dynamic, welcoming France that attracts foreign visitors no less than before. In fact, they travel to France by planeloads, and when they take the time to discover the real France, that is to say not only Paris, but also the French provinces, their majestic mountains, quaint villages, and if they talk to the French people, few come back disappointed. Those who return enchanted, and they are the majority, have surmounted the prejudices that they may have held before their visit, and have been touched by the country and its people who have survived so many accidents in the course of their history.

Yes, at the eve of the Third Millennium, with all its scars, faults and peculiarities, France remains a civilized and dynamic nation as well as a welcoming and fascinating place. This we shall hopefully discover in the following pages of this book.

The Book; Its Nature and Conception

This book is aimed, first and foremost, at students, hence the abundant endnotes, but at a larger public too, indeed to all persons interested in knowing some basic facts about France, whether preparing for a trip or wanting to have an update on the country as it is approaching the Third Millennium.

As the values of the French language are being questioned in universities and colleges, we thought that it might be useful to show that, even if the language is no longer the *number one* international tongue, French culture remains prominent. Because, no matter what is being reported by the media, French is still spoken in hundreds of places in the world. And France is not an island in itself, even if some people say so; it is at the center of Europe and an important part of the world. Writing a book on France is like setting down an important piece in the giant puzzle of global diversity, and diversity is certainly a part of France's problems as well as its greatest charms and achievements.

Our colleague Mario B. Mignone has already written a brilliant introduction on contemporary Italy, a book titled *Italy Today. A Country in Transition.*[4] Our goal, in turn, is to write a companion guide about France. As with professor Mignone's book, this is only an introduction to France and does not require any previous knowledge of the country, its economy, politics or mores.

My readers will no doubt notice the love I have for the country where I was born and spent my youth until my twenties. In spite of this, I have attempted throughout this book to be impartial and even critical when I thought I had to be. And perhaps the fact that I am writing this book in America, and from the point of view of an American university professor, has helped me to remain honestly informative.

The University of Michigan
Ann Arbor, 1999

Notes

1   For some examples see *Xenophobe's Guide to the French* by Nick Yapp and Michael Syrett, Ravette Publishing, 1993.

2   France is labelled an *hexagone* because of its six-sided shape and, better yet, because it is bordered by six countries: Spain, Italy, Switzerland, Luxembourg, Belgium and Germany. The U.K. lies across La Manche, which is the French word for the English Channel.

3   See Michel Faure, "Birds of Paradox", *France*, No 43, Fall 1997, p. 13: "Everyday, in fact, we French do things that seem abominable to you. We flirt in the office, take two-hour lunches, smoke in public places, look indulgently upon the sexual escapades of our leaders. And yet-and yet- men and women still get along pretty well. Our morale is good, we enjoy a good discussion. True, we don't follow the rules, we don't cross at the crosswalk, and yet our French paradoxes promote a certain happiness." (*France* is a quaterly magazine published by the Maison Française, 4101 Reservoir Rd, NW. Washington DC 20007–2182 USA).

4   Peter Lang Publishing, *Studies in Modern European History*, vol. 16, 1995, 253 pages.

Introduction

France: A Diverse Land of Many Contrasts

With a population of 61.3 million, France is a country of Western Europe, bordering on many waters, the Bay of Biscay, the Atlantic Ocean to the west, the English Channel or *La Manche*. It borders the Mediterranean Sea in the south, between Italy and Spain, and is situated north/south between Belgium and Spain.[1] France enjoys a temperate climate, very similar to that of the eastern seaboard of the United States, and even milder near the Mediterranean.

Mainland France, including the island of Corsica off the western coast of Italy, but not including its overseas territories, covers a total area of 551.670 square kilometers (about 220,668 square miles), that is to say, twice the size of the state of Colorado and four fifths the size of Texas. It also has an impressive coastline, measuring 2,783 kilometers (or 1,729 miles) on the mainland, with 644 additional kilometers (400 miles) in Corsica. The total comes to 3,427 kilometers or 2,129 miles. Anyone traveling in France cannot help being amazed by the topographic variety of the country. The landscape changes, sometimes radically, within miles, with vast plains and hills in the north and west, mountains in the east (Ardennes, Vosges, Jura, Alpes).[2] If one leaves the ocean-swept coast of Bretagne (Brittany), one is soon taken by the incredibly soft luminosity of the sky of Touraine, by the gentle landscape and mild climate of Anjou and Touraine. Then, if you press on across the Massif Central, a rounded volcanic mountain of the center of France, you find yourself past the Rhône valley at the foot of the Alpes (Alps), with their high snow-covered peaks and the impressive Mont Blanc summit, 4,807 meters high (15,771 feet), France's highest point, in Haute-Savoie. The country's lowest point (minus two meters) is not far, by the Rhône river delta in the south, as it flows into the Mediterranean.

If you turn to the south-southeast, you immediately find the warm climate of the Côte d'Azur and Provence. From there, if you travel westward, you soon reach the majestic chain of the Pyrénées mountains, older than the Alpes, with more eroded summits, but no less impressive. They form a natural barrier between France's Languedoc and Spain. Then if you push on toward the Atlantic Ocean, you reach the Pays Basque with quaint, attractive towns, villages and resorts such as Biarritz, St. Jean de Luz, Ainoha, south of Bordeaux and Arcachon, another area of France known for its mild and pleasant climate.

But France's variety is not limited to its physical topography. It has small and majestic rivers such as the Loire and the Seine in the north, the Rhône in the east, flowing north/south from Lyon, and the Garonne in the west, to mention only the main ones. France has also very varied faces represented by its different original architectural styles, typical of the various regions. In fact, each region in France has a specific color, personality and distinction. There is no similarity between a Normand and Breton house and a Provençal *mas* (the name of a farmhouse in Provence), and there is no common measure between the alpine chalets and the Alsatian houses. Similarly, Toulouse and Bordeaux are generally opposed, the first one called the Grey City and the other the Pink City according to the color of their respective roofs and façades. Each region of France has also its distinctive monuments, churches, abbeys, châteaux, cathedrals, some in typically Romanesque style like in Burgundy, others in Gothic style like in Paris, Chartres, etc. Even the roofs vary from region to region. Northern roofs are often steep and covered with grey slates, while in the south roofs are moderately slanted and covered with flat or rounded red tiles. It is impossible to cover exhaustively the subject of France's variety, but variety is everywhere, even in the way people speak. The French spoken in Paris is fast clipped; it is crisp and clear in Touraine, a bit rigid or sharp in Lyon and, as you go south, it turns much more lilting and musical. And when you reach Marseille, you cannot miss the *accent du midi* (southern accent) with its melodious tone that Parisians like to mock.

After you leave Paris, and drive several hours outside the French capital, you begin to really perceive France's great variety. In fact, if you leave Bordeaux and drive to Strasbourg, you will no doubt think that you are crossing several different countries, but no, you will still be within the borders of France! The French have a "*je ne sais quoi*" (I don't know what-distinctive feature) that is different. You may hear this frequently, and you may also hear of *the French paradox*. It would appear that, contrary to Americans and many other populations of our planet, the French can eat fat, butter, *foie gras* (liver pâté) and wash it down with a few (or more) glasses of red wine and remain totally healthy and even relatively thin. But that is only a part of the "*French paradox*": There seems to be a French paradox in politics, society and economics as well. It would appear that the French do the opposite of what the Americans consider sane, healthy and reasonable, and they survive just the same and they seem to be happy.[3] Maybe it is the reason why some people dislike the French or call them snobs, and why so many foreigners want to settle in France.

In fact, despite all their problems, worries and fears that I'll be presenting in the forthcoming pages of this book, the French, even if they grumble often, still appear to be a fairly content people, adaptable and willing to play their part in the new era beginning in 2000. Surely, figuratively speaking, there remain for France many land mines to sweep and many storms to weather. France will be surely confronted by many other crises and will suffer disappointments and even periods of despair. The fact is that the *Trente Glorieuses* are not about to return and that France's prestige is not shining as bright as it used to. So the French, at the entrance of the Third Millennium, must find new dreams, new daring visions. Fortunately, the good-old French character is still strong, and in spite of all their faults and frustrations, I trust that the French have it in them to steam ahead successfully into the Third Millennium. This is precisely what the following pages will hopefully demonstrate.

Notes

1   See the map on page xxi.

2   Throughout the book, I am giving the names of towns and regions as they are spelled in France. For instance, Marseilles (US spelling) is given as *Marseille*, and Lyons (US spelling) as *Lyon*.

3   See the interesting and humorous article *Birds of Paradox*, by Michel Faure, published in the magazine *France*, Fall 1997, Washington DC, p. 13.

Chapter 1

Historical Survey of the French Nation

The present chapter offers a concise historical survey of the French nation, that is, the history of French civilization, including the history of the French people and their life from the distant past to modern times. When dealing with ancient times it must be remembered that for a very long time, even past the Renaissance period, nothing which shaped France and the life of the French was specifically *French*. To this extent we can say that there existed rather a medieval civilization than a French one. It is only gradually that a distinct French nation was formed, a reality that has been in constant evolution, as we shall see.

The Dawn of France's History: The Origins

Summary
21,500 BC: Period of prehistoric populations; cave art and stone monuments.
1,200 BC: Settlement by the Gauls; populations related to the Celts.
59–52 BC: Celtic Gaul; Conquest of Gaul by Julius Caesar; Beginning of Gallo-Roman Civilization.
500 AD: Barbarian invasions. End of the Pax Romana after the fall of Rome.
600 AD: Settlement by the Franks, the barbarian tribe from which France derives its name.

Prehistory

During the prehistoric period primitive men lived mostly in caves; they hunted and gathered food around their dwellings. One of the most impressive traces of these inhabitants on the present territory of France is the *Cave de Lascaux,* which dates back to about 20,000 BC. Between 2000 BC and 1500 BC the inhabitants of Western Europe erected *mega-lithic monuments,*[1] and in France many traces of these stone monu-ments can still be found in *Bretagne* (Brittany), particularly around Carnac, where about 2,000 *menhirs* or *dolmens* dating from 4500–4000 BC can still be seen.[2] Around the Mediterranean, the Phoenicians settled around the city of *Massilia* (today's Marseille) and from there they spread all along the coast. At about the same time they named the country *Gallia,* la Gaule (Gaul).

Before the Roman Conquest: Celtic Gaul: Gallia

Celtic Gaul was the name given by the Romans to the region of Europe populated by a group of Ibero-Celtic people. The pre-Roman Celtic tribes that settled on the territory of France around 1000 BC, came from north-ern and central Europe. They also crossed the Channel into England, crossed the Alps and invaded Italy. They even burned Rome in 390 BC. Until the time when the Celts were pushed back by the Romans, they established their culture for four centuries, from southern England to Italy. They practiced a druidic[3] religion worshipping mistletoe and nature (moun-tains, rivers, and forests). Aside from their religion, the Celts had no na-tional unity and so they were unable to resist the Roman legions when they entered Gaul during the second century BC (around 120 BC). The Romans were to remain in control for six centuries.

Rome Conquers Gaul

It is actually wrong to say that the Romans invaded Gaul, because, in reality, Julius Caesar was invited by the Celts to help them contain the Germans. But once in Gaul, Caesar proceeded to conquer the land be-tween 58 BC and 50 BC. It is true that one brave Arvenian chief, Vercingétorix, proclaimed head of the Celtic coalition against Rome, tried to fight Caesar, but he ended up being surrounded in Alesia and was forced to surrender. Vercingétorix was taken prisoner, dragged in chains for Caesar's triumph, and executed in Rome in 52 BC after remaining six years in captivity.[4]

Caesar Romanizes Gaul

Julius Caesar proceeded swiftly to romanize Gaul. And if the conquest by the Romans deprived Gaul of its liberty at first, in the end they gave it in exchange peace, prosperity and a great many material comforts. It can be said that it was thanks to Rome that the future France owed the beginnings of its civilization. And Romanization was not only swift, it was also easy because the people of Gaul actually welcomed the *Pax Romana* and appreciated the superiority of Roman culture. Rome also made a lasting impact on art, architecture and monuments. Still today, many Gallo-Roman structures and vestiges of the genius of Roman civilization remain standing. For instance, the impressive monument of La Turbie near Monaco, the theater of Orange, the Roman temple in Vienne, the amphitheater in Arles, the Pont du Gard, the Arènes of Nîmes built at the end of the first century AD and still being used today.

Vulgar Latin Takes Over

Celtic dialects died rapidly while Latin spread even among common people. The Latin that spread was not the well-known Classical Latin of Cicero, Virgil, Tacitus, but the spoken tongue of the Roman soldiers, colonists, merchants, *Vulgar Latin*.[5] The transformation of Vulgar Latin into French took quite a long time. It first became Old French during the Middle Ages, then Middle French in the fifteenth and sixteenth centuries and it became Modern French, as we know it, beginning with the Classical Period. In fact it was not until 1539 that French was recognized as the official language for administration and justice. Even at the beginning of the sixteenth century, French was still considered an inferior tongue to Latin.

After the Collapse of the Roman Empire

Great as it was, Rome's domination was not to last forever. In the fourth century, under the impact of barbarian invasions, Rome was overrun and soon, in the fifth century, its political, administrative and military structures were destroyed. Nevertheless, Rome's influence was to prevail,[6] all the more because those who are called barbarians were not all fierce unruly vandals like the Huns of Attila.

Many, in fact, were Christians. Christians were severely martyred at first, but were saved in 313 when Constantine the Great embraced the Christian faith and made it the official religion of Rome. Among the barbarians who invaded Gaul, there were the Visigoths (West Goths) in Aquitaine, their kinsmen the Ostrogoths (East Goths), the Vandals, the Burgundians in the Rhône-Saone valley down to the river Durance, the Alemans in Alsace, and the Franks between the river Somme and the Rhine. These Frankish tribes had settled around the Meuse and Moselle rivers, around Tournai and Cambrai in northeastern France. The king of the Salian Franks, Merovaeus (Merovech),[7] founded a dynasty that re-united Gaul into a great Frankish kingdom. It is with the domination of the Franks that the foundations of France were laid, and thus *Gallia* became *Francia*.

Beyond Rome: The Merovingians.
Clovis (481–511)

If the conquest of Gaul by the Romans was a first important event in the history of France, the invasion of the Franks under Clovis was of equal importance. In 486 Clovis (*Cholodovech*), king of the Salian Franks, de-feated the Roman king Syagrius and became the needed sword of the Christian faith. He married a Catholic Burgund princess, Clotildas, in 493 and accepted baptism by Bishop Rémi (*Remigius*) in December 496 in the Roman church of Reims.[8] The oil with which Clovis was anointed was supposedly brought by a dove in the holy ampoule, and from this time on the priestly character of French monarchs was consecrated. By adopting Catholicism along with three thousand other Franks, Clovis was joining the religion of the overwhelming majority of the peoples he was about to rule.[9] He was the first Merovingian king and his dynasty during the next century was able to add Burgundy and Provence to the royal domain.

The High (or Early) Middle Ages:
The Carolingians.
Charles-Martel; Pépin-le-Bref

Charles Martel was named *"the hammer"* for crushing in 732 the Mus-lim armies of Abd-al-Rahman in Poitiers, thus saving the Christian world and the West from the conquering Arabs.[10] His son, Pépin-le-Bref (the short), was proclaimed king as Pépin III in 751 (714–768). He was the first Carolingian to assume the title of king of the Franks. He warred against the Burgundians and Aquitanians, the Saxons, the Alemans and administered Austrasie[11] from 741 to 747, received the unction from Saint Boniface in Soissons. He was called "the Word of God," that is to say "supreme protector of the Church." When he died, his domains were divided between his two sons, Charles (Charlemagne) (742–814) and Carloman, who soon died (751–771)[12].

Charlemagne (Carolus Magnus 742–814 AD)

Summary

April 2,742: Birth of Charlemagne, elder son of Pépin-le-Bref.

768 AD: Charlemagne, 26 years old, is named Emperor of the West.

He attempts to bring back the Roman Empire by creating an empire based on a strict aristocratic rule.

800 AD: By 800 AD Charlemagne is the undisputed ruler of Western Europe. On Christmas Day, Pope Leo III in Saint Peter's Rome crowns Charlemagne.

987 AD: Hughes Capet founds the Capetian Dynasty, which lasted until 1328. The Monarchy attempts to assert its power over feudal lords.

11th and 12th centuries: It is the central period called the Middle Ages During that time Romanesque and then Gothic art flourish. The Crusades take place.

14th and 15th centuries: French-English rivalries culminate in the Hundred Years War.

Epidemics of the Black Death (the plague).

Although it would seem that Germany and France could claim Charlemagne, Germany did not keep his deeds or memory as alive as France did. In France, on the contrary, Charlemagne's memory was revered very early and he soon became a national hero. Charles,[13] who was soon to be known as Charlemagne or Charles Ier le Grand (the Great) (742–814), ruled from 768 to 814. He was crowned Emperor of Rome on Christmas Day 800. The eminence of Charlemagne is undeniable and there is no doubt that he was the greatest of all the Carolingian rulers.[14] He was responsible for creating a lasting administrative structure to the kingdom and for establishing a strong central government. He organized with care and precision the administration of the empire with the assistance of his *missi dominici*, local representatives of his authority throughout the empire. He was also responsible for spearheading a real cultural renaissance, creating a School of the Palace (*Ecole du Palais*), inviting scholars from abroad (the famous Alcuin, for instance) and urging on the construction of monasteries and churches (although his architects still limited themselves to copying Byzantine models) and art workshops. He also encouraged monks to copy all the known works of Latin antiquity and promoted the use of the more legible Caroline minuscule in the writing of manuscripts. In fact many beautifully illuminated manuscripts date from Charlemagne's era. Throughout his reign he watched carefully over the Christian world and encouraged the development and preservation of the faith. Charlemagne was also interested in expanding the empire, and by the end of the eighth century, his territories included most of the old western Roman lands.[15] Unfortunately his great work practically disintegrated after his death in 814. So the decline of the Carolingian empire began almost immediately, and throughout the ninth century the situation grew worse with the pestering invasions of the Northmen (*Normands*).[16] Finally in 987, the direct line of Charlemagne came to an end when Hughes Capet (938–996) was chosen king (987–996).

To Hugues Capet

Chronological summary from the fifth to the tenth century

407: Invasion of Gaul by barbarians, Vandals and others.
409: The Burgonds settle in Gaul.
410: Alaric, king of the Wisigoths takes Rome.
420: Beginning of the Frank monarchy.
448: Mérovée is king 452: Attila is defeated.
496: Clovis becomes Christian.
527–565: Justinian is emperor of the East.
568: The Lombards settle in northern Italy.
595: Mahomet preaches a new religion.
628: Dagobert Ier is king of the Franks.
631: The Arabs take Jerusalem.
693–700: The Arabs conquer North Africa.
732: Charles Martel beats the Arabs in Poitiers.
751: Pépin le Bref becomes king of France.
771: Charlemagne becomes king.
800: Charlemagne is proclaimed emperor of the West.
830: Beginning of the Norman invasions.
842: Strasbourg Oaths.
911: Normandy is given to the Normans by the treaty of Saint-Clair-sur-Epte.
987: Hugues Capet is king.

Hugues had to fight with many of his vassals,[17] particularly the *seigneurs* (lords) of Blois, but in the long run all the feudal lords recognized him as their suzerain. The king's fief, the Ile-de-France, was far smaller than many of his vassals' domains, but in spite of this the king benefited from the sanctity of kinship he acquired with the coronation ceremony and the ecclesiastical unction with holy oil. Thus the king was a partner of the Church, a partnership that was to protect the Capetian kings when confronted by more powerful lords or other enemies.

The Creation of Modern France

The creation of modern France came from the reconstitution of the kingdom of Charlemagne and subsequent additions of territorial units by some of the emperor's successors. This process took a long time because of the constant feuds between the king and his rebellious, powerful and arrogant vassals. State power, instead of being unified and strong, was fragmented during the heydays of feudalism when powerful lords could mock royal power. It can be said that it was Saint Louis who first started to consolidate royal power, a task that was pursued by Philip Augustus and Louis VI. It took centuries for the kings of France to reassert their authority, and they succeeded only because the Church helped them, as it was anxious to secure social order.

The Capetians[18]

Without oversimplifying, we can say that the country that is today called France was born around 842 when in Strasbourg the two grandsons of Charlemagne, Charles the Bald and Louis the German, pledged to aid to each other against their elder brother, Lothaire (Lothair).[19] From that point on, the Frankish Empire was divided, and out of its cleavage France began to form. France surely was not born in a day. Even in the thirteenth century the area of France was still divided into two zones: the North, roughly above the Loire with Paris where the language of Oïl was spoken, and the South, Occitania, with a brilliant civilization and a language (*Provençal* or *Occitan*) of its own.

As late as the fifteenth century, it was not certain whether France would fall in the hands of the English and whether Burgundy would become a separate realm. So it is clear that France did not appear fully formed for a long time. It grew gradually but with many ups and downs. Before the Capetians, it can be said that there was no consciousness of France as a nation, and one has to wait until the fifteenth century to note the appearance of some form of national feeling. The Capetian monarchs in general, surely not all of them equally, struggled to expand the royal domain, but in the end with sporadic efforts the kingdom of France finally became the main power of the Christian West. Some of Hugh Capet's successors were weak or incompetent or both, and their only merit was that they did not let the royal domain be dismembered again, and they achieved this simply by making sure that their eldest sons were crowned before their death.

Chronological Summary from Hugh Capet[20] to Saint Louis (987–1226)

987: Hugues Capet becomes king.
1066: Conquest of England by the Normans.
1078: the Turks conquer Jerusalem.
1095: The First Crusade is preached.
1108: Louis VI is king of France. Suger from Saint-Denis becomes councilor of the of king.
1137: Louis VII marries Eléanor of Aquitaine.
1147: Louis VII takes part in the Second Crusade.
1152: Eléanor of Aquitaine divorces Louis VII and marries Henry Plantagenet, Duke of Normandy.
1163 The Cathars are denounced as heretics.
1166: Brittany recognizes Henry II of England as its suzerain.
1180–1223: Philippe II Auguste is king of France.
1187: Saladin takes Jerusalem. Beginning of the Third Crusade.
1189: Richard the Lionhearted is king of England.
1199: Death of Richard the Lionhearted.
1200: Foundation of the Université de Paris.
1202: Preaching of the Third Crusade.
1204: The Crusaders take Constantinople.
1208: Crusade against the Albigenses.
1220: Creation of the faculty of medicine in Montpellier.
1223: Louis VIII, king of France.
1226: Saint Louis, king of France.

Louis VI le Gros

Louis VI le Gros (1081–1137) reigned over France from 1108 to 1137 assisted by his minister, the wise abbot of Saint-Denis, Suger.[21] They began to put some order in the administration of the royal domain, fought Henry I, king of England, and held back the German emperor Henri V who menaced to invade France in 1124. He married his son Louis VII le Jeune to *Aliénor d'Aquitaine* (Eleanor of Aquitaine), heiress of Guyenne, Gascony and other fiefs in France including Poitou (1137).[22] This marriage unfortunately ended tragically: Louis VII had his marriage annulled in 1152, and Eleanor remarried Henry Plantagenet, count of Anjou and duke of Normandy who became king of England in 1154, assuming the name of Henry II. Thus Aquitaine fell in the hands of England, and as a consequence for close to a century the Hundred Years War was to oppose the Capetians to the Plantagenets.

Philippe II Auguste (1165–1223)

The only son of Louis VII, Philippe II Auguste was crowned king when he was only fifteen years old in Reims.[23] He grew to be a very skillful and realistic statesman, though quite unscrupulous at times. As such, Philippe continued the struggle against the Plantagenets[24] and his victory at Bouvines[25] on July 27, 1214, greatly increased the prestige of the king and allowed him to consolidate the fruit of his conquests, a very enlarged royal domain. Bouvines is often recorded (with some exaggeration) as the first national victory of France. In any case Philippe Auguste had more than quadrupled the size of the domain of the Capetians, and he established Paris as the permanent capital of the monarchy. Philippe also took part in the Albigensian Crusade[26] against the Cathars and he thus added a large chunk of the South to the Capetian domain.

At the time of Philippe Auguste's death, the monarchy acquired hereditary rights in the male line. France owes its early unity to this concept of hereditary monarchy. It also helped the Capetians to further strengthen their power.

Louis VIII (1223–1226)

Louis VIII le Lion, son of Philippe Auguste, became king in 1223 when he was 36 years old, and reigned only a few years until 1226. He managed, however, to continue his father's work. Before being king, he defeated *Jean sans Terre* (John the Landless) and pursued him back to England. After becoming king, he took back from the English the provinces of Limousin, Poitou, Saintonge, Angoumois, Périgord and a part of the Bordeaux region. He also took part in the Albigensian Crusade and put the Languedoc under his control, with the exception of Toulouse.

Chronological Summary from Saint Louis to the Beginning of the Hundred Years War (1226–1337)

1226: Louis IX king. Regency of Blanche de Castille.

1235: Louis IX reigns.

1244: Louis IX goes to Crusade. Jerusalem is taken.

1249: Seventh crusade. Damiette is taken.

1250: Defeat of Mansourah. Saint Louis remains in Syria.

1254: Saint Louis returns to France.

1270: Eighth Crusade. Saint Louis dies in front of Tunis. Philippe III le Hardi becomes king of France.

1285: Philippe IV le Bel becomes king of France.

1294: War with England.

1296: Philippe IV quarrels with the papacy.

1307: The Templars are arrested and accused of heresy.

1309: The popes in Avignon.

1314: Louis X, king of France.

1317: Philippe V le Long, king of France. The loi Salique (Salic law) is proclaimed.

1322: Charles IV, king of France.

1328: Death of Charles IV. Philippe VI de Valois is chosen.

1329: Edward III secretly prepares the war but accepts to pay homage to the French king in exchange of Guyenne and Ponthieu.

Louis IX or Saint Louis (1214–1270)

Louis IX was the son of Louis VIII and of Blanche de Castille[27] and reigned from 1226 to 1270, although he first reigned under his mother's regency (1226–1236) since he was only twelve at his father's death. Blanche de Castille ruled the kingdom wisely and with a firm hand. She was regent of the kingdom for five years while Saint Louis was away with the Seventh Crusade. Saint Louis was nevertheless regarded by many as the greatest of all medieval kings, and he was surely a remarkable person and a deeply devout Christian. When he began to rule by himself, Saint Louis followed the Christian teachings of his mother and his reputation of thorough honesty made of him frequently the arbiter of Christian Europe. Upon his return from the Holy Land, Louis worked hard at bringing peace, justice and order to his subjects, and he spared no effort to reinforce royal authority. He also ended the long conflict between the Capetians and the

Plantagenets with the Treaty of Paris in 1258. Following this treaty, Henry, king of England, paid homage to Saint Louis and gave up his claims to the domains that he had taken from Philippe Auguste. Saint Louis also managed to recover the county of Toulouse from the king of Aragon. The royal domain of the Capetians had never been as large. In 1270, prompted by Charles d'Anjou, his brother, he undertook the Eighth Crusade, but he caught the plague and died in front of Carthage, where he was going to convert the Moslem king of the country to the Christian faith. After his death he was revered as a holy man and a legend.[28] He was canonized in 1297 and the great medieval chronicler Joinville, who had accompanied Louis to Egypt, wrote his life in his *Memoirs.*

Saint Louis' Successors:
Philippe III le Hardi (1245–1285);
Philippe IV le Bel (1268–1314);
Philippe V le Long (1294–1322)

Philippe III le Hardi, son and successor of Saint Louis does not seem to have done much to deserve his name of *"le hardi"* (the bold). He was a weak, hesitant prince who let his father's advisers take care of all the affairs of the kingdom, and he proved incapable of stopping the incessant intrigues of his second wife, Marie de Brabant.[29] His greatest achievement perhaps, aside from having participated in the efforts to reunite the county of Toulouse to the Crown, was to declare war on Pierre III of Aragon, who was an instigator of the *Vêpres Siciliennes* (Sicilian vespers).[30] The Pope had excommunicated the king of Aragon and given his kingdom to Charles de Valois, third son of Philippe le Hardi. The king of France failed in his Aragon Crusade, and thus was not able to support the claims of his son. Philippe III died in Perpignan as he returned from one of his latest failed expeditions in December 1285.

Philippe IV le Bel (1285–1314)

Philippe was eighteen years old when he began to reign. He was tall, handsome, hence his nickname of *"le Bel"* (the Handsome One). He had an imposing stature, but many of his contemporaries did not admire him. They felt that he had only hunting on his mind, that he was weak, morose and dominated by his entourage. The truth was quite different. He was on the contrary aware of his power, of his rights and he did not tolerate any trouble or dissension around him. Most historians agree that Philippe was ambitious, crafty, jealous of his authority and frequently cynical. Above all he was dedicated to continue the work of Saint Louis. In order to do that, he surrounded himself with able jurists such as Pierre Flote, Enguerrand de Marigny and Guillaume Nogaret. They all contributed to reinforce royal power. Philippe believed so deeply in the holiness of his cause that he punished heresy, real or imagined, with utmost cruelty. For him the end justified the means no matter how arbitrary. With his strong will and personality, and with his unbending conception of royal power, he soon clashed head on against the Pope, Boniface VIII, himself a very ambitious man and with an equally unbending conception of his supreme papal authority over kings. Philippe's war against England was costly and the royal coffers badly needed cash. Philippe decided that he would levy a tax (*fouage*) on each "*feu*" (household), and he also decided to tax the clergy as well (1294). Upon hearing Philippe's decision, the Pope fulminated against the French king and told him that he was not allowed to tax the clergy. He ordered Philippe to back down on his decision, or else. But the Pope himself did not want to provoke the anger of Philippe, so he backed down a little, saying that he would allow the clergy to contribute to the expenses of the kingdom. To further placate Philippe's feelings, the Pope agreed to canonize Saint Louis. But peace between the two men was not to last long. Philippe accused the bishop of Pamiers, Bernard Saisset, of conspiring with the English and Aragon. Philippe arrested the bishop and demanded his destitution by the Pope (1301). Boniface VIII immediately demanded the bishop's release and said that he would excommunicate and depose the king if he disobeyed. Philippe refused to obey the Pope who excomunicated him. Furious, Philippe dispatched his aid, Nogaret, to Agnani to arrest the Pope and to accuse him of all sorts of crimes, including magic and sodomy. Nogaret did manage to arrest the Pope, but the population released him the next day (September 7, 1303) and Nogaret had to flee, fearing for his life. Boniface, nevertheless humiliated and shaken, died several weeks later. His successor, Benoît XI, absolved the king but refused to pardon the Agnani affair and Nogaret. Philippe managed to have a new Pope elected more favorable to his cause, Bertrand de Got, archbishop of Bordeaux (who took the name of Clément V (1305). Philippe wanted the resumption of the pursuits against Boniface in order to bury the Agnani affair and make sure that Nogaret was rehabilitated. As the Pope hesitated, the Templars affair broke out.[31] The king had them arrested, tortured, judged and executed, and he could thus put his hands on the important wealth of the order. Philippe forced the Pope to abolish the Templars order and obtained the exoneration of Nogaret. For the first time in the Middle Ages a conflict between a Pope and a king ended to the advantage of the king. With this event, the papal theocratic doctrine of superiority over kings was ended, Philippe's power reinforced, and the preeminence of France in Europe further consecrated.

In spite of his unjust and inhuman treatment of the Templars, Philippe le Bel remains a great figure of French history, for he is the first among modern sovereigns to have stood against the power of the Church. In addition, he greatly enlarged the royal domain and contributed actively to the development of the administrative and judiciary institutions of France. After his death (1314), his three sons reigned one after the other. The first one, Louis X (1314–1316),[32] spent most of his time fighting feudal revolts, and the two others, Philippe V le Long (1316–1322)[33] and Charles IV le Bel (1322–1328), both childless, were the prey of multiple intrigues in view of the succession. In 1328 (February 1) Charles IV died, leaving the Crown to his cousin Philippe VI de Valois (1328–1350)[34] since women were ineligible to govern.[35] This ended the Capetian dynasty and marked the beginning of the Valois dynasty.

The Capetians, however, had brought about great changes both in economy and society. Agriculture progressed thanks to new technical innovations (the horse collar and the water mill, for instance) and better methods of tilling the land (crop rotation and expansion of cultivated areas). This agricultural progress was followed by an important rise in population (4 million in 1086 and 12 million in 1328). Both agriculture and population helped the growth of trade and industry. In construction, stone began to replace wood; new harbors were constructed which helped improve trade within and outside the country. Important fairs, in Troyes and Provins, for instance, were instituted giving a further boost to the country's economy. As a consequence, urban life developed and gave rise to a new middle class made up of wealthy merchants, craftsmen and administrators. The Church also played a very important role, for it was the very foundation of society and since all considered themselves Christians. It was the Church that created the first intellectual centers such as the *Université de Paris* with the *Sorbonne*, and it inspired art, architecture and watched over the preservation of culture. The monastic institutions of Cluny and Citeaux set the example. Their orders spread throughout the medieval world. The Church also organized pilgrimages to holy sites built around relics of saints and along pilgrimage roads such as those leading to Santiago de Compostela in northern Spain. Crusades were a special type of pilgrimages made to the East, to the Holy Land, to the tomb of Christ. These crusades allowed the knights who were eager to fight to spend their warlike energies outside of France and, upon their return, they brought back home a taste for luxury items and spices.

Chronological Summary: 1337–1453

1337: Beginning of the Hundred Years War.

1346: Defeat of Crécy.

1347: Calais is taken by the English.

1350: Jean le Bon, king of France.

1356: Jean le Bon defeated and taken prisoner in Poitiers.

1358: Revolt and death of Etienne Marcel. The Dauphin is regent.

1360: The king is freed in exchange of a ransom.

1362: Philippe le Hardi, youngest son of Jean le Bon receives the Duchy of Burgundy.

1364: Charles V is king.

1367, 1373: Du Guesclin wins victories against the English.

1377: Edward III dies.

1378: Le Grand Schisme. End of the papacy in Avignon.

1380: Du Guesclin dies. Regency of the uncles of the future Charles VI.

1388: Charles VI gets rid of his uncles.

1392: Madness of the king. Regency of the duke of Burgundy. Rivalries between the houses of Burgundy and Orléans (Armagnacs and Bourguignons).

1404: Jean sans Peur, duke of Burgundy.

1407: Murder of the duke of Orléans by the Bourguignons.

1415: Defeat of Azincourt.

1418: The Armagnacs are murdered in Paris. The Dauphin flees.

1419: Jean of Burgundy is assassinated on the bridge at Montereau.

1420: Treaty of Troyes. Henry V of England becomes heir of the French Crown.

1422: Death of Henry V and of Charles VI. Charles VII proclaimed king.

1429: Jeanne d'Arc delivers Orléans. Charles VII anointed king in Reims.

1431: Joan of Arc burned in Rouen.

1436: Paris opens its gates to Charles VII.

1450: The English are thrown out of Normandy.

1453: End of the Hundred Years War. England keeps only Calais and the Channel Islands. Fall of Constantinople and end of the Byzantine Empire.

On the Eve of the Hundred Years War[36]

The Capetians had left the Valois a rich and powerful kingdom, an efficient administration, a tradition of respected authority and a bright civilization that was a model to the rest of Europe. However, within a few years these brilliant results were to be menaced because of a renewed conflict with the Plantagenets leading to unprecedented military disasters.

The Reigns of Philippe VI (1328–1350) and Jean le Bon (1350–1364)

Philippe VI, founder of the Valois dynasty, was a rather mediocre person, vain, dreaming of armed feats, glory and honors, but totally unrealistic and certainly unable to cope with the grave economic crisis of his time. In addition the feudal taxes could no longer cover the increasing expenses of the monarchy, and the king was no longer able to raise taxes at his will; he had to have the consent of the States.[37] The king's need for money was made all the more urgent since he faced a series of major problems. First, there was the situation of Guyenne that opposed the king of France to Edward III of England. Guyenne belonged to England and the king of France wanted to intervene in the affairs of that province. As a result the English king withdrew his homage to Philippe in 1331, a major feudal slap of the vassal to his suzerain. Next, there were the claims of Edward III of England to the French Crown.[38] The nobles of France rejected these claims and Edward III declared war against France. Furthermore in Flanders the population revolted against their count, Louis de Nevers, of French origin and supported by Philippe. The people of Flanders recognized Edward III as king of France (February 6, 1340), and from this day on, Edward called himself "King of France and England" adding the *lys de France* to his blazon. Naturally after this, the relations between the two kings further deteriorated. The Hundred Years War was unavoidable. England was far less rich than France, but it had an excellent army, while the French army, made up almost exclusively of nobles, lacked discipline and fought on horses with heavy armor. The English archers were more swift and light. In addition, the two kings were quite different. Edward III was an intelligent and crafty man while Philippe was weak, hesitant, and had little talent as a leader.[39]

Philippe was beaten at sea (in the harbor of L'Ecluse in 1340) and on land at Crécy (August 26, 1346).[40] Then Edward III put the siege to Calais and the town surrendered the following year. To make things worse, France was devastated by a plague epidemic (1347–1348). France was in a terrible position, but thanks to the mediation of the Pope, a truce was finally concluded; however, it was not to last long. After eight years and several truces, and after the death of Philippe VI (August 1350), the war resumed.[41]

After Philippe's death the Crown passed to his son Jean le Bon (1350–1364), who, unfortunately, was almost as mediocre as his father. When the Black Prince, elder son of Edward III, resumed the hostilities and attacked the army of Jean le Bon along the Loire River, Jean launched an attack against the English near Poitiers (September 19, 1356), but he was sorely defeated. Worse yet, Jean found himself prisoner of the English (September 19 1356). With the king away in captivity, the power passed to his elder son, the *Dauphin Charles,* who was only a frail adolescent, eighteen years old, intelligent but totally lacking in experience. And there were plenty of people who were waiting in the wings to take advantage of the young Dauphin. The Parisians found an ambitious energetic leader in the person of Etienne Marcel, provost of merchants. Marcel, with the support of the States, pushed several reforms that had for real purpose to put the Council of the King under the control of the great bourgeois. In order to intimidate the Dauphin, Etienne Marcel organized an insurrection, but Charles left Paris (March 25, 1358), isolated the city and cut off its food supply. Eventually Marcel fell out of favor and was killed in July 1358,[42] thus allowing the Dauphin to return to Paris and take back the reins of the government. He was able to negotiate with Edward III, and on May 8 of 1360, a preliminary peace was agreed upon in Brétigny, near Chartres, and signed in Calais the following October. The king was freed in exchange of a hefty ransom of three million *écus* payable in six years. Edward on his part renounced his claims to the French Crown, but received (without having to pay homage) Guyenne, Poitou, Saintonge, Limousin and Périgord, about one third of the French kingdom. Jean le Bon wanted to follow the steps of his father and direct the new crusade that Pope Urban V was organizing against the Turks. But first the ransom had to be paid. In the meantime, Jean had left behind in London some hostages of royal blood, one of them Louis d'Anjou. Louis finally managed to escape and Jean made a point of honor to go back and constitute himself prisoner, hoping to be able to be freed through direct negotiations. But he died in London after a brief illness on April 8, 1364.

France's Recovery under Charles V (1364–1380)

The Dauphin Charles became King Charles V in 1364 and immediately decided to put some order in the kingdom. He surrounded himself with wise, hard working and honest counselors and took as leader of his armies an excellent Breton knight, Bertrand du Guesclin,[43] particularly success-ful in guerilla warfare. With these brilliant men at his side, Charles V succeeded in bringing about a serious but, alas, only temporary recovery of the royal finances. In 1368 Charles resumed the war against Edward III and managed to reconquer some lands, Rouergue, Agenais, Quercy, Périgord. The English, however, still held Calais, Cherbourg, Brest and Bordeaux. The war was not over! And anarchy was lurking again over France!

For some reason Charles V felt that his death was approaching, so as early as 1374, he organized the regency in favor of his younger son Charles, born in 1368. On his deathbed, September 16, 1380, Charles was taken by sudden scruples; he felt that he had overtaxed his subjects, and so he abolished the *fouage* tax. Unfortunately this tax was the most important contribution to the royal coffers. By eliminating it, the king deprived the monarchy of one of its most important and needed financial resources.

The Reign of Charles VI

Charles V's successor was, unfortunately, a mentally unstable king, Charles VI (1380–1422), also called *le Fou* (deranged, crazy). He had not reached his majority when he began to reign, so the government was put in the hands of two paternal uncles, the dukes of Burgundy and of Anjou and Berry, and his maternal uncle the duke of Bourbon. This triumvirate soon met with great financial difficulties. When they tried to levy new taxes there were revolts in many large cities such as Paris, Rouen, Reims, Orléans, Laon and also in Languedoc (1382). It was a bad beginning for the new king.

When Charles VI reached his majority, he married Isabelle de Bavière, called *Isabeau,* and decided to rule without his uncles. Unfortunately, in spite of his good intentions, the new king began to show signs of his mental illness and was unable to follow a straight political line. In 1392, as he was riding with his men to Brittany, he had a fit of madness while crossing LeMans forest. He was taken back to Paris, where he recovered for a while, but he remained subject of more and more frequent fits of madness. Naturally, under these conditions, all sorts of intrigues, quite disastrous for the country, took place behind the king's back.[44] It seemed at this point that the king was weak enough to be menaced again by England, but Richard II, grandson of Edward III, unexpectedly decided not to resume the war against the French king.

Armagnacs against Bourguignons

In 1404, Philippe le Hardi (the Bold) died and his son, Jean sans Peur (the Fearless), became Duke of Burgundy. Suddenly violent quarrels erupted between the new duke and Louis d'Orléans, his cousin. Both wanted desperately to lead the French political affairs. The two men were totally different: while Louis liked to play and spend money, and was more interested in Italian affairs (perhaps because he was married to the daughter of a great Milanese lord), Jean, on the contrary, was intelligent, brave, and well versed in politics. On the other hand he was a man without scruples and known to be brutal and stubborn. In November 1407, Jean, who was tired of his quarrels with his cousin, had Louis d'Orléans killed by his men. This murder started a civil war between the partisans of Louis' widow, who formed a coalition headed by Bernard d'Armagnac, hence the name of the party: *les Armagnacs*. Opposed to them was Jean sans Peur ruling over Burgundy and Flanders, and receiving the support of several towns, including Paris. They were called *les Bourguignons*. At first the Bourguignons were victorious. Jean sans Peur returned to Paris and forced the king to declare him non-guilty of Louis d'Orléans' murder.[45]

In 1413 Jean called a meeting of the States General *(Etats Généraux)* and agreed to make draconian reforms (which he did not make). At the same time, the Parisians revolted and killed many of the Armagnacs.[46] Jean sans Peur was powerless and could not stop these street disorders, so Charles VI's elder son, the Dauphin Louis, asked the help of the princes, and so the duke of Burgundy was forced to leave Paris, and the Armagnacs returned to Paris in August 1414. Civil war was at its height, and so the English decided that it was a good time to invade France.

The Hundred Years War

Since 1399 English politics had changed. Richard II was in favor of peace, but he was soon replaced by his cousin, Henry IV of Lancaster, who was eager to resume the war against France. However, he never was able to start the hostilities because he died in 1413. His son, Henry V, excellent war chief, was also eager to carry out a campaign against the French, all the more willingly that Bourguignons and Armagnacs asked for his help, promising him several territories as a reward. So, in June 1415 Henry V landed in Normandy and took Honfleur. On October 25, 1415, Henry was attacked by the French at Azincourt[47] in Artois, but he succeeded in crushing the French chivalry, taking prisoner Charles of Orléans (Louis' heir) and the duke of Bourbon. Henry V spared the knights who could pay ransom, but slaughtered all the others. This bloody and disastrous defeat for France actually marked the end of French feudal society. Azincourt, however, would be the last English victory of the Hundred Years War.[48]

In the meantime, Jean sans Peur, whose only goal was to bring down the Armagnacs, did nothing. Thanks to a Parisian revolt in May 1418, Jean was able to return to Paris with his queen Isabeau, and there he took charge of the government while Charles VI let him act unopposed. Henry V finished to conquer Normandy and took Rouen in January 1419. From there, he decided to move on to Paris, but Jean sans Peur organized the defense of the capital. Confronted by this danger, the French factions agreed to put an end to their civil war in order to be able to fight the English. A meeting was set between the duke of Burgundy and the new Dauphin Charles, the future Charles VII who was considered head of the Armagnacs, who had fled from Paris to the south of the Loire when Jean returned to Paris. On September 10, 1419, a meeting was held on the bridge of Montereau. There, Jean sans Peur was assassinated by the men of Charles. This murder had terrible consequences for France. The new duke, Philippe le Bon, who wanted to avenge his father's death, allied himself with the English king Henry V (December 1419). But Charles VI was still in Paris and wanted to make peace with Henry V in order to put an end to the war against the English. His negotiations succeeded, and the Treaty of Troyes was signed on May 21, 1420,[49] and to complete the agreement Henry V married Charles VI's daughter. Henry was designed as the successor of Charles VI to the throne of France, and until Charles' death he was Regent of the kingdom. The Dauphin Charles was cut off from his inheritance, but Henry died suddenly in an accident on August 31, 1422. Several months later Charles VI died too. So the young son of Henry V, Henry VI, still a nine-year-old child, became king. In spite of his young age, the partisans of Dauphin Charles still recognized him as king.

Joan of Arc (Jeanne d'Arc)

In 1429 France was divided, weakened by both the civil war and the English invasion, totally at the mercy of the king of England. It seemed then that there was no one to resist except Charles VII, a fearful indecisive prince. From 1422 to 1428 the Bourguignons and chiefly the English regent Bedford inflicted serious defeats on Charles. The English entered the Maine and the Anjou provinces, and in 1428 they put the siege to Orléans. It was then clear that if Orléans surrendered, the English would easily conquer the center of France and Berry, areas that were still faithful to Charles.

Then, almost miraculously, Charles seemed to recover from his lethargy and decided to fight the English. This sudden change was in great part due to the arrival of Jeanne d'Arc on the scene.[50] In Chinon Jeanne had met Charles, who, after some hesitation, agreed to let her fulfill her God-inspired mission and allowed her to go and fight at Orléans.

Once in Orléans, Jeanne organized attacks against the English, who were so taken aback that they lifted the siege on May 8, and withdrew from the Loire valley. On June 18, the French defeated an English army at Patay. These were the first victories of the French for a very long time, and so the French troops regained courage and hope. Jeanne d'Arc, then, decided that it was time to have Charles VII consecrated king in Reims, in accordance with the tradition of French monarchs. On July 16, 1429, Jeanne and an important escort arrived in Reims with Charles, who, once he was consecrated, became the *true* king of France (because Henry V had not been consecrated). From then on, everybody knew that they owed obedience to Charles alone. Unfortunately for France and for Jeanne, Charles remained weak and indecisive. His entourage managed to convince him that the war had lasted too long. Charles still took back Laon, Soisson and Compiègne, but failed to take back Paris. At this point, Charles gave up the fight and sent his army home. Jeanne, meanwhile, continued to fight with some faithful soldiers, but she was finally surrounded in Compiègne and captured by a Burgundian chief on April 23, 1430. Shortly after, he sold Jeanne to the English. After a long and painful trial, Jeanne was declared a heretic and put to death on the pyre in Rouen on May 30, 1431. Even those who had remained faithful to Charles VII were discouraged. Nevertheless, something important had happened thanks to Jeanne d'Arc:[51] There emerged among the French a feeling of common solidarity, something that would be later called *patriotism*, born from the miseries of the war and from the desire to chase the English out of France.

The End of the Hundred Years War

The struggle was not over for the French king. From 1431 to 1435 he did not win any fight and he was aware that what he really needed was to be reconciled with Burgundy, because the province surrounded the French territory in the south and in the east. At this juncture, it happened that Philippe le Bon was ready to negotiate because he was afraid of the victory of the English and of the possibility of a peace between England and France. So, in 1435 Philippe proposed a negotiation that would lead to the end of the war. But these negotiations hardly started were stopped on account of the English's excessive demands that the French refused to satisfy. So the French continued to oppose the Bourguignons for a while, but they finally agreed to reconcile. So, on September 20, 1435, they signed the Treaty of Arras, and Burgundy withdrew from the war. According to the treaty, the French king agreed to leave to the duke of Burgundy all the territories the latter had conquered, and Charles VII further agreed to punish the murderers of Montereau.[52] In addition, the duke was dispensed from paying homage to the king of France as long as he lived. The duchy of Burgundy was reaffirmed as an independent state and Philippe le Bon appeared to be the most powerful prince of Europe. Charles VII, under these conditions, realized that he had to put some order in the administration and army of France before trying to reconquer the provinces he had lost. Fortunately, Charles had become stronger and more energetic than he was earlier. He even managed to surround himself with faithful and competent people. With them, Charles tried to improve the country's finances, but he was not very successful, as he met resistance in many regions.[53] Charles VII then decided to reform the army, which he did rather well. In fact he abolished the feudal army and replaced it by a royal army paid by the government and under his sole command.[54] His efforts with finances and his reorganization of the army helped in reestablishing his authority as king over France. But that was not enough to end the war. France, even with the improvements brought about by Charles VII, remained poor and fairly discouraged. Charles took back Paris in 1436, but, fearing for his security, he took refuge in his Loire châteaux. In 1441, however, confident in his powerful reorganized artillery, Charles resumed the fight and reconquered Champagne, the Oise valley, the Maine and Normandy. Finally in April 1450 Charles crushed the English at Formigny. Then he reconquered Guyenne (1451–1452), beat the English at Castillon and freed Bordeaux. The result of these last French victories was that the English were practically out of France, keeping only Calais. This technically marked the end of the Hundred Years War, although no treaty was signed to end the long struggle officially.[55]

Consequences of the Hundred Years War

All in all, the war had lasted at least 138 years and thus it affected five and even six generations of Frenchmen. Even if the military operations were sporadic and short, the war kept coming back in incessant skirmishes. It took a very long time for France to recover from the various traumas of these wars. Many lands had been destroyed, roads were dangerous, haunted by former soldiers turned bandits and murderers, and the depressed economic situation of the population of France reached a new low. But at least the fateful consequences of the marriage of Eleanore d'Aquitaine to the English king Henry Plantagenet were on the whole obliterated, and with a more stable royal power, the French had begun to feel for the first time something close to a sense of national unity.

Chronological Summary: 1461–1515

1461: Louis XI, king of France.
1467: Charles le Téméraire, duke of Burgundy.
1468: Péronne. Charles le Téméraire forces Louis XI to sign a humiliating treaty.
1477: Death of le Téméraire at Nancy. Louis XI is master of Burgundy.
1483: Regency of Anne de Beaujeu.
1491: Anne de Bretagne marries Charles VIII, king of France.
1495: Charles VIII at Naples.
1498: Louis XII, king of France, marries Anne de Bretagne, widow of his cousin Charles VIII.
1499: War against Milan.
1504: France abandons Naples to Spain. Treaty of Blois.
1507: New expedition in Italy.
1513: France loses Italy.
1515: François Ier, king of France.

The Reign of Louis XI (1461–1483)

When in July 1461 Louis XI,[56] Charles VII's son, became king, the situation of France seemed to be about to change.[57] Louis was 37 years old when he took place on the throne of France thanks to Philippe le Bon, who paid for the expenses of his anointing as king. He was a character, dressing like a merchant, detesting any luxury and all in all not hand-some. He was clever, but often two-faced and cunning. Believing strongly that people are fundamentally crooked and that they can be bought, he surrounded himself with such people, his only goal being to be obeyed and served. In intention at least, Louis XI was the first absolute sovereign of France.

When Louis XI began to rule, he had a great deal to do to achieve his goal of becoming the absolute master of the kingdom. The high nobility could not accept that the power be left in the hands of one person, the king. They wanted to be involved in the government. But the king wanted to govern alone, and soon the anger of the nobles led them to form a coalition called *Ligue du Bien public* (League of the Public Good) (1465). One of the leaders happened to be the very brother of Louis, Charles de Berry allied to the duke of Brittany, the duke Jean de Bourbon and Charles de Charolais known as Charles le Téméraire (the Bold). Louis XI fought against the coalition with all his might, but his means were insufficient. After the battle of Monthléry (July 16, 1465), Louis XI had to capitulate and pacify his enemies by granting them a number of provinces and by humiliating himself in front of them. An optimist at heart, Louis XI thought that he could rapidly repair his first disaster. But in June 1467 Charles le Téméraire became duke of Burgundy. Louis XI, crafty as he was, decided that it was time to negotiate with le Téméraire and agreed to meet him in Péronne in October on the Somme river. There, le Téméraire held Louis XI prisoner until he signed a humiliating treaty when he learned that Louis was supporting a revolt of the Liégeois against him. Louis XI then decided that it was time to destroy the duke of Burgundy at any price. Crushing Charles le Téméraire and destroying his States were from then on the single preoccupation of Louis XI.

At first le Téméraire seemed about to succeed, but he eventually was beaten and killed in front of Nancy by the duke of Lorraine (January 1477). Louis XI then felt that nobody could stop him, and he occupied Burgundy, Picardie and Artois. However, the only daughter of le Téméraire, Marie, married Maximilien de Habsbourg, son of the emperor Frederic III (August 1477). War would have resumed, but Marie de Bourgogne died suddenly, and Louis XI jumped at the occasion to conclude an agreement with Maximilien. Soon they signed the Treaty of Arras (December 23 1482). The king of France was allowed to keep Burgundy, but Artois and Franche-Comté passed as a dowry to Marguerite d'Autriche while

Luxembourg was given to Maximilien, who was then the tutor of Philippe Ier le Beau (the Handsome). Louis XI had lost some lands, but in reality he had consolidated his power. So, before long he recovered Anjou, Provence and Burgundy. Only Flandre (Flanders) and Bretagne (Brittany) remained outside the king's influence. However, Brittany would return to the royal domain shortly after Louis XI's death, when his son (Charles VIII) married Anne of Brittany in 1491.[58] In any case, at Louis XI's death,[59] he was the master of the almost entirety of the kingdom as defined by the Treaty of Verdun in 843, and he also had Provence and Dauphiné. In addition, Louis XI's financial politics had positive benefits, particularly with the assistance of Jacques Coeur.[60] However, Louis XI died unloved by most because his court was full of intrigues and chiefly because his taxes were very unpopular. No regency was set up, although Louis XI's son, Charles VIII, was only thirteen years old. Instead, Anne de France and her husband, Pierre de Beaujeu, assumed the direction of the government. And France, hardly freed from the English wars, started to be fascinated by the mirage of Italy. This fascination would bring France substantial benefits, but much grief too.

Crisis and Calamities in the Fourteenth Century and Beginning of the Fifteenth Century

Throughout the fourteenth century to the beginning of the fifteenth century, the West knew a series of serious critical situations. First an economic and financial crisis, then a social crisis that was aggravated by natural calamities and epidemics that led to a general moral, religious, intellectual and artistic crisis.

The worst of calamities was the advent of the plague or Black Death that was particularly severe between 1348 and 1350.[61] Because of its devastating nature, this plague received the name of Great Plague. It was brought from the East on an Italian ship coming from Crimea, and it spread like wildfire throughout Europe. Just in France, it was estimated that at least one third of the population died. In Burgundy, for instance, the village of Givry lost half of its inhabitants (680 out of 1,500) within a three-month period, from August to September 1348. The consequences of the plague were many, but the worse was a rapid depopulation that created a tremendous lack of working hands and therefore a severe economic crisis. These disasters had a deep impact on minds, and since religion was at the center of people's minds and hearts, people decided that it was a punishment of God. As a consequence, religious faith became more sentimental and mystical. And unfortunately, the Church itself experienced a series of crises at the same time, the shift of residence of the popes from Rome to Avignon, *Le Grand Schisme* (the Great Schism) as well as the crisis brought about by an Oxford professor, the ancestor of Anglicanism, John Wyclif.

The Papacy in Avignon

When Pope Boniface VIII died in 1303, the cardinals chose, mostly to please the French king Philippe le Bel, the archbishop of Bordeaux, who assumed the name of Clément V (1305). This Pope never settled in Rome, residing most frequently in Avignon, a town that was on papal land. Clément's successors continued to remain in Avignon perhaps because the town had a better climate than Rome, but more importantly because Rome was then troubled by a series of revolts. Only in 1377 Pope Grégory XI decided to return the papacy to Rome. During their Avignon stay the Popes managed to reinforce the power of the papacy and to make it a kind of absolute monarchy. The Popes began to control the clergy every-where and to levy taxes in order to replenish the coffers of the Church. So, the higher clergy began to live in luxury, building rich manors and châteaux, such as the famous *Palais des Papes* in Avignon. But the Avignon papacy did not bring back peace and order in the Church. On the contrary, it spurred religious dissensions. The Church was accused of concentrating on material affairs, and the Popes were accused of playing favorite with France. The most severe accusation was that the Church was too rich and the clergy too interested in money and luxuries.

With the miseries of the war and epidemics, all sorts of heresies began to spread. The Franciscans of Saint Françis accused the Church of being too rich, and the order was therefore accused of heresy. In order to counter heresies, the Popes instituted the Inquisition, with its well-known brutal means.

The *Grand Schisme* (the Great Schism) and Its Consequences

The return of the Pope to Rome in 1377 did not improve the situation. When Grégoire XI died, the cardinals elected an Italian Pope mostly through fear of a revolt. But a few days later another group of cardinals elected another Pope, a Frenchman, and thus suddenly Christendom was divided between two Popes. While England and the Empire recognized the Italian Pope, France and Spain recognized the French Pope, who settled in

Avignon. This Schism lasted forty years, until 1409, when a solution was suggested. The two popes in conflict would be deposed, and a third one would be elected. Unfortunately the two deposed Popes refused to leave, and so the Schism grew worse with three Popes! As a result, the papacy lost more of its prestige and more heresies surfaced. An Oxford professor named Wyclif violently criticized the papacy and in his books rejected the most basic beliefs of the Catholic dogma. His ideas spread rapidly, particularly in Prague (Czechoslovakia) with the priest Jean Huss.[62] Worried by this escalation of heresies, a large number of bishops and theologians met in Constance (1414–1418) in order to end the Schism. The Constance Council decided that the three Popes should abdicate, and when under great pressure they finally left, a new pope was finally elected thus ending the *Grand Schisme*. However, the end of this crisis did not settle much. The internal situation of the Church was not improved by the election of a new Pope because the Constance Council proclaimed that it had supreme power over the Pope himself. The decision of Charles VII that bishops should be chosen only by the clergy and the king without intervention from the Pope, who in addition had no right to levy taxes, marked the triumph of the Council over the Pope. In the interim, no real reform of the clergy took place. They continued to live in luxury just like noble laypersons. Some believed to obtain a serious reform they might have to leave the Roman Catholic Church. In fact, that is exactly what happened during the sixteenth century!

While the high clergy and the Popes continue to wade in luxury and wordly pleasures, at the other end of the spectrum there was an increasing malaise among all ranks of the population. This malaise was reflected in art with the triumph of a new theme, spurred on by the fear of death, the *Danse Macabre*, written in poems and often painted on cemetery walls and churches. In art the new style became pathetic, teary and baroque, reflecting their fear that nothing could protect them from the plague, wars, hunger, death and decay. The personification of death with dancing skeletons was developing everywhere, in poems and in paintings too. By the end of the Middle Ages men became more and more haunted by macabre visions.[63] People began to fear that the end of the world was approaching, and hence there was a resurgence of religious fervor, as reflected in many works of art.[64] The literature of the time was also replete with imageries of skeletons and worms represented crawling in open wombs. As an example let me quote this extract from Chastellain's *Le Pas de la Mort* (Steps of Death).

Il n'a membre ne facture
Qui ne sente sa pourreture.
Avant que l'esperit soit hors,
Le coeur qui veult crevier au corps
Haulce et soulième la poitrine
Qui se veult joindre à son eschine.
-La face est tainte et apalie,
Et les yeux treilliés en la teste.
La parole luy est faillie,
Car la langue au palais se lie.
Le poulx tressault et sy halette.

. . . .

Les os desjoindent à tous lez;
Il n'a nerf qu'au rompre ne tende.[65]

France's Sudden Attraction to Italy: Why?

The French kings who sent their armies into Italy did not really have ambitions of conquest. Rather, they gave in to family claims and sometimes to calls from Italian heads of state seeking allies to fulfill their personal ambitions. More than anything else, they were attracted by the prestige of the land and by the brilliance of its civilization that was so far in advance of its neighbors. They were also attracted, it is true, by a certain taste of adventure and by money.

Charles VIII:[66] His Italian *"Castles in Spain"*

As soon as Charles VIII was freed from Anne de Beaujeu's regency (1494), he was ready to launch his own Italian expedition. Unfortunately Charles was crippled with a misshapen body and a degenerate mind. He was frequently overcome by fits of epilepsy and had aged prematurely. In other words, Charles VIII had all the degenerate features of the men at the end of the Valois dynasty. As an education he had devoured a large number of romances of chivalry and he could not wait to imitate these fictional heroes. With such a mind, Charles was an easy prey for all sorts of intrigues, particularly those of the Italian heads of state. Charles VIII had inherited from the Anjou line and from his father the rights over the kingdom of Naples that was then held by the bastard Ferrand of Aragon. Upon the invitation of Ludovic le More, duke of Milan, and urged on by his own advisers, among whom bishop Briçonnet, Charles decided to fulfill one of his fanciful dreams, to conquer the kingdom of Naples. Even before leaving France, Charles assumed the title of king of Naples and Jerusalem, the latter because he also intended to launch a crusade against the Turks!

In order to finance his expedition, Charles obtained the assistance of some Lyon bankers, and in July 1494 he led 40,000 men into Italy. Thanks to his superior artillery, Charles advanced with ease through Tuscany and entered Rome, where he made a solemn entrance. The kingdom of Naples fell shortly after in March 1495. Charles thought that France was settled in the south of Italy, but he did not count on a coalition that soon forced him to retreat to France. Unrealistic as he was, the king swore that he would return to Italy as soon as conditions would be more favorable. But he never carried out his dream because he died on April 8, 1498, from a banal accident.

Louis XII

After Charles VIII's death, the heir of the French throne was Charles' cousin, the duke of Orléans, who became king under the name of Louis XII.[67] Louis was in poor health and like his cousin had aged prematurely, but at least in appearance, he seemed prudent and careful with the finances of the country. In reality he was dictatorial and always ready to listen to the least reasonable advice. In order to remain popular, he was overly generous with the writers and artists of his entourage, which gave rise to the legend that his was the golden age of the sixteenth century.

Next to Italy, Louis wanted to add Brittany to France, and he was not sure of what Queen Anne, Charles VIII's widow, could do, so he had his marriage with Jeanne de France, daughter of Louis XI, annulled. Then he married Anne de Bretagne (Brittany), totally indifferent to the horrible court scandal it caused. What counted for Louis was to be free to pursue the Italian expedition. At first he was lucky, and Milan was conquered in 1499, but Ludovic le More took back the land, and Louis had to reconquer Milan in 1500. After that, Louis sent Ludovic le More as a prisoner to France, and never let him free. Louis, proud of his victory and urged by his entourage, decided that he could conquer the rest of Italy. His (temporary) Spanish allies took Naples, but eventually kept the town for themselves, and Louis had to be satisfied with Milan. But then Louis made a series of errors, and in the long run his allies abandoned him to form the *Sainte Ligue* (Holy League), which only purpose was to oust the French from Italy. In fact, Louis had to leave Milan and all his further attempts into Italy failed miserably. Soon he died, and on January 1, 1515, François Ier replaced Louis XII on the throne of France.

Historical and Cultural Survey of the Middle Ages

The Name *"Moyen Age" ("Middle Ages")*

The name *Moyen Age* is traditionally given to the 10 centuries of history between the fall of the Roman Empire (476) and the formation of a new world with the Renaissance (end of the Hundred Years War (1453) and the beginning if the Italian wars (1494). When dealing with French litera-ture it is customary to give the name of *Moyen Age* to the period of five centuries beginning with Hugues Capet (987) and ending at the end of the fifteenth century. Some historians like to end the Middle Ages with the fall of Constantinople to the Turks in 1492, and others state that the end comes in France with the death of Louis XI in 1483. What is certain is that during the course of this period, the Middle Ages, the world was totally transformed and France shrunk and expanded according to the more or less good governments of the different kings.

Europe, at the beginning of the Middle Ages, appeared to be in total chaos, and the powerful Roman Empire itself disappeared to make place to populations which had no unity, and no desire to be united; they were still fairly uncivilized and badly organized. At the end of the Middle Ages the situation was quite different: there were unified kingdoms with bor-ders which would not change much in the future.

The improvement was also noticeable in the institutions and in society. Gradually a noble class and a bourgeois class had formed and the disorder of barbaric groups was replaced by organized governments and monar-chies assisted by strong political and administrative organisms. Finally the greatest originality of the Middle Ages is to be found in the varied aspects of its culture, in its languages, literature, architecture, sculpture and art, inspired and penetrated by a profound faith in God, and unified under the strong influence of the Catholic Church. It was the *Age of Faith.*

The Feudal System

At the end of the Carolingian period new relationships were established between men and this brought about a new social regime which survived until the end of the Middle Ages. This new social regime was called *la féodalité* (feudal system). Since the end of Antiquity men got more and more accustomed to be linked between themselves by a sort of social contract according to which the weakest was protected by the strongest, in exchange of certain services and an allegiance owed to the more powerful by the less powerful. This social contract took real shape under Charlemagne, who saw in this a way to impose his authority and to be assisted by those he protected. The most powerful person was called the *suzerain* and those who swear allegiance to the suzerain were called *vassals*. In the course of history the kings who would in principle be suzerains were not always able to impose their authority because many vassals became stronger than their suzerain, as they possessed far larger domains. In addition many vassals began to transmit their domains and power directly to their sons, a tradition that removed much of the king's power. The invasions of the ninth century further complicated the relationship of the king and his vassals. Many times the king was unable to come to their help, and so the noble vassals turned their allegiance to other lords who could better assist them.

Feudalism has also profound economic roots. In the Middle Ages the main source of wealth was the land and these lands were ruled by aristocratic landowners called *seigneurs* (lords), who exploited the land thanks to the help of peasants or serfs. The feudal domain was generally called a *fief*. It was often a land given by a suzerain to his vassal in exchange of the latter's homage or oath of allegiance and service. This homage was sworn in a religious ceremony that linked a vassal to his suzerain to whom he owes service, advice and assistance in case of need such as war. The vassal became *l'homme-lige* (liege) of his suzerain. This feudal system gradually developed from the ninth century and became really organized in the eleventh century. However, not all the lands were fiefs; some remained free and were called *alleux*.

Life within the Feudal System

Life within the feudal system was fairly identical everywhere. The lords (*seigneurs*) were busy fighting wars, whether they fought for themselves or to help their suzerain or sometimes the king. In order to defend his domain, the lord lived in a fortified castle at the center of which was the lord's residence, the *donjon*. The castle was frequently set on a hill or mountain and surrounded by a moat. The rooms of the castle were generally obscure and cold, and social life was extremely limited. Since war or warlike enterprises were the occupation of the lords, they spent a great deal of time training for fighting, and that since the age of 18 when they become knights (*chevaliers*). The ceremonies of knighting were one important social event in the castle. When the young knight was dubbed, his lord sponsor gave him a horse, an armor and, before embracing him and giving him his sword, he would strike him on the shoulder with his sword. This was called *"la colée"* and it served to show that the young man could stand blows. The young knight also had to show his faith in God and allegiance to the Church by spending an all night watch in prayer after hearing mass and having his new arms blessed by the priest.

The lords were not always fighting a war, but aside from organized feasts and banquets, they enjoyed the sports of tourneys and hunting. In the evening, in winter mainly, troubadours would come and sing. Jugglers would display tricks, or poets would recite poems like the *Song of Roland,* or courtly tales, those of Chrétien de Troyes, for example.

In the meantime the peasants or serfs lived a very different life. Most of the day they worked for their lord or tilled the land to feed themselves. They depended much from the weather to survive and feared periods of drought, harsh winters or rainstorms that devastated the crops and condemned them and their animals to starvation.

The Church

Land was the main wealth of the Middle Ages, and so the Church had to count on large rural domains that it exploited in order to survive. Benedictine abbeys following the rule of Saint Benoît (Saint Benedict) settled in the country as they were dedicated to manual labor and studies. Thus many peasants as well as lords became monks, and monasteries became the most active agricultural centers of the time. Monasteries were the major civilizing force of the Middle Ages, and among them the Benedictine Abbey of Cluny was the most active and prosperous. It was also the most powerful religious and financial institution in France and the largest monastery ever built, with 1,400 sister institutions throughout the world by the twelfth century. As a result the order of Cluny became immensely rich, so rich in fact that many people condemned its wealth and chose to leave Cluny to join other more austere orders, condemning Cluny's sumptuous rituals and beautiful ornate churches. Those who after 1130 were seeking less ostentatious ways to express their faith in God turned to the religious orders of the *Chartreux* founded by Saint Bruno. In 1084, Saint Bruno founded the *Monastère (monastery) de la Grande-Chartreuse* near Grenoble. There was also the Cistercian monastery of Citeaux near Dijon, founded in 1098 by some monks from the abbey of Molesmes, under the leadership of Robert de Molesmes. Citeaux soon became famous particularly after the arrival of Saint Bernard who strictly applied the rule of Saint Benoît (Benedict), emphazing manual labor, sometimes even at the expense of intellectual work. Saint Bernard preached utmost simplicity, an austere life and the quiet contemplation of God. The most famous Cistercian monastery was the monastery of Clairvaux created in 1115 near Troyes in northeastern France. Contrary to Cluniac buildings, Cistercian buildings had to have a simple architecture without any decoration. Both Cluny and Citeaux played a major role in feudal society at least until the end of the twelfth century.

One of the main civilizing and religious actions of the Church was to organize pilgrimages to the most famous sanctuaries of Christendom: Rome, Le Puy, Santiago de Compostela in Spain. The great monasteries and churches, like Conques and Moissac, were refuges to the pilgrims walking along the main pilgrimage roads. The Church also played a major role in trying to moderate violence among the knights of feudal society. It established the Truce of God (*Trêve de Dieu*) that prohibited fighting from Thursday to Monday and the Peace of God (*Paix de Dieu)* that prohibited to harm women, children and clerics. Finally the Church established the Right of Asylum (*Droit d'asile*) protecting persons who took refuge in churches and monasteries. No less importantly, the Church encouraged the reconquest of the Holy Land, of Palestine, and preached crusades against the Turks and other infidels.

The Medieval Crusades

The origin of the crusades was the desire of the Christians of the West to travel freely in pilgrimage to the Holy Land where Christ lived, in Jerusalem and Bethlehem. With this goal, they organized regularly, since the end of the eleventh century, military operations in order to free the Holy Land, that is to say, Palestine, from the infidels. Many important men and the greatest kings of the time took part in these crusades. The Popes organized this crusading movement because they could accept that the country of birth of the founder of Christianity be occupied by non-Christians. If at first crusades were inspired by religious motives, soon economic causes and human greed were added to these motives and corrupted them. The merchants and sailors of Italian towns who traded with the Orient wanted to see Westerners more favorable to them settling in Asia Minor in order to develop their businesses. Some political causes also came into play: it was one way for Popes to increase their power and, at times, the Byzantine emperors called upon Western crusaders to come help them fight the Turks, promising in exchange to put their clergy under the authority of the Pope. There were also some psychological causes for this crusading enthusiasm, the love of adventure and fighting of the knights.

Popes and kings were also in favor of crusades because they knew that, while the most turbulent elements of their society were fighting far away from Europe, they were not causing trouble at home. So, one must admit that if crusading was inspired by deep and sincere religious motives at first, other motives eventually corrupted the cause.

The First Crusade (1096–1099)

Of the eight crusades to the Holy Land, the First Crusade was the one that was almost entirely inspired by religious motives. When the papacy learned that the Turks had taken Jerusalem in 1078, it conceived the idea of a crusade to expulse them from this holy place. In 1095 Pope Urban II preached the *First Crusade,* traveling throughout France in order to urge knights and bishops to join in the expedition. It was then that the knights adopted the sign of the cross on their armor, and it is the origin of the word "*crusade.*" At first the Pope succeeded in stimulating the enthusiasm of the poor people of France, who engaged in the crusade under the leadership of a Picard monk, Pierre l'Ermite, and of a certain Gauthier-sans-Avoir. They left first, shouting "*Dieu le veut*" (God wants it) but, lacking discipline, in fact totally disorganized, they never reached the Holy Land and were devastated by the heat, hunger and the Turks. The knights, contrary to the poor people crusaders, carefully organized their expedition. Four armies set out, the first under the direction of Godefroy de Bouillon and made up of northern French knights and some from Lorraine. The second army was made up of Normans and of French knights from the center of France. It was led by the king of France's brother, Hugues de Vermandois. The third army, made up of southern knights, was led by Raymond, Count of Toulouse. Finally the fourth army, led by Bohémond de Sicile, was made up in majority of Normans from Italy.

These four armies gathered in Constantinople, and from there marched toward Palestine. After beating the Turks in 1097 at Dorylée (Dorylaeum, Phrygia) they managed to take Antioch. After a fight, they took Jerusalem on July 15, 1099. This First Crusade by the knights was victorious, and the men immediately organized the conquered country into the Kingdom of Jerusalem that adopted the feudal institutions of Europe and started to build castles and churches. Godefroy de Bouillon was the first king, and after him the crown went to Godefroy's brother, Baudoin (1100). The rest of the crusading knights became vassals and were granted fiefs according to feudal tradition. But the Moslems, Turks and Arabs were still a menace and so, in order to protect themselves, the crusaders created religious orders of knights-monks such as the *Hospitaliers* (Hospitalers) and the *Templiers* (Templars), who provided shelter, medical treatment, horses when necessary, and money too.[68]

The Second and Third Crusades (1147 and 1189)

In spite of their first victory and organization, the crusaders still felt the menace of the Muslims. In 1144 a Moslem *emir* from Mossoul conquered the county of Edessa that had been given as a fief to Bohémond de Sicile. So Saint Bernard immediately preached a new crusade in Vézelay in order to fight the infidels. The emperor Conrad III[69] and the French king Louis VII joined this Second Crusade (1147–1149). Unfortunately the two sovereigns acted independently and were both beaten. So during the following years the Muslims formed a powerful empire under the direction of an excellent chief, *Salah-ed-Din* (Saladin). Saladin, exasperated by the incessant plunders of some Christian knights, attacked the Kingdom of Jerusalem in 1187, crushed the army of Guy de Lusignan in Tibériade and took the Holy City. The Christian crusaders only held Antioch, Tyr and Tripoli. So the papacy decided to launch a Third Crusade. At first it was led by Frederic Barbarossa,[70] but he unfortunately drowned in Cilicie (Cilicia, SE Asia Minor) in 1190. Philippe Auguste and Richard Coeur de Lion left together, took Chypre and reconquered Saint-Jean-d'Acre in 1191. However, the French king returned suddenly to France under the pretext that he was ill. But the king was not really ill. He left because he wanted to settle the succession of the count of Flanders, who had just died. So Richard alone was not able to beat the infidels, and this Third Crusade ended in failure.

From the Fourth to the Eighth Crusade

The Fourth Crusade (1202–1204) preached by Foulque de Neuilly and led by Baudoin Ier also failed not so much because of military troubles, but because the Western crusaders were beginning to lose enthusiasm for this religious pursuit. Political and economic considerations began to prevail over faith. *The Fourth Crusade* was preached by Innocent III, who wanted to take back Jerusalem from the infidels. The Pope also hoped to bring back the Byzantine Church under his authority by helping a deposed Byzantine emperor who had promised his allegiance to the Pope if he was helped to recover his throne. But things got complicated because the crusaders lacked money. They were promised financial help and transportation by Venice if they took the town of Zara. The crusaders and the Pope agreed, but by doing so, the main goal of the crusade was changed. The crusaders took Zara and marched on Constantinople, where they did what they had promised, returned the deposed emperor to his throne. The town of Constantinople revolted against the crusaders who, had to take back the city and plundered it, thus losing all desire to go on and fight in Palestine. Byzantine wealth rapidly supplanted the crusaders' religious fervor.

The Last Crusades (from the Fifth Crusade to the Eighth)

In spite of the failure of the Fourth Crusade, Innocent III called for another crusade at the *Concile de Latran* (1215). Few knights answered his call; however, a small troop volunteered to go and help the king of Jerusalem, Jean de Brienne, who wanted to attack Egypt. It was the *Fifth Crusade* (1218–1221). It also ended in failure.

Shortly after, the emperor Frederic II led a *Sixth Crusade* (1228–1229) preached by the Pope Grégoire IX, who reminded the emperor of a previous promise to fight in a crusade.[71] Frederic went, but instead of fighting the infidels, he negotiated with them and obtained from Egypt the return of Jerusalem, Bethlehem and Nazareth, as well as the freedom to conduct pilgrimages. But neither the Pope nor the Muslims respected this agreement, and in 1244 the Turks took back Jerusalem.

Then, urged by Innocent IV, Saint Louis, a very pious king, decided to organize a crusade to fulfill a wish he had made. In 1248 he sailed from the town of Aigues-Mortes in southern France to lead the *Seventh Crusade*. Saint Louis attacked Egypt, took Damiette (June 1249), but he was defeated at Mansourah in December 1249 and taken prisoner. Saint Louis, after paying a huge ransom, was liberated, but he chose to remain in Palestine, spending his time in pious works and in paying ransoms to free Christian prisoners. In spite of this, one can say that this crusade also failed. In 1270, however, Saint Louis decided to go and convert the Bey of Tunis to Catholicism, hoping to attack Egypt again from Tunisia. That was the *Eigth Crusade*. But, hardly on Tunisian shore, the king was struck by the plague, and he died in Carthage on August 25, 1270.

There were some later small expeditions, but none can be ranked among the major crusades. In the meantime most of the cities of Palestine fell to Muslim hands, and the fall of Ptolemais in 1291 marked the end of the Crusades, and Christ's tomb remained in Muslim hands.

Consequences of the Crusades

In spite of many failures, and the fact that the Holy Land was finally lost by the Christians, the Crusades had some positive consequences: the Muslims began to let pilgrims travel freely to the holy places, and gradually the idea of fighting the infidels was replaced by a missionary spirit. More importantly perhaps, the Crusades opened the knowledge of the East to the West; they enriched scientific knowledge, literature and the arts and they fueled the economic activity of the Mediterranean basin and of the West. In the long run Christians and Muslims discovered each other as men and no longer as enemies. Feudal Europe had discovered all sorts of luxuries in the Orient, and thus the austere life of the *châteaux* became more pleasant with the addition of sumptuous tapestries, carpets, rich coffers, jewelry and gold. So one can say that the Crusades, after giving individual faith an outlet, opened the East to the West and brought about an extraordinary renewal and expansion of the economy in Europe. Of no less importance, the Crusades gave rise to the first two historical masterpieces of Geoffroy de Villehardoin and Jean, sire de Joinville.[72]

A Time of Cultural Renaissance: Birth of Universities, Improvement of Teaching, Fantastic Progress in Sculpture and Architecture: Romanesque and Gothic Literature Bloomed

Birth of Universities

Until the twelfth century the clergy taught in the monastic schools of the great abbeys and in the cathedral schools in cathedral churches where teaching was done by a canon. In the eleventh and twelfth centuries some of these schools were famous, such as the school of the Normand abbey of Bec, the schools of the abbeys of Saint-Victor and Sainte-Geneviève in Paris, the school of the Saint-Felix monastery in Bologna, Italy, the cathedral schools of Chartres, Laon, Paris etc. . . . Some of the well-known and famous professors were Saint-Anselme at the Bec Abbey, and Abélard in Paris, etc. . . . But in the twelfth century most of the abbey schools no longer attracted students because they were situated too far from cities. Another reason was because Saint Bernard did not want to encourage his young disciples to be interested in intellectual pursuits, afraid that they would neglect their religious ideal. In fact all monasteries became off limits to those who were not monks. From that time on, the monastic schools were forgotten. On the contrary, the cathedral schools flourished, but they had many problems too. First they had to cope with a considerable increase in the number of students, and a corresponding increase in the number of professors. Those who granted degrees, bishops and canons, became afraid of the competition, and therefore there were frequent clashes between them and the other members of the professorial corps.

As a result of these oppositions, the professors and their students wanted to be free from the school directors and wanted the teaching degrees to be granted, not according to the whim of some bishop, but only to those judged worthy of teaching and having passed an examination. In order to succeed, they united under the name of *universitas*, the origin of the word *université*. These unions soon received the support of Pope Innocent III, who saw a way for him to oversee and control teaching. Many kings also supported these new learning centers. Thus the Université de Paris was born in 1200, specializing in theology. At the same time the school of medicine opened in Montpellier, as well as Oxford in England.

The Organization of Universities

Universities were divided in four *facultés*: The Arts, Theology, Law and Medicine, and at the head of each *faculté* was a Dean (Doyen) and the Dean of Arts was also the university *Recteur*, officially representing the university. The university professors were accredited by examination and like their students recruited internationally.[73]

Studies

Medieval universities taught what we are presently teaching in Lycées and universities (secondary and higher education). Medieval students tended to be older than our current students, and it was not rare to have persons over 30 years old or more attending universities. They began by attending the *Faculté* of Arts, where they followed a program of general culture including seven subjects divided in two cycles, the Trivium (Grammar, Rhetoric, Philosophy) and the Quadrivium (Arithmetic, Geometry, Music and Astronomy). At the end of both cycles they took the *baccalauréat ès arts* and they became *bacheliers ès arts*. After they had the choice to pursue advanced studies in Theology, Law, Medicine or at the *Faculté* of Arts where they took the *licence* and could go on to the *doctorat*.

In these universities the great medieval masters of the time taught, such as Abélard, Saint Thomas d'Aquin, Saint Bonaventure, etc.

Brief Survey of French Medieval Literature

Like most other Romance literatures, French literature was at first exclusively composed of religious texts. All the texts anterior to 1100 were mostly hagiographic, that is to say, dealing with saints' lives. But from the twelfth century on there was a real renaissance of letters and a great variety of genres began to appear, epic texts, lyric poetry, drama, history and romances. In fact one can say that the real beginning of French medieval literature took place in the twelfth century and, from then on, it never ceased to develop. The thirteenth century has been acclaimed as the real classical age of medieval literature, but both the fourteenth and fifteenth centuries produced many varied masterpieces too.

Hagiographic and Epic Texts[74]

At first and from the end of the ninth century literature was exclusively restricted to religious edifying texts such as the *Séquence or Cantilène de sainte Eulalie (end of the ninth century)*, the *Vie de saint Alexis (1040)*, the *Voyage de saint Brandan* (1112) and many more. The number of hagiographic texts produced was so considerable that we cannot list them here, and we must also add numerous sermons because most of these texts were produced around abbeys and church and monastery schools.

As hagiographic texts were copied, more and more were produced even at the expense of combining several texts to compose other saints, lives, some of these being pure fiction. As the texts expanded the adventures became more complex, and with the prevailing feudal spirit new heroes were born, no longer saints, but knights. This gave rise to epic songs called *Chansons de Geste*. These epic texts are narratives using some historical fact or background and transforming them into marvelous legends. The epic heroes date from the time of Charlemagne or of his son. The oldest epic songs, among which the famous *Chanson de Roland*, do not go back further than the first half of the eleventh century with an extensive production starting in the twelfth century and expanding in longer cycles in the thirteenth, fourteenth and even the fifteenth century. These epic texts are imbued with a strong feudal spirit and exalt faith, crusades and knightly adventures. At first the songs were frequently sung by jugglers but in time they were transcribed in order to be read. In their first forms they were in verse, but after the thirteenth century many began to be written in prose. In the thirteenth century the epic production was divided in three *gestes* (gestae) or cycles, each one with a characteristic inspiration: (1) The *Geste du Roi* with Charlemagne and the holy war against the infidels as main themes. (2) The *Geste de Garin de Montglane* exalting feudal fidelity. (3) The *Geste de Doon de Mayence* dealing with revolting feudal barons.

The most famous epic text and the oldest of *the Geste du Roi* cycle is without a doubt the *Song of Roland*.[75]

The second group of Chansons de geste deals with the poetic history of William of Orange (Guillaume), his brothers and nephews, father and grandfather. The masterpiece of this group is the *Chanson de Guillaume* dating from the mid-twelfth century.

The third group of Chansons de geste is united by a common epic theme, the rebellion and repentance of a tragic hero. The oldest text of this group is *Gormont et Isembart* (about 1130) but *Raoul de Cambrai* (before 1160), *Doon de Mayence, La Chevalerie Ogier, Renaud de Montauband* and *Girart de Roussillon,* all of the end twelfth century/ beginning thirteenth century are worthy of note.

With these epic stories the medieval public was getting more and more interested in adventures and the public was no longer exclusively feudal knights enjoying war and proud violent deeds. The elite of society had become more refined and enjoyed tales of love, women included. From 1150 on a new spirit was born, *l'amour courtois* (courtly love) that soon developed its own themes and literary laws under the triple influence of the *Romans Antiques* (Romances of Antiquity), the Celtic legends, and the lyric poetry of troubadours born in the middle of the eleventh century in the south of France (Occitania, Provence).

Romances

Starting in the mid-twelfth century some romances appear in Old French inspired by antiquity: the romances of the *Alexandre* cycle, the *Roman de Thèbes* (1150), the *Roman d'Enéas* (1160), the *Roman de Troie* (1165). The *Roman d'Enéas* telling of the loves of Lavinia and Eneas represents the new public taste for feelings, love and passion in a universe which is now far removed from the harsh world of epic.[76]

In addition the new courtly literature was also inspired and greatly enriched by Celtic tales and legends, such as the famous legend of King Arthur and his Round Table knights. The first traces of these courtly and marvelous tales are found in Wace's *Roman de Brut*, in Marie de France's *Lais* and in the romances of *Tristan* by Beroul and Thomas, both dating from the twelfth century.

Furthermore, the beautiful lyric songs of the Provençal troubadours had a profound influence on the new courtly public of France.[77] They extolled the service of love, the virtues of the lover, the joy of being granted love by the lady. Under the influence of the songs of the great troubadours (Guillaume IX, Marcabru, Cercamon, Bernart of Ventadour, Jaufre Rudel, Bertran de Born, Arnaut Daniel, etc. . . .), courtly love flourished in the great courtly romances of Chrétien de Troyes (1160–1190),[78] *Lancelot or Le Chevalier de la Charrette, Erec et Enide, Yvain or Le Chevalier au Lion* and *Perceval.*

The destiny of Chrétien de Troyes' *Perceval* was extraordinary and it gave rise to the continuous development of the *Grail Legend*, with its masterpiece *La Queste del saint Graal* (1220).

During the first half of the thirteenth century there appeared an interesting and somewhat unique romance of adventure, called *Aucassin et Nicolette* named "*chantefable*" because it is a mixture of prose and of sung poetry.

Lyric poetry practically died in Provence, ruined by the Albigensian Crusade (1208–1209), but it passed on to neighboring countries, in Sicily, Spain and Italy and in the north of France. The French *trouvères* continued the tradition of courtly poetry, but it was less erotic, less passionate than the songs of the troubadours. Some of the great northern *trouvères* were Thibaut de Champagne (1201–1253), Colin Muset (thirteenth century), and Rutebeuf (+ 1280).

Prose began to be used extensively only near the mid-fifteenth century, and then it produced a number of interesting prose works of imagination such as *Les Quinze joyes de mariage, Les Cent nouvelles nouvelles, Le Livre des faits de Lalaing, Le Petit Jehan de Saintré,* all attributed to Antoine de la Sale, *Le Jouvencel* by Jean de Bueil, and the romance of *Jean de Paris.*[79]

Poetry during the Hundred Years War

In spite of the violence of the war some poetry continued to flourish, even if with some rare exceptions the war seems to have paralyzed the poetic muse. But fortunately there are some exceptions that are worth mentioning:

The poems with music of Guillaume de Machaut (1300–1377),[80] lais, motets, ballads etc.; a didactic poem (1342) called *Le Remède de Fortune* after Boethius' *De Consolatione philosophiae*; a *Dit de la Fontaine Amoureuse* (1360–1361) in Jean de Berry's honor.

Froissart (1337–1404), author of the *Chroniques*, also wrote some allegorical poems, *L'Orloge amoureux, Le Traité de l'Espinette amoureuse, le Paradis d'Amour,* none of them real masterpieces.

Eustache Deschamps (1346–1406) wrote a great variety of works, many poems (virelais, ballads, rondeaux) and satirical poems like his *Miroir de Mariage,* against women and marriage.

One of the most brilliant and famous women of the Middle Ages was Christine de Pisan (1363–1430),[81] who composed a great many poems (*rondeaux, virelais*) and allegorical poems, but she is better known for fighting for women against Jean de Meun. Her poem on Joan of Arc also deserves mention, *Ditié de Jeanne d'Arc* (July 1429); Christine wrote it in the enthusiasm of Jeanne's victory at Orléans and as Charles VII was being anointed in Reims.

Alain Chartier[82] became in his time as famous as Ronsard or Hugo will be in theirs. He was not only the author of the *Quadrilogue invectif*

(1422) against the English, but the author of delicate amorous poems. The *Livre des Quatre Dames* (1415) is an echo of Azincourt and a judgment of love. Chartier's most famous poem, however, was *La Belle Dame sans Mercy*.

Charles d'Orléans (1391–1465),[83] father of Louis XII, was one of the last truly courtly lords of the Middle Ages. He was taken prisoner at the battle of Azincourt, and taken to England. There, he composed many poems, songs and ballads, singing of his regret to be held prisoner, his joy to be able to see the coast of France from his jail, and his hope of return- ing soon to France. After his return from captivity, Charles wrote mostly melancholy rondeaux or poems on nature.

Fifteenth-century poetry is dominated by a great poet, François Villon, author of the *Lais* (1456), of the *Testament* (1461), *L'Epitaphe Villon* (1463).[84]

Bourgeois Literature

As early as the twelfth century, the feudal world reached its apex, but at the same time produced signs of its forthcoming decay. As early as the first half of the twelfth century urban communities developed and their power began to challenge the feudal world. In addition the Crusades had opened the East for the West, creating many commercial opportunities for merchants, thus giving rise to a bourgeois class, rich, dynamic and eager to rise in status and power. It is not surprising therefore that by the end of the twelfth century a new literature began to surface in order to satisfy the tastes of the new bourgeois public. This literature tends to be realistic and often mocking and satirical, particularly with the *Fabliaux*. A masterpiece of the genre is certainly the *Roman de Renart* with the *goupil* (fox in Old French) as the main character.[85]

Medieval Drama[86]

At the beginning of the Middle Ages the theater was not only serious but a complement of the ceremonies of the Church, either commemorating the various times of the liturgical year or celebrating the Virgin and the saints. Liturgical dramas can be divided into three genres, liturgical dra- mas, Miracle plays, that begin to appear as early as the eleventh century and Mystery plays that appear later in the fourteenth and fifteenth centu- ries. The *Jeu des Vierges Sages et des Vierges Folles or Sponsus* (end eleventh century) and the *Jeu d'Adam* are two examples of the liturgical drama. The second branch of the religious theater is composed of *Miracles* that draw their theme from the saints' lives. One of the most famous of these *miracles* is Jean Bodel's *Le Jeu de saint Nicolas* including realistic parts and tavern episodes.

Near 1260, a dramatic miracle dedicated to the Virgin Mary was written by Rutebeuf, *Le Miracle de Théophile* (1260), the first of the *Miracles de Notre-Dame*.

Comic Theatre

The first manifestations of this dramatic genre, *Comic Theater*, appeared in the XIIIth century, but it grew rapidly during the fourteenth and fifteenth centuries. Among the masterpieces of the genre, it introduced *la farce* in French dramatic literature. One of the first traces of the comic theatre is Rutebeuf's *Le Dit de l'Erberie* (1260), a parody of charlatans trying to sell all sorts of odd remedies on the marketplace. Some of the real comic plays that deserve mention are: *Le Garçon et l'Aveugle* (1266), the oldest farce known, *Le Jeu de la Folie* (formerly called *Jeu de la Feuillée*) by Adam le Bossu, a satirical review of the people of Arras and *Le Jeu de Robin et Marion* by Adam le Bossu (1283), a dramatic *pastourelle*.

In the late Middle Ages the comic theater survived and flourished again in the late fifteenth century, and particularly from 1500 on with farces, *sotties,* joyous sermons and dramatic monologues. A famous example is the *Farce de Maistre Pathelin* (1464). The *sotties* produced during the last third of the fifteenth century are not a well-defined genre and they really belong to the repertoire of oral literature and farces. Dramatic monologues are the oldest form of comic theater. The most famous from the fifteenth century is *Le Franc-Archer de Bagnolet*.

During the fourteenth century and through the fifteenth century the taste for dramatic representation remained in favor. The public of the time still attended with pleasure the traditional miracles that were then performed by companies called *puys*. Some of these miracles composed during the second half of the fourteenth century were the *Miracles de Notre Dame* that always ended with the final intervention of the Virgin and the defeat of Satan and his henchmen.

During the fifteenth century and even during the first half of the sixteenth century Mystery plays (*Mystères*) became in favor. They were huge plays, huge in length (from 30,000 to 60,000 lines), and their subject was very broad. Some, for instance, covered a huge period, starting with Adam's Creation and ending with the Redemption. These performances could last from four to ten days. Famous among those is Arnoul Gréban's (1420–1471) *Mystère de la Passion*.

Didactic Literature[87]

All along the twelfth century appeared a prolific scholarly didactic literature made of proverbs, religious meditations, bestiaries, lapidaries and herbals, and treatises of etiquette. Out of this numerous production a meditation on death stands out, the *Vers de la Mort* (1197), anticipating similar meditations on death in the fifteenth century.

During the later Middle Ages, encyclopedias, religious meditations, considerations on man's salvation were plentiful. During the thirteenth century many didactic and allegorical works were written, among the most famous the *Roman de la Rose,*[88] composed in two parts. The first part, composed around 1225–1240 by Guillaume de Lorris, is a kind of courtly *Art d'Aimer* (art of love) with the symbol of the rose representing the lady lover. The continuation or second part was written by Jean de Meun forty years later (1275–1280) and is a compilation of erudition, social satire, alchemy, with a violent irony against love and women. For Jean de Meun, love was not a subject of devotion nor the source of courtliness; it was a dangerous evil and a vice.

History[89]

The Crusades were a great historical event and we have seen that they had some very positive consequences, economic and social mostly, for the Middle Ages. They also created medieval history thanks to the genius of our first chroniclers-historians, Jeoffroy deVillehardoin (1150–1215), who wrote *Histoire de la Conquête de Constantinople*, Robert de Clari (1170–1216), who also wrote *La Conquête de Constantinople* dealing mostly with the Fourth Crusade and thus completing Villehardoin's work.

One of the great historians of the Crusades was Joinville (1224–1317) who accompanied Louis IX to the Holy Land in 1249. At the request of Jeanne de Navarre, wife of Philippe le Bel, Joinville started his masterpiece, the *Livre des saintes paroles et des bons faits de notre saint roi Louis or Histoire de saint Louis,* a book written when Joinville was eighty years old and ended in 1309.

Next to the Crusades, another rich topic for historians was the Hundred Years War. The great historian of this war was Froissart (1337–1404) who wrote a detailed account of salient aspects of the war in his *Chroniques* (Chronicles).

There were other chronicles written during the fifteenth century, and one of the most interesting was *Le Journal d'un Bourgeois de Paris*, a chronicle day by day of the years 1405–1449 by an anonymous Parisian, probably a cleric. After the defeat of Azincourt, the narrator describes in graphic details the misery of France, with the English pressing at Paris' walls and starving the people.

Azincourt (1415), it is true, marked the end of French chivalry. The Dauphin was mocked and called *roi de Bourges* because in fact he fled from Paris to go and hide south of the Loire. It is then that Alain Chartier wrote his *Quadrilogue Invectif,* a masterpiece of oratory prose by the Dauphin's secretary who vented the anger of the French against the English.

Philippe de Commynes is without a doubt the most famous historian of the fifteenth century. He is truly the father of modern history. Contrary to his predecessors, Commynes tried to understand the events and to draw lessons from them. His masterpiece is certainly his *Mémoires* in which he examines Louis XI, reflects on the world and affirms the necessity of Providence to maintain peace and the stability of the world. Commynes is one of the first modern political scientists.

The Fabliaux[90]

The fabliaux are tales, the purpose of which is to cause laughter, but by the same token many also become social satires. The oldest fabliau known is called *Richeut*, composed around 1170. It treats with cynism feminine cunning. Most fabliaux are concerned with people, usually of the lower orders, country folk or church clerics. They are tales aimed at making people laugh. Some of them are bawdy, provoking ribald belly laugh and most of them end with a moral like in fables. The genre *fabliau* flourished in northern France, particularly in Artois and Picardie during the thirteenth century, but it began to lose favor during the fourteenth century.

Translations

Starting in the fourteenth century and continuing afterward there was a great interest in translations from Latin into French. At the court of Burgundy the position of translator was official and well paid. This vogue for translation certainly contributed to the development of the sixteenth century Renaissance Humanism.[91]

The Art of the Age of Faith:
Romanesque and Gothic Art and Architecture[92]

After the turn of the millennium (year 1000) there was a tremendous renewal of religious architecture. Churches were restored and many were built, at first according to the Roman models. It is Romanesque art. Romanesque art marked the appearance of the carved stone, of stone vaults. Since the weight of the vault rested on the ribs, massive, thick and windowless walls were needed, hence the Romanesque buildings of the eleventh century looked like fortresses as they were first conceived as protective places and places where pilgrims could find quiet and peace. Before 1100 the Romanesque churches were plain, unadorned, with rare windows and low doors that created an atmosphere of quiet stillness.[93] After 1100 with sculptors and painters of frescoes,[94] churches became more expressive, and shortly after, from the second half of the twelfth century, Romanesque style was replaced by the high, bright, slender and lighter Gothic style. With the advent of Gothic art, churches lost their severe, austere look and became bright, open with thinner walls, many high stained glass windows and adorned with monumental sculptures outside.[95] Gothic style changed with the years and the lightness, slenderness and height of the constructions became somewhat exaggerated with the creation of the *Gothique rayonnant*, the first example being Paris' Sainte Chapelle (1242–1248) and the churches of Troyes (Saint-Urbain and the cathedral). When further exaggerated in the fifteenth century, the *Gothique rayonnant* became *flamboyant* with large, high windows letting in more light, and therefore they were often dangerously delicate. It was the urge for more light and height that marks this mature Gothic style. Vaults could reach 98 feet or 29.5 meters above the ground. Notre-Dame de Paris reached 107 feet or 32.6 meters, Chartres 118 feet or 36 meters, Amiens in 1240 reached 138 feet or 42.1 meters and Beauvais 157 feet or 47.9 meters. The church of saint-Maclou in Rouen is a good example of flamboyant Gothic.

Conclusion: France at the End of the Middle Ages

At the end of the Middle Ages France was still far from being a synthesis, and the French did not have yet a real sense of belonging to a united nation. The common feeling remained regional, not national. The end of the Middle Ages was also a period of great mobility; students, lawyers, merchants and even peasants moved, either because they had to or because they were seeking better jobs. Some people even traveled for the pleasure of seeing other places, but those were in fact very few and they had little impact on their contemporaries. If some rare mavericks looked to the future, most people still clung to the past. The common feeling among most people was pessimism. Suffering dominated the minds of most, fear of illness, fear of Hell, but at the same time they hoped to be granted eternal happiness in Heaven. In the fifteenth century people were still deeply religious, even if there were heretics and if some were more fascinated by sorcery and astrology than by God and his saints. Many powerful men consulted astrologers, but the same thing happens in our own time.

One characteristic of the end of the Middle Ages is certainly insecurity; insecurity of roads, but also economic insecurity and insecurity brought about by epidemics, by the plague, by wars, by the fear of death.[96]

It was said that Joan of Arc's example and leadership stimulated the birth of a national spirit, a kind of patriotism among the French. The victory against the English certainly created a kind of national feeling because the war had forced the French, more so than in the past, to think "French" as they fought against a common enemy, the English. But if there was a hint of national feeling, it was still a feeling in its infancy. South of the Loire, people living in Occitania did not speak the same language as the people living in the north, who spoke the language of Oïl. Even today, the Occitans still resent the role of northern France in the Albigensian Crusade. In the north too, people felt more Norman, Bourguignon etc. . . . than French. In the fourteenth century the kings wanted to impose their law over the whole country, but no later than the fifteenth century they had to backtrack and recognize some autonomy to the provinces. But some positive things too happened at the end of the Middle Ages; if there were occasional revolts, there was no revolution, no desire to change society. Besides, people after the miseries of the Hundred Years War were convinced that nothing was worse than a revolt, than disorder or war. In other words, people obeyed the king as long as he brought them bread and peace. People were tired of suffering, tired of war, of fighting, and by siding with their king they hoped to be able to finally live better. Hence the fifteenth century saw the birth of a society of compromise, believing that things would be better if everyone kept to his own rank and affairs. Some had the power, others the money; the people had peace in exchange, and the king knew how far he could go in exercising authority.

The Sixteenth Century: The Renaissance

Although we seem to make a clear-cut distinction between the end of Middle Ages and the Renaissance period, it must be remembered that in reality there was no obvious sudden change between the two periods.

Before the sixteenth century Renaissance, there was in fact a Medieval Renaissance as early as the twelfth century, with the humanist work of clerics copying in manuscripts the works of Antiquity. So it must be understood that this medieval humanism prepared the way for Renaissance humanism. Naturally Renaissance humanism came about under new influences and brought about a new spirit and ideas.

The Renaissance was a period of literary, artistic and scientific renewal under the influence of the culture of Antiquity transmitted by the Italian humanists and artists who were much in advance of their other European brothers. The invention of printing also greatly helped the spread of knowledge. The Renaissance was also a period of discoveries, of travels. New frontiers were discovered, new horizons sought in art, literature, science and astronomy thanks to the enthusiasm of adventurers, erudite scholars, poets and artists. The Renaissance with its huge appetite for knowledge could have been an even greater century if it had not been damaged by fanaticism and intolerance that led to the disastrous wars of religion.[97] Some good, however, came out of them, if nothing else the human reaction of great minds like Erasmus, Montaigne and others, and the fact that it inspired many of the greatest works of the sixteenth century.[98]

Some Dates
1539: Latin was replaced by French as the official language.
1562–1589: The Wars of Religion between Catholics and Protestants.
1598: The Edit de Nantes grants freedom of worship to Protestants.

Renaissance Humanism

Renaissance Humanism was born in Italy around the mid-fourteenth century. The Italian elite was attracted by all the glories of Classical Antiquity. Latin was praised as the richest and most cultured of all languages. Humanists sought knowledge with boundless energy and dug relentlessly into the remains of Greek and Latin cultures. Renaissance clerics searched without pause to find copies of the great works of Antiquity so that they could copy them and make them available to the scholarly public.

From Italy, the Italian Renaissance first passed to Germany, flourishing at the court of Maximilian I in the last years of the fifteenth century and early sixteenth century. But the Reformation silenced the movement because Reformers believed that man was basically sinful, while Humanists thought the opposite. So the Reformation brought the German Humanist movement to a rapid close.

France was more receptive to Italian Humanism as early as 1500 with scholars like Lefèvre d'Etaples[99] and Guillaume Budé,[100] who fostered the study of Greek works and moved François Ier to establish the *Collège de France.*

French Renaissance was greatly advanced by the Italian artists who were brought to France by the king. Almost naturally, there rose in France schools of poets, writers and painters who were emulated by their Italian brothers: The group of poets, *La Pléiade,* headed by Joachim du Bellay (1524–1560) and Pierre Ronsard (1524–1585), the writers and philosophers Rabelais (1494–1553) and Montaigne (1533–1592) are famous representatives of French Humanism.

A Renaissance Prince: François Ier

Louis XII's successor was a very different person. While Louis XII was sickly and often morose, François Ier[101] was a handsome, radiant, charming man, connoisseur of art and fond of beautiful things. As such he was a humanist, a Renaissance prince, an intelligent protector of the arts and letters who brought some great Italian artists to France such as Leonardo da Vinci. As a great patron of scholars, artists and poets, François Ier enhanced the magnificence of monarchy and also its power. The last feudal barons soon lost whatever little power they had, and the court of the king became the new cultural and political center of the kingdom. François Ier would have been one of the greatest French kings, but he had an unfortunate dream: he wanted to gain glory in wars. And indeed, he fought five wars, against Henry VIII of England, against Charles V of the Holy Roman Empire and against Italy. In fact he wanted to conquer the duchy of Milan, and if he obtained it in the end, it was only in exchange of giving up his claims over Naples. All in all the Italian wars were a great waste, but as it happens frequently, there were some positive consequences to these evil wars: they contributed to the discovery and influence in France of the Italian Renaissance. Not only did François Ier bring the great Leonardo da Vinci to France, but also Benvenuto Cellini, Francesco Primaticcio, Andrea del Sarto and others. The reign of François Ier was surely a period of rebirth of classical learning, of creation of new art forms, of building beautiful *châteaux* along the Loire, Chambord, Blois and others. The king was also responsible for the renovation of the Louvre, for founding with Guillaume Budé[102] the National Library of France *(La Bibliothèque Nationale).* François Ier encouraged freedom of intellectual thought and encouraged great minds such as Rabelais and Erasmus (1466–1536). In 1530 the king created a new college teaching a variety of new subjects such as Hebrew, Greek, Latin philology and science, thus protecting them from the criticism of the Sorbonne. This college is the ancestor of our *Collège de France*.

After this mostly successful and even brilliant reign, François Ier died with heavy debts and after inaugurating the persecution of Protestants by his massacre of the Vaudois (Waldensians).[103]

The Reformation and the Wars of Religion

The Sixteenth century was a time of powerful religious vitality that culminated in the development of Protestantism in the Age of the Reformation, a period of momentous changes in almost all aspects of society. It mainly saw the abolition of the religious status quo. Grievances against the Catholic Church grew in number and bitterness. It was criticized for its worship of saints, for its wealth and above all for granting indulgences.[104] Spiritual Reformers and preachers believed that the Church and society were corrupt and that a return to true piety was necessary. The Conciliarists and Humanists were less rigid, but they too demanded a reform of the Church from within, and the knowledge of the Bible. They thought that if men were educated, since they were basically good they would improve. The "Dean" of Humanists was Erasmus, born in Rotterdam in 1466. He thought that education was the supreme key to a changed world and a change in the ethics of men. He even wished that every plowboy could whistle the Psalms while furrowing the soil. Erasmus' wisdom certainly touched many among the elite, but education is a slow process, so he did not touch the hearts or beliefs of the masses. However, Luther and his disciples did. In Zurich, Switzerland, Ulrich Zwingli, John Calvin in Geneva, William Farel and Pierre Viret in France[105] had one purpose: to challenge the Church of Rome. After the promulgation of the Edict of Nantes (*Edit de Nantes*) in favor of the Huguenots, the Catholic Church started to take steps to stop the Protestant tide. During the period called the Counter Reformation, Catholic bishops met at the Council of Trent (1545–1564) seeking to redefine Church dogma. Catholic missionaries were also sent all over the world to make converts, and the Jesuits, a new strict order of priests, started to teach and preach. A new set of churchmen began to rule, strong and severe Popes like Paul IV. Under the guidance of these Counter-Reformation spiritual leaders, and afraid of their ire, Catholics began to embrace more humble, pious lives. Monks no longer could keep concubines and bishops were expected to be more frugal. It was in 1547 that the confessional boxes that can still be seen today were introduced so that the priest had less opportunity to be tempted by women penitents.

Both the Renaissance and Reformation movements contributed to the most incredible revolution in letters. The major contributions of the six-teenth century letters were made in France as well as in Spain and En-gland. The Reformation movement caused the reexamination of the early versions of the Scriptures and the Renaissance rediscovery of Greek and Latin Classics. Aside from Erasmus,[106] whose *Bible* was translated into German by Luther, the French monk François Rabelais was a brilliant second, ridiculing the indolence, the greed of the clergy, while at the same time calling Calvin "a mad devil" and "the impostor of Geneva"! Rabelais' main contribution was surely to confront the new humanistic trends with the old medieval ways. He rejected the pessimistic views of Reformers, declaring that far from being sinful, men could be good through learning and pleasure. Montaigne, like Rabelais,[107] contributed to France's resis-tance to Protestantism. Erasmus, Rabelais and Montaigne are just the first string of many other great thinkers, philosophers of the Renaissance such as Machiavelli in Italy, Cervantes in Spain, Edmund Spenser and Shakespeare in England.

Interestingly, the cultural revolution of the sixteenth century ended with the waning of Greek and Latin learning and the rise of vernaculars. By the close of the Renaissance and the Reformation, letters were no longer the sole privilege of scholars, the clergy or the very rich. They were more and more accessible to the people and the development of printing largely contributed to this swift dissemination of ideas to a larger public.

The Wars

The introduction in France of the Protestant religious movement called the Reformation[108] unleashed a series of fierce religious civil wars. During the fourteenth and fifteenth centuries, the Church faced many problems, the main one being the Great Schism, but there were many others, the corruption, the luxury of great Church leaders, the Church's sale of indul-gences,[109] etc. The Reformists claimed that drastic changes and a renewal of faith were necessary. Martin Luther, a monk like Rabelais, believed that a new faith supported by strict values was needed. The Reformation movement therefore was to religion what Humanism was to arts, letters and philosophy. Conceived as a new freedom for man, the Reformation soon turned out to be something different, veering away from freedom and joy. Papal authority was totally rejected and the Bible replaced the Church as a rule of faith and life. In other words, austerity and Puritanism became the new moral and religious codes. The Huguenots were not seeking a new freedom, they demanded a righteous life. While Humanism sought a new freedom for thought, Calvinism that invaded France with the publication of Calvin's *L'Institution chrétienne,* preached the infallibility of the Scriptures and condemned free will. It preached Christian simplicity and required the elimination of all superfluous sacraments. The result of the Huguenots' unbending tenacity was both war and misery. The reaction of the Catholics was just as violent as that of the Huguenots. The Protestants were considered as rebels against the Church and State, and Calvinism was perceived as a threat and even a heresy, and as such condemned by severe edicts.

While François Ier was a rather tolerant king,[110] his successors were not, and from 1560 to the abjuration of Henri IV in 1593 France knew no rest from the religious wars. Henri II fought the Protestants without mercy, chiefly under the influence of the Guise clan, and neither François II, Charles IX nor Henri III were able to put an end to the conflict. In fact under the last Valois, Charles IX[111] and Henri III,[112] France was ravaged by civil discords. Catherine de Médicis at first tried to maintain peace between the two factions and played the two parties against each other, but in 1572, seeing that it was impossible and fearing the growing influence of Gaspard de Coligny over the king, she decided to strike a major blow against the Huguenots. Taking advantage of a great gathering of Huguenot leaders in Paris to celebrate the marriage of Henry of Navarre, Catherine de Médicis decided to rid herself of the heads of the Huguenot party at a single blow. In the resulting massacre of St. Bartholomew some thousands of Huguenots were dragged from their beds after midnight and brutally murdered. On August 24, 1572, Coligny was taken out of his house, castrated, decapitated and torn into pieces. Similar massacres were perpetrated across the country and only a few Huguenots escaped, with the exception of those who converted to Catholicism, a sword to their throats. These outrageous murders aroused the fury of the Huguenots and led to a renewal of the religious civil war, with ever increasing atrocities on both sides. Companies of foreign mercenaries were hired: Spanish troops, at the invitation of the Guise clan, invaded France, and Protestant towns like Rouen and La Rochelle appealed to England to invade France. But England had other problems, and in the long run neither side seemed able to win. Consequently, there were many truces that always expired into further wars because the Huguenots felt no security and the Catholics did not want to recognize what they considered heresy. The Huguenots' cause would have been desperate, but 24-year-old Charles IX died on May 30, 1574, sick with remorse for having been too blind and too weak to prevent the St. Bartholomew slaughters. The Crown then passed to the Duke of Anjou, Henri III, who was to be stabbed in the stomach by a Dominican monk on August 1, 1589. His last words were to exhort Henri IV to convert to Catholicism. Henri de Guise, the Catholic party chief who was trying to depose Henri III, was also assassinated by a Protestant fanatic. The throne then became legally vacant for the Huguenot chieftain Henri de Navarre, who assumed the royal name of Henri IV.[113]

Before Henri IV sat on the throne, Catherine de Médicis was still in power, but more interested in astrology, poetry, music and ballet than in crushing heretics, so she decided to lean toward moderation and accepted the Peace of Beaulieu in 1576. That gave back the Huguenots their right of worship. However, Henri III questioned the right of worship and thereby stirred more violence. The civil war did not stop with the accession of Henri IV. The Huguenots, although a minority, were a minority determined to survive, but on the other hand the majority of the French people had no desire to accept Calvinism. The Catholics of Paris, the majority, could not accept a heretic king within its walls. So, Henri IV decided to abjure the Protestant faith and to convert to Catholicism on July 23, 1593, in the St. Denis Basilica, promising a fight against the heretic Huguenots. Henri IV is reported to have said at this occasion: "Paris is well worth a mass." The Huguenots, naturally, who were elated to have one of theirs king, felt betrayed and alarmed for their own safety. Henri IV tried to reassure the Huguenots, and to bring peace between the two factions, he promulgated the *Edit de Nantes* on April 15, 1598.[114] The Huguenots were thereby granted freedom of cult, conscience, worship and equitable justice. The Huguenot minority, somewhat reassured, became less rebellious, but the rest of the French viewed the *Edit de Nantes* with suspicion, and some towns even refused to recognize the edict as the law of the land. Henri IV then decided to impose the edict and succeeded in reducing Catholic opposition by granting favors to the Jesuits. Thus, the Huguenots were protected by the king, but certainly not accepted by the people. Having appeased the religious controversy, Henri IV brought an end to the wars by the Treaty of Cateau-Cambresis that granted full liberty of religion to the Protestants. He also did everything in his power to help the country recover from the civil wars and he is said to have wanted for every French family "*la poule au pot*" (a chicken in the pot). Henri IV worked hard putting back together the ruined government; he collected taxes, disciplined the army and supervised carefully the administration of justice. He can be said to have laid the foundation of the future royal absolutism of the Bourbons. But, on May 14, 1610, a crazed fanatic, François Ravaillac,[115] who thought that Henri IV was a menace to the Catholic Church, assassinated the king. Henri IV was remembered by most Frenchmen as the "good king Henri" because they recognized his personal kindness and that he tried hard to improve their life by repairing the country's economy and launching great construction projects (bridges, roads, canals).

Unfortunately, all the efforts of Henri IV to settle the Protestant problem proved to be intolerable to the Catholic majority. Under the king's widow, Marie de Médicis, the nobility and the upper Catholic clergy grew restless again and forced the summoning of the Estates-General. But Marie, seeing nothing but distrustful and conflicting interests among the participants, dismissed the Estates in 1615. In fact no meeting of the Estates-General took place until the French Revolution. It was therefore the king alone who conducted the affairs of the national government.

After Henri IV:
Marie de Médicis, Cardinal Richelieu and Louis XIII

When Henri IV died, Louis XIII was only nine years old and therefore too young to reign, so Marie de Médicis hurried in having herself recognized as Regent of the kingdom, but she brought along her foster sister's husband, an Italian adventurer named Concini.[116] For all practical purposes Marie and Concini became the rulers of France. Unfortunately, Concini was a social climber without scruples and a very poor statesman. He succeeded in winning over the nobility by showering money upon them, and thus held his undeserved power even when Louis XIII became increasingly jealous of his power. With Concini the finances of the kingdom, which had been so well managed by Sully,[117] practically vanished. When Louis XIII was fourteen, he was declared "of age" and capable of assuming his royal responsibilities. His most ardent desire was to get rid of Concini, who held on, fighting back with heavy bribes. So, Louis XIII, enraged, decided to join a plot with Charles de Luynes,[118] against Concini and have him killed. On August 24, 1617, a captain of the guards, captain Vitry, shot Concini in the Louvre.[119] Immediately Luynes took Concini's place, but as he became as greedy as Concini, he was sent away to restore order among some revolting Protestants, and there, Vitry fell ill and died in December 1621. Marie de Médicis, who had been removed from the Court, was still waiting in the wings. Upon Vitry's death, she came back somewhat in favor and managed to have her confident, Cardinal Richelieu, accepted by Louis XIII, first as member of the king's council, but soon after as the king's prime minister. Although Louis XIII did not trust Richelieu, he recognized his political genius.[120] Thanks to Richelieu, Louis XIII defeated the Protestants, who lost most of the benefits and freedoms they had acquired with the *Edit de Nantes*. Richelieu prohibited individual fighting (duels), and ordered the destruction of all castles that were not serving the king. The Huguenots lost their fortified cities, their military and territorial rights but still retained their religious and civil rights. But the Protestant problem was only a small affair next to the *Thirty Years War*, a political and religious conflict that affected most of central Europe. It began in 1618 and ended in 1648 by the Treaty of Westphalia. The cause of the war was the antagonism of Protestants and Catholics and the ambitions of the House of Austria. France was involved directly in one of the periods of the war, as Richelieu intervened against Austria. It was thanks to the victories of France that the Austrians decided to sign the Peace of Westphalia (1648).

When Louis XIII died and after Richelieu's death in 1642, France reverted to a regency and Cardinal Mazarin (1602–1661),[121] a shrewd diplomat like Richelieu, pursued the cardinal's objectives, which placed the new king, Louis XIV, on solid political grounds and assured his uncontested authority. Louis XIV could and did become an absolute monarch. Mazarin prepared Louis XIV for the succession of Spain by arranging his marriage with Marie-Thérèse, but in the end, Mazarin, who left France in perfect order to Louis XIV, while retaining his considerable political power, became very unpopular because of his self-serving greed.[122] Louis XIV, himself, although declared of age in 1652, never dared to claim the Crown as long as Mazarin lived.

The Seventeenth Century, the Classical Period, Louis XIV (Sun King)[123]

Louis XIV was born on September 5, 1638, in St. Germain-en-Laye. He acceded to the throne in 1643 and died in Versailles on September 1, 1715. He was buried in St. Denis. He had married Marie-Thérèse of Spain on June 9, 1660, in St. Jean-de-Luz. From her, he had one child, the Dauphin Louis de France. He married a second time on June 12,

1684, in Versailles Françoise d'Aibigné, with whom he had one child, Mademoiselle Françoise Marie de Blois.

Louis XIV inherited his throne in 1643 at the age of five, but assumed the direction of affairs only at the age of twenty-three in 1661. He went on to reign for seventy-two years until his death in 1715. It is clear that no king in modern history held a similar position of power for as long a time as Louis XIV. As he inherited the splendid achievements of Richelieu, Louis XIV was able to make of France during his long and brilliant reign the most powerful and admired country in Europe. During his lifetime and thanks to his efforts and taste, the French language, French ideas, literature, architecture, style and way of life became the models for Europe. Louis XIV was called Louis le Grand (the Great), the Sun King.[124]

Louis had a sense of his destiny; he became convinced that he was God's agent on earth, and this belief was reinforced by Bishop Bossuet,[125] who in his sermons told the king's subjects that the king ought to be obeyed as if he were God himself. With such a reinforcement of his belief, there was little room for humility in Louis. This explains why he developed his court life around him so that he could control his nobles by making them increasingly dependent on the king and on Versailles' brilliant life.[126] Louis XIV was an energetic ruler and anxious for glory. He organized carefully the institutions of the government and worked tirelessly for the growth of France's industry and commerce. The king was assisted in his task by two excellent men, Fouquet and Colbert. Colbert "carried a big stick": he prohibited strikes, increased work hours and eliminated many holidays. Always trying to develop France's commerce, Colbert encouraged colonial enterprises, and purchased slaves in Africa to make them work on sugar plantations in the West Indies. Unfortunately, in spite of his zeal, Colbert could not prevent huge deficits in his treasury, deficit mainly due to Louis XIV's ambitious foreign policy.

In the domain of religious affairs, Louis XIV was a strong Catholic and therefore he detested the Jansenists and the Protestants. His motto was "One king, one law, one faith." It is no surprise then that on October 18, 1685, he signed the Revocation of the Edict of Nantes, removing from the Protestants their right of worship. As a consequence up to 300,000 Protestants left France.

It was in his foreign policy that Louis XIV's ambition and arrogance appeared as excessive as they were futile in the long run. Louis XIV had clear expansionist ideas; first he wanted to push the borders of France eastward and he wanted to obtain the Spanish inheritance for himself. To these ends, Louis XIV intrigued with some German princes and with

England even. Louis XIV thus became a menace in Europe as his ambitions became clearer and bolder. One man decided to resist Louis XIV; it was the Dutch William III, Prince of Orange who would later become king of England and Scotland. When Louis XIV, in 1667, decided that he could legally claim and take the Spanish Netherlands and Franche-Comté,[127] the Dutch allied themselves with England and Sweden. Louis XIV was temporarily intimidated and renounced his claims, keeping nevertheless a few Flemish towns. Louis XIV then intrigued, bribing the English and the Swedes away from their alliance with the Dutch, and in 1672 Louis XIV crossed easily into the Spanish Netherlands and occupied three of the seven Dutch provinces. It was then that William of Orange allied himself with Denmark, Brandenburg, and the Austrian and Spanish Habsburgs. Louis XIV again had to give up his ideas of conquest and in 1678 signed the Treaty of Nimwegen by which he retained the Franche-Comté and a few more towns of Flanders, but had to abandon the Dutch territory he had conquered. In spite of some failures, the main one being his inability to achieve his grand plan of universal monarchy, Louis XIV managed to die with great dignity on September 1, 1715, and remained in the eyes of the French and of Europe a great monarch.

French Civilization under Louis XIV: The Classical Period

Louis XIV reigned over a country of 21,000,000 inhabitants, which made it four times as populous as England and twice as populous as Spain. The French nation was the most powerful of Europe, the wealthiest, the strongest commercially, trading in India, Madagascar, the Levant and discovering Canada, the Great Lakes, the Mississippi valley and the West Indies. France, with the Sun King, was at the forefront of civilization; its art and literature were admired and emulated throughout Europe. In fact it was not the armed forces of the king that swept Europe in the seventeenth century, but French thought, the French language, Descartes and the great Classical authors, Molière, Racine, Corneille, La Fontaine.[128] The ideal man of the Classical period was the *honnête homme* and the classical writers, poets, artists are the *honnêtes hommes*, who wrote or painted for the *honnêtes gens* (civilized, cultured people). Grandeur, magnificence and splendor, these three words qualify the XVIIth century, an age dominated by finesse, elegance, order, reason, good taste, clarity and authority. All these values peaked under Louis XIV, but were soon menaced by new trends. Very much in the same way that Classicism replaced the

Baroque Renaissance, Classicism was replaced by less high, more natural tastes and styles ushered by the Age of Enlightenment (*Le Siècle des Lumières*), the eighteenth century.

Louis XIV's Royal Absolutism

While French culture dominated Europe, the regime of absolute monarchy of Louis XIV reigned over France, represented by the king's motto:"*L'Etat c'est moi*" (I am the state). According to Louis XIV and Bishop Bossuet, law was the will of the king so long as it conformed to the law that was the will of God. In other words the divine right of the king was established and popularly accepted in France at the time.

If Louis XIV had dreams for France beyond its borders, he had similar dreams for France within the borders. First of all he made sure that he was in full control of the army, which he reorganized completely and increased its size to about 400,000 men. Second, Louis XIV reorganized the administration of the government and made it more efficient by hiring a large number of assistants, inspectors, supervising agents of the central governments and clerks.

Colbert and Finances

With all his dreams and with the expenses of war and of Versailles, Louis XIV needed money, so he turned to one great minister, Colbert,[129] who succeeded in efficiently streamlining tax collecting, improving the finances of the state and strengthening French commerce in general.

Louis XIV, with Colbert's assistance, greatly improved the economy of France and similarly greatly improved the life of the French middle and even lower classes. For the common people and peasants, Louis XIV did protect them from the lords that exploited them and thus freed them from the burden of serfdom. On the other hand Louis XIV showered the nobles with privileges and thus kept them quiet, but at a prohibitive cost. So, all in all, Louis XIV was popular with most social classes. What made this popularity wither in the end was the sufferings and deaths caused by his wars.

Louis XIV and Religion

Louis XIV had also a religious dream: he considered that religious unity was necessary to the strength of his rule and of monarchy. Therefore, since he was a Catholic king, he repressed the Protestants and the Jansenists, whom he saw as heretics among his subjects. These views naturally led Louis XIV to revoke the Edict of Nantes, making the life of Protestants close to unbearable and forcing many to leave the country.

The Reign of Louis XV

Louis XV was born in Versailles on February 15, 1710. The great-grand-son of Louis XIV, he was only a five-year-old orphan when he began to reign in 1715.[130] The Regency therefore was entrusted to Louis'elder cousin, Philippe, Duke of Orléans, who was then forty-one years old. He immediately met the opposition of the nobles who had resented Louis XIV's absolute power. The Regent, who did not have the authority of a monarch, had to let many nobles who had been ousted by Louis XIV back in the government. In fact, under Louis XV many nobles who had been deprived of power under Louis XIV regained powers. In addition the Parliament of Paris and many provincial parliaments that had been silenced by Louis XIV reasserted themselves. With Philippe, incredulity and licentiousness emerged. The Court was brought back from Versailles to Paris and, following the Regent's example, went wild with pleasures.

Louis XV, as he came of age, proved to be indolent and selfish and he left most of the public affairs in charge of the Abbé de Fleury, Louis XV's old tutor, who was seventy-three years old when he took office, and ninety when he left it. The Duke of Bourbon, who thought that Fleury was too old, made an attempt to dismiss him, but it made Louis XV so furious that he dismissed Bourbon and gave Fleury,[131] soon to be made cardinal, the task of governing with the title of Minister of State. Louis XV, who was basically lazy, saw that in this way he could postpone assuming his responsibilities. And Louis XV did just that until Fleury's death in 1743. Fleury, in fact, had not been a bad choice; he was a shy, quiet, peaceful man whose main interest was to reorganize the state finances and keep peace in France and abroad. His long service was a good thing considering that Louis XV was not really apt at governing the country. But in 1743, when Fleury died, Louis XV had to begin to rule himself. He was then forty-three. Since his main passion was women, the king soon fell under the spell of several of them who were to have a great deal of influence on him. He fell for a certain Jeanne Poisson, whom he made Marquise de Pompadour and lodged her close to him in Versailles. She was a beautiful and intelligent woman, but most of all crafty, and she used her charms on the king, who could not resist her. She encouraged the pleasures at the Court and soon began to meddle in political affairs.[132] Before dying in 1764, Madame de Pompadour kindly introduced several young ladies to the king and, not surprisingly, he fell in love with a certain Jeanne Bécu, whom he soon made Countess Du Barry, and settled her in the Versailles palace. Under the Du Barry's influence, the king became even more disinterested in state affairs. Because of his indifference, Louis XV began to destroy the bond that existed between the king and the country and, in fact, prepared the way for the total breakdown that was to occur between people, state and monarchy when monarchy rolled off the guillotine with Louis XVI's head. The king's behavior with the Du Barry[133] became so scandalous and shameless that, when he died on May 10, 1774, of smallpox, he was hated so much that his men had to sneak his body out to St. Denis at night.[134] In consequence, very few positive achievements can be attributed to Louis XV, perhaps with the exception that he managed to reunite Lorraine and Corsica to France.

In spite of his disinterest in government, Louis XV had to fight several wars. One against Austria to support Stanislas Leszczinski in the war of succession of Poland (1733–1735), one against Austria for the Austrian succession (1740–1748), the Seven Years' War (1756–1763) that began in America and was a phase in the long dispute between France and England. Louis XV, as usual, negotiated at any price and the price was for France the loss of a part of its overseas colonies, including India, and the loss to the British of the land of Canada. In addition the territories west of the Mississippi were surrendered to Spain in compensation for their loss of Florida because they had fought on the side of France.

The irony of it all is that with Louis' laziness, indifference and corruption, France appeared to be a prosperous country, even under the king's dubious government. The administration prospered, the population increased, agriculture became more productive and France even became a major industrial power. This prosperity benefited the bourgeois, who became wealthy and grew in number and influence. Paris at the same time was becoming the hub of culture and arts and the French language became the international aristocratic tongue of Europe.

Louis XV died in 1774.

Louis XVI (1774–1792)[135]

Louis XVI, though far superior in personal habits than his grandfather and possessed with a genuine desire to govern, was pious and virtuous, but he was fat, rather clumsy[136] and lacked sustained willpower. He also ate in excess so that he would often fall asleep during meetings or other functions in Versailles. Contrary to Louis XIV, Louis XVI had a very common appearance and, even when dressed in the best garments, never looked elegant. His big love was hunting and aside from this sport, Louis XVI had little taste for the arts and music, and he was too clumsy to dance. In spite of these drawbacks, Louis XVI was liked by the French people. He appeared to have a good heart[137] and to be worthy of trust. His wife, Marie-Antoinette, was beautiful, charming and at ease in society, in contrast with Louis XVI, who was clumsy and very ill at ease with people. Louis XVI adored his wife to a fault, while Marie-Antoinette had only contempt for him, seeking frivolous pleasures away from him. She was also a spendthrift, so much so that she was soon nicknamed "*Madame déficit.*" The fact that she was the daughter of the Austrian empress alienated her from the affection of the French, who remembered that for three hundred years Austria had been France's enemy. In fact, Marie-Antoinette never became French. She looked at the French from an Austrian point of view, and so the French were very unhappy, not only because they hated the queen, but because France faced crisis after crisis, mostly due to the national debt, which was huge and which tripled after 1774. Between 1775 and 1778 there were many violent riots because of food shortages and heavy taxes. Louis XVI was faced with an emergency situation, but he could not cope with it. The finances of the state were further drained by France's involvement in the American War of Independence,[138] a way for France to get back at England. Of course there was a more positive aspect to France's assistance to young America. A number of young noblemen, the famous Marquis de Lafayette among them, went to the help of the American patriots. Soon Benjamin Franklin came to France and dazzled the Court, its women and Parisian salons. But when the war ended in America, France did not gain much. First of all the Americans signed a unilateral treaty with England, and France only managed to recover later a few minor territories, the islands of St. Pierre et Miquelon off Newfoundland, that it had lost through the Treaty of Paris in 1763. The consequences of the American war were serious for France, particularly because it showed the French people a model of government founded on democratic principles. In addition it drastically emptied the coffers of France to the point that it required a meeting of the Estates-General to examine what measures could be taken. Ironically, this meeting did not do much for France's finances, but more importantly, it precipitated the fall of the Old Regime.

Background of the French Revolution.
The Eighteenth Century: Age of Enlightenment.
New Ideas Germinate.

If the reign of Louis XIV marked the apex of French Monarchy, the eighteenth century would bring it down. Already under Louis XV, Versailles gradually ceased to be the center of social, political and intellectual life. Versailles was abandoned in favor of Paris, and gatherings started to take place in Parisian cafés and fashionable salons, where all sorts of new "philosophical" ideas began to circulate, often under the disguise of wit. These "philosophical" ideas would become in time subversive and revolutionary under the pens of great minds such as Voltaire, Montesquieu and Diderot.[139] Under the intellectual leadership of such men, new ideas began to circulate, rejecting tradition, metaphysics and theological dogmas. In the same way as Classicism was a new humanism in the seventeenth century, the Enlightenment ushered in a new humanism called *L'Esprit Philosophique* that opened the minds of the time to such ideas as freedom and denounced intolerance and despotism. This *esprit philosophique* also brought about an incredible enthusiasm for everything that contributed to man's happiness. Science took the place that had been held by metaphysics, and Royal Absolutism was seriously questioned. This change in mood, fashions and beliefs did not cause a decline in civilization; on the contrary, it brought about a brilliant new civilization called the Enlightenment.[140] France remained a model for Europe by its language, literature, elegant life, and the sharp wit of its intellectuals. This age opened France to the outside world and many foreign monarchs became admirers of France and invited many of its writers and philosophers to visit their Court. Voltaire was invited to Prussia, and Diderot to the court of Tsarina Catherine II.[141] Ideas of tolerance from England began to take root in France, ideas that would soon explode in the 1789 Revolution. People no longer wanted gardens like Versailles, finding them too perfect, too cold, too symmetrical. They now liked gardens "*à l'anglaise*" (English style) with stones, streams, flowers, irregular, in short a disorganized nature. All these ideas matured and laid the ground for the great crisis which was to radically upset the conception of government and society in France, the French Revolution. In art and literature, reason was replaced by sensibility, emotions, all precursors of the pre-Romantic intellectual and esthetic revolution that was to accompany the social and political revolution. In fact the intellectual life of France was rejuvenated and exploded into various movements such as Romanticism, Realism and Symbolism. *Romanticism,* with Chateaubriand, Lamartine and Victor Hugo, favoring sensibility, imagination and emotions. Soon after *Realism and Naturalism* reacted against *Romanticism.* They no longer emphasized the soul, but became more interested in dreams, in the material world, the environment, physiology, psychology and society. Such interests appear in the novels of Balzac, Flaubert, Stendhal and Zola. The *Symbolist movement* that followed brought a new taste for idealism. Baudelaire stressed the hidden connections between the world of emotions and sensations and the supernatural world, with the mysteries of the unconscious. Among the great poets of this school were Verlaine, Mallarmé and Raimbaud. This poetic movement in turn opened the way to the great *impressionist movement* in art with Monet, Renoir, Degas, etc., all in quest of the mysterious qualities of light and forms. Reality was no longer so much represented but transposed through the veil of the unconscious and the interplay of light.

All in all, the Age of the Revolution was a period of social and political upheaval and global change for France and Europe. It can be said that 1789 marked the end of a form of civilization that would never return and to this day has not returned.

France at the Eve of the Revolution

On the eve of the Revolution, France was hardly less large than today; however, Mulhouse, the Duchy of Savoy and the County of Nice were outside the kingdom. Montbéliard belonged to the Duke of Wurtenberg and the Venaissin around Avignon belonged to the Pope. In 1785 the population of France was estimated at about 26 million[142] while England had only 12 million inhabitants, Spain 10 million and Prussia 6 million. In 1789 the French were the most numerous of all European peoples under a single government. The French birthrate was high, and families with 15 children were not rare among the paesants and bourgeois. The death rate was comparatively high due to the lack of hygiene (33 per 1000; however, during the second quarter of the eighteenth century the population had increased by 30%. This increase was due in large part to the disappearance of large-scale famines. The French as a whole were the wealthiest in Europe, but not per capita. It has been said that most of the gold circulating in Europe was French. French exports were greater than those of England. However, commercial exchanges within the kingdom were difficult and slow because there were only 48,000 kilometers of roads and by horse-driven carriage travel took a long time. For instance, it took three days to go from Paris to Lille and five days at least from Paris to Lyon and eleven days from Paris to Marseille. Waterways were used too for the transportation of goods, but circulation was also slow because many times barges had to be pulled by horses when going against the current. In spite of its apparent wealth, France was suffering from some severe economic problems due to the torrential rains and hail which ruined the crops in 1788, causing a steep increase in prices. Furthermore the large contributions of the French Crown to the War of Independence in America[143] made the situation even worse.

The French Revolution.
Declaration of the Rights of Man and the Citizen.
End of the Monarchy.

The Old Regime

The essential fact about the Old Regime was that it was legally aristocratic and in many ways feudal. That meant that everyone in society had a certain place according to a division in three estates or levels. The First Estate was the clergy, the Second Estate was the nobility, and the Third Estate included all those inferior to the first two, from the business and professional classes to the poorest peasantry. Out of the 26 million inhabitants of France there were over 20 million peasants. The nobility was on top of the pyramid with the higher clergy. They constituted about 1% of the population,[144] but they were the social elite because of their wealth and because of their position they enjoyed many privileges. They could levy taxes, hold important offices in the government, the Church and the army. They also dominated the country's cultural life. The clergy constituted an even smaller percentage of the population, less than 1%. They were between 110,000 and 120,000. But there were huge differences of status between the lower and the higher clergy that was often as rich as the nobility and enjoyed as many privileges. They also owned vast portions of land that brought them taxes, dues and in general vast incomes. The lower clergy enjoyed few privileges although they were those who did most of God's work in the towns and small villages of the provinces. As for the middle class, the bourgeois, wealthy city dwellers, rich merchants and bankers, they were perhaps more than two million and represented about 8% of the population. The bourgeois, even those with money, were scorned by the nobility, who feared that they would finally reach noble status. Conversely, the bourgeois' main aspiration was to eventually join the ranks of the nobility. In other words the bourgeois, even more than the oppressed lower classes, resented the privileged status of the nobility and it is no surprise that the most ardent leaders of the Revolution came from the bourgeoisie.[145] The lower classes, the peasants, represented roughly 80% of the population. Most of them possessed no land and were subjected to heavy taxes both by the king, clergy and nobles. The lot of the rest of the population, urban workers, household servants and small wage earners, was often worse than that of the peasants who at least could feed themselves.[146]

Under these conditions, apart from the happy few of the high clergy and nobility, most French people were suffering and unhappy with their social and economic situation. They were hoping that the king would do something to improve their lot, and almost to the end, many remained confident that Louis XVI would understand their plight and improve their life. Perhaps the king understood, but he did not act, and tried to forget the problems of state by hunting or playing locksmith. He was a kind man but acted like an ostrich when faced by a crisis. He stuck his head in the sand, rather than trying to confront problems.

The Financial Crisis Precipitates the Revolution

The Revolution was precipitated by a financial collapse of the government. Thus, although the country was prosperous, the government treasury was empty with a debt amounting to almost four billion *livres*. Louis XVI, unfortunately, had neither the ability nor possessed the required leadership qualities to deal with the terrible and worsening financial situation of the country. The nobles and the rich bourgeois did not want to lose their privileges and were even more reluctant to pay taxes, and they were furthermore exempt from the most important direct tax, *la taille*.

Finally the government was brought to a standstill, unable to collect taxes, unable to borrow money with army officers, intendants, administrators refusing to serve. The situation remained tense and blocked until July 1788 when representatives of the three orders (nobility, clergy and *tiers état*) met in the Château de Vizille in Dauphiné and declared that no taxes should be paid unless the king would convene the Estates-General.[147] In the meantime each electoral assembly drafted a list of grievances to be handed to the king. The consensus was that people wanted reforms, a less arbitrary government, equitable taxation and above all a constitution.[148] Louis XVI then promised to call the Estates-General and they met on May 5, 1789, in Versailles under the leadership of two men, Siéyes and Mirabeau.[149] By declaring itself the National Assembly, it repudiated the Old Régime. Louis XVI, under the pressure of the nobles, tried to close the meeting, but the members escaped to another hall, a neighboring tennis court. Once there they signed the *Serment du Jeu de Paume* (the Oath of the Tennis Court) on June 20, 1789, stating that they would not disband until they had drafted a constitution. The king tried to force them to disband, but in vain. The Assembly did not back down and the king found himself at a loss. Unfortunately, he gave in once more to the demands of the nobles and summoned a large contingent of soldiers to Versailles. There was no doubt that he was hoping to dissolve the Assembly by force. The result of the king's action, however, was that the Revolution gained momentum. People were afraid, so they armed themselves in self-defense. Riots erupted in Paris and all over France.[150] On July 14 a large crowd came to the *Bastille*, a prison for people with enough influence not to be put in common jails. The governor of the Bastille refused to give arms to the people, and did not want to remove a single cannon turned in the crowd's direction. So, in a confusing moment, the people assaulted the fortress, which was only defended by a handful of soldiers,[151] killed six soldiers, murdered the governor and the mayor of Paris. The capture of the Bastille was a minor incident, but became a momentous symbol. It appeared as if it had saved the Assembly of Versailles, freeing it from the menace of Louis XVI's soldiers.[152] And so the National Assembly restored order by meeting the demands of the people, by getting rid of all manorial obligations and consequently it abolished feudalism. The next step was taken on August 26, 1789, with the proclamation of the *Declaration of the Rights of Man and Citizen* that became the revolutionary rule in France and a model for the rest of Europe.

The king and his family tried to escape from Paris, but were recognized before reaching the border and brought back in shame to the capital. This failed attempt was to have serious consequences for the royal family and the monarchy: it provided a motive to those who wanted to get rid of Louis XVI and abolish the monarchy.

On September 30, 1791, the Constituent Assembly dissolved itself and was replaced by a new assembly that declared war against the king of Bohemia and Hungary on October 1, 1791. In the end, the revolutionary armies forced the Prussians to retreat at Valmy, but there was another insurrection in Paris that ended in the replacement of the current assembly by an executive council made up of revolutionary extremists who would soon begin a reign of terror.[153] The new assembly, the Convention, was to govern for three years from September 1792 to October 1795. Urged by the leader of the extremists, Maximilien de Robespierre,[154]

Louis XVI was put on trial, accused of being a traitor and condemned to death and shortly thereafter executed on the guillotine on January 21, 1793, on the Place de la Révolution, the current Place de la Concorde. The king's execution brought two new enemies against Revolutionary France, Spain and England. In order to face the foreign menace, the government remained revolutionary, that is to say, of an emergency character and the Reign of Terror increased in violence. It abolished Christianity and the Church Calendar. Instead a Republican calendar was adopted, its main purpose being the blot out from men's minds any reference to saints' days, Christian holidays and traditional names of the months. This was a part of the government's program of dechristianization.[155] Another part of the program of dechristianization was the founding of the Cult of Reason, reason being impersonated by a pretty young woman dressed in white flowing robes. In 1794 Robespierre introduced another cult called Worship of the Supreme Being, a sort of naturalistic cult which was supposed, in Robespierre's mind, to reconcile Catholics, agnostics and free thinkers. By the spring of 1794 the Revolutionary government had managed to gather an army of 800,000 men that was to earn some victories against the allied forces. These successes made the French aware that they no longer needed the Reign of Terror and that it was time to get rid of Robespierre. In fact on the 10th Thermidor (July 28, 1794) Robespierre was arrested and sent to the guillotine along with his sympathizers. After Robespierre's downfall, terror subsided and a new assembly was called with a new constitution, the Constitution of Year III; it was called The Directory (le Directoire) (1795–1799).

Under the Directory, Paris became a place of uncontrolled pleasures with extravagant fashions,[156] gambling, scandalous behaviors and general corruption. The Directory, while it managed to improve the situation of France internally, was unwilling or unable to end the war against the coalition. On the contrary, the new government thought it could improve its prestige by pushing beyond its borders. That is when Napoleon Bonaparte came into active play. He was a twenty-six-year old Corsican who had rendered services to the Convention, and who had previously driven the English out of Toulon and broken up demonstrations by Royalists. In 1796, he drove the Austrians out of Italy and forced them to agree to the Treaty of Campo Formio on October 17–18, 1797, that recognized France's possession of Belgium, of the Rhine boundaries and the creation of a Cisalpine and Ligurian Republic bound to France.[157] Even though Bonaparte had acted against the wishes of the Directory, he was a hero when he returned to France. The Directory was irritated and was happy to send him away on an expedition to Egypt. Bonaparte went and conquered Malta on the way, and after landing in Egypt, he defeated the Mamelukes near Cairo. After that victory, Bonaparte reorganized the country and grew confident that he could recapture Saint Jean d'Acre. But his attempt was a failure, which coincided with the destruction of the French fleet by the English Admiral Nelson in the Bay of Abukir. Naturally this victory gave new hopes to the coalition. At that point, however, Bonaparte, hearing that the Directory was in trouble, decided to return to France.[158] The French lost their previous conquests except Italy, but they forced the Anglo-Russian troops to surrender.

In the spring of 1797, there were elections and they were won by those who wanted peace, and most of those were Royalists. The Directory in panic called for Bonaparte's help and sent one of his generals to Paris with a military force. On September 4, 1797, there was a big purge: two of the Directors were ousted, and the elections were annulled. The old Republicans of the Convention took power on the ground that they were defending the Revolution, preventing the return of the Old Régime with Louis XVIII, who was waiting in the wings. That was the Coup d'Etat of Fructidor.[159]

A Cultural Survey of the Eighteenth Century

The Eighteenth century was a period of movement, of great change, ending in a violent crisis that brought monarchy to an end and introduced a new order. Cosmopolitanism was also a mark of the century. In politics a long period of intellectual and social fermentation led to the French Revolution while in literature Pre-Romanticism replaced the seventeenth century Classicism. Most of the literature of this period is closely linked with the ideas that inspired the French Revolution.

The Royal Court was no longer the intellectual and social center nor the source of ideas and opinions. Salons, cafés and clubs were the new hubs. The salons of prominent Parisian women like the Duchess of Maine, Mme Lambert, Mme Geoffrin, Melle Julie de Lespinasse were places where brilliant conversation shone and where poets, artists, writers and philosophers made their reputation. In the cafés, new modern ideas were exchanged and circulated. These cafés were the meeting place of many writers, thinkers and philosophers who there spread the revolutionary ideas which eventually led to the Revolution. Diderot attended the *Café de la Régence,* while the *Café Procope* was frequented by a host of philosophes and writers such as Voltaire, Fontenelle, Diderot, Marmontel.

Other cafés like the *Café Gradot* and the *Café Laurent* were also famous meeting places. The clubs, imported from England, also played an important part in the circulation of modern revolutionary ideas. Among these clubs, *Le Club de l'Entresol* was attended by thinkers interested in political ideas, men like Montesquieu and the Abbé de Saint Pierre.

In addition, the *philosophes* had the *Encyclopédie* as their main organ of expression. Started in 1751, this *Encyclopédie* was most influential because its aim was to expose what was wrong in the existing order, including religion, and it demonstrated the virtues of tolerance, natural law and science. The main contributors of the *Encyclopédie* were the lighthouses of the French Enlightenment, Voltaire, Diderot, Montesquieu, Rousseau and Condorcet.

The eighteenth century was also called *Le Siècle des Lumières* (Enlightenment). It was a period of frantic passion for new ideas, confident in human reason, science and progress. This philosophical spirit was the new humanism of the period, and all the more important that France then was a model for Europe with its art, literature, fashion and language. Most courts prided themselves of speaking French. Frederic II, King of Prussia, spoke French and admired Voltaire. France, on the other hand, opened itself to foreign ideas and influence. For instance, Voltaire and Montesquieu found their model of tolerance and liberty in England.

The eighteenth century was also a period of reaction against the Jansenist rigor of the seventeenth century. Passions and instincts took the place of reason and in certain circles of society cynicism and immorality were in fashion. Literature received the influence of England, of Newton, Swift, Shakespeare, Pope and Richardson. A strong current of sensibility, of emotions pervaded the poetry with the development of Pre-Romantic tendencies and feelings.

Among the great artists of the time were Watteau, Boucher, Fragonard and David for painting. In politics, revolutionary ideas were spoken and circulated by eloquent men like Mirabeau, Vergniaud, Danton and Robespierre.

The Rise of Napoleon Bonaparte

After the Fructidorian *coup d'état,* the Directory became an ineffective dictatorship increasingly relying upon the army. Bonaparte, meanwhile, was quietly observing the situation and waiting for his time. When he returned from Italy, he was greeted as a savior and given the command of the army that was to invade England. A wise general, Bonaparte thought that the landing of French troops in England was premature, and it is then that he went to Egypt. But we know that he suddenly came back from Egypt to France particularly because he had heard that the government looked for a general. Bonaparte, thirty years old, was chosen. No time was to be wasted: Napoleon executed the *Coup d'Etat* of Brumaire (November 9, 1799). That is how Napoleon proclaimed a new form of Republic that he called *Consulate*, with three consuls at its head and with Bonaparte as the First Consul.

The Consulate (1799–1804)

So, with the *Coup d'Etat* of 1799, France fell into the hands of a general, Napoleon Bonaparte,[160] who was, in the long run, to put an end to the French Revolution. Under the Consulate, France was governed by an enlightened despot who immediately set up a new constitution that did not give much room to parliamentary institutions. In reality, it was the First Consul who ran the country and made all the decisions. Napoleon did not meet much opposition because he promised, and obtained, what most people wanted, peace. And indeed, Napoleon defeated the Austrians at Marengo in June 1800 and made them sign the Treaty of Lunéville in February 1801. In March 1802 Napoleon made peace with England. He also restored order within the country by improving the administration. Bonaparte also judged that it was in his interest to settle with the Church, so he signed a *Concordat* with the Vatican in 1801. If it is true that he met some opposition from the old Jacobins Revolutionaries, he gained friends among the counter-revolutionaries. Obviously, Bonaparte was an eighteenth-century rationalist who did not believe in religion except as a means and convenience. This being done, Napoleon turned to introduce in-depth reforms within France. He established a Civil Code, also called *Code Napoleon*, and codes of civil and criminal procedure as well as commercial and penal codes, all applied uniformly all over France.[161] Napoleon also reformed education in order to prepare France's elite to be his best servants.[162] He brought order to French finances and encouraged the creation of the *Banque de France* (Bank of France).

As a sign of gratitude for his achievements in France, Bonaparte was asked to remain Consul another ten years, but typically this offer was not enough to satisfy his growing ambition, and instead he chose to declare himself Consul for life on August 2, 1801. But that was not yet enough for Bonaparte. Three years later, on May 18, 1804, he proclaimed himself hereditary Emperor under the title of Napoleon I.

The Emperor at the Zenith of His Glory (1809–1811)
His Fall (1812–1814)

In 1809 the French emperor was forty years old, having weathered many crises, defeated many enemies and signed many treaties. He became master of Italy, made peace with Russia, set up a blockade against England, but had to abandon the plan of conquest of the country. But Napoleon had no heir from his wife Josephine. A practical man, the emperor divorced Josephine in 1809, and in 1810 he married Marie-Louise, daughter of the Austrian emperor and niece of Marie Antoinette. She bore him a son whom he entitled the King of Rome.

By 1811 Napoleon had Europe in his grip, and he then felt that he could push his conquest a step further. In June 1812 Napoleon led his army into Russia. He wanted a *Blitzkrieg*, but soon things went wrong; each victory was at the cost of massive losses, but, almost by miracle, Napoleon entered Moscow on September 14, 1812. The problem was that the Russians had withdrawn, but they were still strong and unwilling to negotiate. Then winter came, unusually severe. The Grand army began to withdraw and soon was reduced to a mass of frozen, hungry, harassed, starving fugitives. Of the 640,000 men who went to Russia, 400,000 died during the retreat. The Prussians joined the fight against the French, and at the same time the Spanish troops chased the French out of Spain. On March 31, 1814, the Czar and his army entered Paris. Napoleon abdicated and was sent into exile to the Mediterranean island of Elba. And the Bourbon dynasty was restored with Louis XVIII.

The Restoration of the Bourbon Monarchy: Louis XVIII
Then the Return of Napoleon: *(Les Cent Jours)*

Since Louis XVI's son had died in captivity during the Revolution, Louis XVIII (1755–1824), Louis XVI's younger brother, who had fled to England, was declared the legitimate heir to the throne. The First Restoration lasted only one hundred days. Once more Louis XVIII had to flee to Gand (Ghent) in Belgium. Napoleon's return renewed Europe's fears of napoleonic wars and French aggression. On June 18, 1815, Napoleon met Wellington at Waterloo, and there the French were routed and Napoleon once more taken prisoner, and this time sent into exile far away to the island of St. Helena, an English possession. Napoleon would never escape and died on the island, probably poisoned,[163] on May 5, 1821.

France suffered much from the Hundred Days (*les Cent Jours*) interlude. The country found itself occupied and heavily taxed.

Louis XVIII's Successors:
Charles X[164] and Louis Philippe,[165] and the
February Revolution of 1848

Fat and ailing with gout, Louis XVIII returned to power, but not for long because he died in 1824. To Louis' credit, it must be said that he succeeded in keeping the ultra royalists at bay, in bringing back a degree of liberty that had disappeared under Napoleon, and, most importantly, he paid up the war indemnity imposed by the coalition, thereby bringing about the withdrawal from France of the foreign troops of occupation.

Louis XVIII's successor was the Count of Artois, crowned in Reims as Charles X in 1825, but his reign was cut short by a three-day rebellion called the "Three Glorious Days" (*les Trois Glorieuses*) which forced him to abdicate and to flee to England.

On August 9, 1830, Louis-Philippe, Duke of Orléans, was proclaimed king. He was fifty-seven years old. With him the monarchy became"bourgeois" and some even said *"petit bourgeois,"* and as such it was often timid and shortsighted in its enterprises. Louis-Philippe wanted to remain above the factions and as aloof as possible from foreign politics. He soon gave in to the aggressive radicals of his government when they decided to launch a colonial war against Abd-el-Kader, a war that in the end brought Algeria to France with far lasting unfortunate consequences for France. Louis-Philippe's reign was not to last long. People wanted reforms and Louis-Philippe unfortunately did not understand the seriousness of his people's needs and demands. He refused to make any changes, so on February 22,1848, barricades were built. The king called the National Guard, but they refused to obey him. Finally on February 24, 1848, Louis-Philippe, like Charles X before, abdicated and left for England. The constitutional reformers hoped to bring Louis-Philippe's young son as king, but the Republicans who had forced out Louis-Philippe also forced the Chamber of Deputies to proclaim the Republic. Violence did not subside immediately. For three days, June 24–26, 1848, also called "Bloody June Days," civil war raged in Paris. The specter of social revolution hung over France and a terrible fear of social upheaval determined the course of events during the Second Republic.

Louis-Napoléon Bonaparte becomes President

After the June Days, the Constituent Assembly drafted a Republican constitution with a strong executive headed by a president elected by universal suffrage.[166] Of all the candidates (Lamartine, Cavaignac, Ledru-Rollin and Louis-Napoleon), Louis-Napoleon was elected on December 10, 1848, with an overwhelming majority. Louis-Napoleon was the nephew of the great emperor Bonaparte, and his father, Louis Bonaparte, was king of Holland when his son was born. When Louis-Napoleon arrived on the political stage, people were already reliving the Napoleonic Legend, and Louis-Napoleon's name was Napoleon *Bonaparte*. He was also supposed to be a friend of the people. With all this, Louis-Napoleon emerged as President of the Second Republic with a very strong popular support. The new Legislative Assembly was a curious mixture of Monarchists (2/3 in fact) and 1/3 of Republicans. But after the euphoria of the elections, disillusionment returned fanned by a serious economic crisis. So Louis-Napoleon saw that the time was ripe for him. On the anniversary of Austerlitz, December 2, 1851, he executed a *coup d'état*. At first the country resisted and hundreds were killed in Paris, but the *coup d'état* was finally accepted with little opposition by plebiscite on December 20, 1851.[167] Louis-Napoleon was elected President for ten years. A year later, however, he proclaimed himself Emperor of the French with the name of Napoleon III, following Napoleon's son.[168]

1852–1870: Napoléon III and the Second Empire

With Napoleon III, the Republic was dead and France ceased to have a parliamentary life. The Second Empire was in fact a modern dictatorship in spite of its apparent popular acclaim.[169] Napoleon III loved to make political speeches and promises. He promised a modern era, with progress. He proclaimed that "*l'empire c'est la paix*" (empire means peace)[170] and he claimed that he would preserve the interest of all equally. But he also said that in order to carry out his program of enlightened progress with new roads, new harbors, canals, railroads, he needed to have order, and that justified the authoritarian mode of government he imposed to the French. Napoleon III knew that people loved pageantry, and so he used it as much as he could, holding a sumptuous Court at the Tuileries and even by marrying Eugénie, a beautiful young Spanish woman who helped him to make his social life even more brilliant. Above all Napoleon III wanted to be known as a social engineer, and as such he managed to do some good for France. He tended to the country's economy,[171] fostered public health and several financial institutions still in existence today, including the *Société Générale* and the *Crédit Lyonnais*. He encouraged enterprises, industry and let financiers speculate to their heart's content. France built everything and everywhere, canals such as the Suez Canal, trains, railroads, tunnels, harbors. Napoleon III even envisaged the construction of a tunnel under the Channel *(La Manche)*, but was forced to back down because of the reticence of England. Napoleon III also modernized Paris, asking the famous Baron Haussmann, prefect of Paris,[172] to open broad avenues,[173] including the magnificent *Champs Elysées*, building train stations, modern sewage systems and parks. Present-day Paris is still basically what Haussmann did with it.[174] The emperor also thought of the working men, he legalized trade unions and even strikes. He saw to it that there were plenty of jobs with decent wages. He also established hospitals and ordered the distribution of free medicines to the needy. Perhaps more importantly, Napoleon III worked hard to bring about freedom of trade. As a matter of fact he concluded a free trade treaty with England. With all these initiatives, France under Napoleon III appeared to be booming; the stock market encouraged many people to invest, and many became very rich, unfortunately giving rise at the same time to a society lacking in morality and with ostentatious new-rich tastes.[175]

If we forget the decline in morals, France appeared to do well under Napoleon III,[176] but that was not to last.[177] By 1860, troubles were brewing, opposition to the emperor grew even after Napoleon was forced to become more liberal.[178] His grandiose foreign policy was mostly unsuccessful, with the exception of a few victories: he completed the conquest of Algeria and joined the English in a military expedition to China in 1860, and Pekin was captured. During the same year Napoleon III sent expeditionary forces to Syria, as he was eager to take part in the Crimean War against Russia. And after a long siege, the French troops forced the Russians out of Sebastopol. Napoleon III did not stop there; he led an adventurous war in Mexico that brought nothing but losses to France, losses in men, prestige and money. Then the war against Otto von Bismarck declared on July 19, 1870, turned out to be a disastrous fiasco. The Germans took Alsace and Lorraine and surrounded the French in Sedan. Napoleon himself was captured and could do nothing but surrender on September 2, 1870. This humiliating defeat brought about the collapse of the Empire and the eventual proclamation of the Third Republic. Napoleon III fled to England, where he died on January 9, 1873.

A Cultural Survey of Letters, Arts and Science under the Second Empire

Science became the queen of the age and influenced every aspect of daily life. Political economy, history, Marx' socialism, all claim to be sciences.

Positivist philosophers expected that science would replace religion as well as philosophy, and as such would transform humanity. The progresses in chemistry and physics served as models for the life sciences. Darwin posed the problem of the evolution of species and Auguste Comte's *Cours de philosophie positive* became the bible of a new philosophy according to which the only criteria of truth were observation and experience. Claude Bernard applied this positivist method to experimental medicine and Fustel de Coulange to history.

In literature, the middle of the nineteenth century was marked by a reaction against the Romantic movement. In fact, with the exception of Victor Hugo, most Romantic authors died (Chateaubriand in 1848, Balzac in 1850, Nerval in 1855 and Musset in 1857). The new cult was the fervent and exclusive cult of art for art *(l'art pour l'art)*. In poetry this new cult was represented by Théophile Gautier, Baudelaire, Leconte de Lisle. The novel became realist, with Flaubert for whom style was supreme, another expression of the art for art cult.

In art, painters were particularly attracted by the problem of light. It was the magical period of Impressionism with great painters like Renoir, Monet, Seurat, Van Gogh, Pissaro, Gauguin. Between 1880 and 1900, some young painters began to conceive painting as a flat surface covered with colors. These painters did not try to translate an impression, but a certain choice of colors and forms. Bonnard recomposed what he saw into an imaginary fairy-like atmosphere; Cézanne avoided contrasts of shadows and light, and constructed forms in general totally independent from reality

The Sequels of the Franco-Prussian War of 1870
The End of France's Hegemony in Europe

A government of National Defense replaced the emperor. It first tried to negotiate with Bismarck, but he demanded Alsace and a third of Lorraine plus Metz. The interim government decided to resist the Germans; however, Bismarck put Paris under siege, hoping that hunger would force them to capitulate. On October 9, Leon Gambetta, Interior Minister, 32 years old, made a brave attempt to go and establish a temporary capital in Tours by flying from Paris in a balloon.[179] He succeeded in mustering a fighting force of 600,000 men, but they failed to move the German army. The troops of Bismarck harassed the Parisians with incessant bombardments and, to make things worse, the winter 1870–1871 was exceptionally cold. Resistance soon appeared futile and many already thought that the war was lost and that it was necessary to have peace. Some even accused Gambetta of being a dictator acting against the wishes of the nation. Bismarck, in the meantime, did not budge: he demanded a total capitulation. On October 27, the Germans crossed the Loire and the temporary government delegation in Tours had to flee again, this time south to Bordeaux. By mid-January all hope of breaking the siege of Paris was abandoned. In the capital people were reduced to eating horses, even rats and cats. On February 12, 1871, a National Assembly met in Bordeaux to sign the peace with Bismarck. Thiers, as head of the executive branch, left for Versailles and met with Bismarck to discuss the conditions of capitulation. They were harsh. German occupation would continue in France until 5 billion gold francs were paid, and the Germans took Alsace and a part of Lorraine with Metz. France retained the Belfort territory. Peace was signed on May 10, 1871. France's crushing defeat made Germany the supreme power in Europe.[180]

France from 1871 to 1914

The new National Assembly elected February 8, 1871 met in Bordeaux and designated Thiers as head of the executive branch of the government. Thiers, 68 years old, was chosen because he wanted peace and also because he was perceived by Monarchists as the best man who would help them to bring back a king eventually. Thiers was indeed a good, reasonable man who had some experience in politics since he was a minister under Louis-Philippe. Unfortunately, Thiers was almost immediately confronted by an insurrection of Parisians enraged by the Sedan defeat. This insurrection was called *la Commune* (March–May 1871), one of the most complex and most serious French revolt in the nineteenth century.[181] These *Communards* were exasperated by France's defeat, and mostly by those who accepted the defeat. They adopted the red flag, proclaimed the separation of Church and State, banished Catholic schools and reverted to the Revolutionary calendar. Fortunately, Thiers had on his side General Mac Mahon and an army of 100,000 men. Under his command the troops crushed the Commune rebellion and twenty thousand Communards were tried and executed, thousands jailed or deported to far away penal colonies. Because of the violence of the rebellion and of its punishment, the moment was named *"L'Année terrible"* (Terrible year). Thiers then appeared as the savior of France and was given the title of President of the Third Republic on August 31, 1871. With new powers, Thiers restored order, reorganized the army and finances and paid off the war indemnity imposed by Germany. In fact, surprisingly, France was still rich and productive and seemed to escape from the depression that was very bad in other countries. Furthermore, social unrest in France was almost absent, even after the experience of the Commune. Thiers at first was not opposed to the restoration of monarchy as it was the wish of the majority of the Assembly, but gradually he began to lean more toward a conservative Republic. Upset by Thiers' change of heart, the conservative majority forced Thiers to resign on May 23, 1873. The Royalists replaced Thiers by Mac Mahon in May 1873, who unfortunately had no political experience, so he left the power to Albert de Broglie (1821–1901), a Catholic, conservative Orleanist. The other faction of the Monarchists, the Legitimists, wanted the Count of Chambord, Henry, while the Orleanists were for the Count of Paris, grandson of Louis-Philippe. The problem, however, was that "Henry V" refused to return unless the French tricolor flag was abolished and replaced by the white *Fleur de Lys* royalist banner. Mac Mahon and others refused to abandon the tricolor flag, and so the two royalist candidates were cast aside, and reelected Mac Mahon for seven more years. The fear of Bonapartists led the majority of the Assembly to accept the establishment of a Republic, the Third Republic, with a president elected for seven years at its head. On December 1875 the Assembly dissolved itself, and finally the Third Republic was born.[182]

· The Third Republic (1871–1889)

At first the new Republic tried to be conservative and as moderate as possible while at the same time imposing "*l'ordre moral*" (moral order) through some political measures: limitation of the liberty of the press, watching the University, and the creation of Catholic institutes of higher education. Still stormy days were to come when Mac Mahon was forced to resign in 1879, replaced by a Republican, Jules Grévy, who represented the majority in the Assembly. One of the first acts of Grévy and his Assembly was to declare July 14 a National Holiday in celebration of the fall of the Bastille; they also established the *Marseillaise* as the national anthem and they freed the *Communards* from jail. The new Republic became Opportunist (1879–1889). The Prime Minister, under the Third Republic, had more power than the president, but the president represented continuity and experience. As an illustration, there were seven presidents between 1879 and 1914, but forty-six new governments during the same period.[183] The Third Republic, however, was marred almost immediately by political instability which was even made worse because

of the rise of political factions, Radicals like Clémenceau (Radical-Socialists), and Opportunists who remained in power twenty years. Jules Ferry,
a fervent Opportunist, and his followers were violently anticlerical. They
removed education from the Church and established a strong secular education for all children 6 to 13 years old, making primary education compulsory and free (1881). Lycées for girls were set up in 1880.

They banned religious education from all state schools and catechism
was replaced by moral and civic courses teaching republican ideals and
patriotism. No member of a religious order was allowed to teach.

Naturally the government of Jules Ferry was attacked for its religious
policies, and instability reappeared with Royalists gaining seats in Parliament. There were new financial problems and the government was criticized for its colonial expansionist policies and for a worsening economy.
The French people, in the meantime, had not forgotten the defeat of
1870, and a new feeling of patriotism and nationalism was fanned by the
teachings in schools as well as by the activities of Bismarck, who brought
to his side most of the other European countries. During 1886–1887
Bismarck appeared to be preparing another war. In France the critics of
the government grew in number, and they united under the leadership of
a general, General Georges Boulanger, who as minister of war advertised
himself as the Republican general who would avenge the defeat of 1870.
A rather mediocre individual, Boulanger drew his support from a medley
of people, Bonapartists, Royalists and mostly workers without work.
Boulanger had no real program, just slogans and demagogic propaganda.
Worse yet, Boulanger did not have any political backbone, and he did not
dare to make a *coup d'état* even though he was strongly encouraged by
Déroulède, who begged him to go to the Assembly and to demand its
dissolution, promising that two hundred thousand men would second
him. But Boulanger did not even take advantage of the electoral victory
his supporters had won for him on January 27, 1889. Threatened with
arrest, Boulanger fled to Belgium, where he subsequently committed suicide on the grave of his girl friend (1891). *Boulangisme* died with the
general in the 1889 elections. Nevertheless, Boulanger had scared many
who immediately brought to power a new Right supported mostly by
angry citizens of large cities. But this new Right was not to enjoy peace
for very long. Even though the financial and economic situation of France
improved with the new more cohesive and stronger republican government, a huge scandal destroyed all the progress made in 1892, the *Panama
Affair*. The company of Ferdinand de Lesseps went bankrupt, losing
money for thousands of investors. Lesseps and many government

personalities were accused of wanting to hush up the affair, so new Socialist, pro-Marxist and Anarchist parties appeared, and they managed to win 37 seats in the 1893 elections. The rise of Socialism was also fanned by a severe economic depression, by strikes and by the actions of a small hard core of Anarchists who assassinated the President of the Republic, Sadi Carnot, in 1894. But even a worse event was awaiting the nation, the *Dreyfus Affair* that brought down the Opportunists and brought to power a coalition of Radicals, Socialists and Republicans who established an anticlerical Republic.

The Dreyfus Case 1894–1906

The Dreyfus case becomes *the affair* of the time. The French army had just adopted new artillery material and modified its war plans, and therefore the military high command was sensitive to spying. In 1894 the "*2e Bureau*" in charge of espionage came into possession of a document stolen from the German military attaché that gave important information about the French army. After several contradictory examinations of his writing, a Jewish staff officer, captain Dreyfus, a member of the intelligence section of the General Staff, was arrested on October 15, 1894, accused and prosecuted for spying for the benefit of the Germans. He was rapidly sentenced by court-martial to life imprisonment on Devil's Island, a harsh French penal colony off the coast of French Guiana.

Dreyfus, meanwhile, steadfastly maintained his innocence, and his family and some other persons demanded the revision of the trial. Dreyfus' main mistake was probably to have made his way into a General Staff that was traditionally exclusively made up of conservative Catholic-Royalists. And Dreyfus was Jewish! In 1896, however, the *2e Bureau* discovered a note addressed by the German military attaché to another French officer, Major Walsin-Esterhazy. Colonel Picquart noticed that colonel Esterhazy's handwriting corresponded exactly with the handwriting of the note previously attributed to Dreyfus, but he never could convince his chiefs, and Esterhazy was promptly acquitted while Picquart was dismissed from service. People continued to think that Dreyfus was guilty and should be hanged. All Picquart could do then was to acquaint the family and friends of Dreyfus of his discovery. For the first time, in 1897, those who still fought for Dreyfus turned public, but nothing was done until suddenly on January 30, 1898, the novelist Emile Zola came out with an explosive letter in the newspaper *L'Aurore,* Clémenceau's newspaper. The open letter was titled "*J'Accuse*" (I accuse). Immediately a host of French intellectuals, scientists and politicians, Clémenceau at their head, rallied behind Zola's flag. That was enough to stir the anti-Dreyfusards, and Zola was condemned. The trial, however, revealed to the public the details of the affair. And in August it was found that one of the secret documents charging Dreyfus was a forgery made up by an officer of the *2e Bureau*, colonel Henry. In turn Henry was arrested, but he committed suicide.

The trial of Dreyfus was revised, and in 1906 Dreyfus was liberated, pardoned, rehabilitated and decorated with the Legion of Honor (*la Légion d'Honneur*), one of France's most prestigious decorations. Esterhazy, in the meantime, had fled to England and eventually confessed to having been a spy for the Germans. Picquart was reinstated and promoted general. Dreyfus subsequently fought in World War I as lieutenant colonel, and died in 1935.[184]

Consequences of the Dreyfus Affair[185]

The ugly controversy was apparently over, the case was closed, but in reality it left deep scars over a whole generation. France was divided, families were divided, friends did not speak to each other and everyone used the affair for political ends. The *Dreyfusards* (i.e., those who defended Dreyfus), intellectuals, writers, teachers, Free Maçons, the Radicals and Socialists, founded the League of Man's Rights *(La Ligue des Droits de l'Homme)* and wanted to put the army under the civil power. On the other hand, the *Antidreyfusards* wanted to preserve the honor of the army and they accused the Jews of trying to plot against the nation. On the *Antidreyfusards'* side new leagues were created, including the *Action Française* with Charles Maurras and Léon Daudet. All these factions reflected a deep political and moral illness in the nation that never quite died and certainly resurrected during the Vichy Years, i.e., during the World War II episode. When Dreyfus was finally pardoned, the *Dreyfusards* clan formed a coalition of Republican defense, alleging that France was in danger and that the Church was a menace. The Radical Republic turned violently anticlerical, accusing the Church of having sided with the army and with the *Antidreyfusards*. Hundreds of Church orders were summarily dissolved, their lands and buildings confiscated, and their schools closed. Nuns and priests were banned from teaching. In fact one can say that at the beginning of the twentieth century, anticlericalism began to dominate politics. In 1902 Emile Combes was called to form a new government and this government proved to be fiercely anticlerical to the point that it broke relations with Rome. When Combes fell in 1905,[186]

Maurice Rouvier tried to mend fences with the Pope, but in vain because the Pope was furious at the proposed laws of Separation of Church and State. In 1902, that the General Confederation of Labor union was formed, in favor of strikes and of the overthrow of the government. It was mostly an anarchist rather than a socialist group. The Radical Georges Clémenceau remained in power from 1906 to 1909, but his actions created a drift between Radicals and Socialists, and he was unable to carry out his vast program. In 1909, Clémenceau was replaced by Aristide Briand, who remained in power until 1911. But during his brief tenure Briand faced many problems: manifestations of May 1, strikes and the revolt of peasants in Languedoc following the devastating crisis of *phylloxéra* killing most of the vines. Finally, in January 1912, Raymond Poincaré became Premier and was elevated to the presidency a year later. He was the very incarnation of the country's program of National Defense, which was then judged imperative on account of the many unsettling international tensions, and the news that Germany was reinforcing its army. Ironically, though, the partisans of peace, the Socialists, won enough seats to have one of them elected to the head of the government precisely when World War I was declared.

Europe at the Eve of World War I

In 1914, at the eve of World War I, Europe counted five major powers, Great Britain, Germany, France, Austria-Hungary, and Russia. France and Great Britain were democratic and liberal powers, while Germany, Austria-Hungary and Russia were three authoritarian empires. More importantly perhaps, the five great European powers were at a different stage of economic development. Russia and Austria-Hungary were just beginning to modernize with few important cities, a mostly rural population and an underdeveloped railroad system. France, conversely, had a modern industry, a very good railroad system, and a solid currency. On the negative side, France still had a large rural population. England and Germany were great producers of coal, pig iron and steel; they had a superb fleet, an excellent banking system, but Germany was ahead and threatening to become the first industrial power in Europe. Soon the Great War of 1914–1918 was going to erupt and become the first World Conflict.

A Conflict Brooding

Since 1905 war was brooding in the Balkans, with the growing Yugoslav nationalism, increasing tension between Austria-Hungary and Serbia, and the formations of blocks of coalitions such as the *Triple Alliance* of Germany, Austria-Hungary, and Italy and the *Triple Entente* of France, Russia and England (eventually). As these blocks were forming, the tension between them increased and led them to engage into an arms race. In 1913, France increased the length of military service to three years, while Germany increased its army, all the more because it was afraid of Russia's power, which was on the side of France. So William II of Germany, who had long wanted peace, had to change his mind, saying, "war is unavoidable and necessary" and "if we don't strike first, our situation will become worse." Peace was therefore hanging by a thin thread.

On June 28, 1914, a Bosnian nationalist student assassinated the Archduke Francis-Ferdinand, heir to the throne of Austria-Hungary, and his wife in the streets of Sarajevo in Bosnia.[187] The Austro-Hungarian government immediately sent an ultimatum to Serbia, but Serbia ignored it, so Austria declared war on Serbia on July 28, 1914, thinking that it was a wonderful opportunity to eliminate Serbia from the political scene of the Balkans. Germany approved the move, thinking that Russia would not intervene, considering that it was hardly recovering from its 1905 Revolution. Poincaré, the French President of the Republic, promised France's assistance to the Czar, and Russia in turn promised its assistance to Serbia. On July 28, 1914, the Austro-Hungarian forces attacked Serbia. Soon most of Europe was engulfed in a bloody war that would kill ten million men by its end in 1918. It was Austria, Hungary and Germany against Serbia, France, Britain and Russia.

Russia mobilized on 30 July, 1914, Germany declared war on August 1 and the same day France mobilized and on August 3 Germany after entering Luxembourg and Belgium declared war on France. On August 4 England went to war. Nationalist feelings on all parts were at their highest pitch and in France nationalism was fanned by the writings of Maurras and Barrès. The French wanted to recover Alsace and Lorraine and take their revenge for their defeat of 1870. In spite of some partisans of peace on each side, people resigned themselves to war as something inevitable.

The War

The Germans were ready, but France and its allies less. So Russia had many men, but their armaments were old-fashioned and mobilization was slow. England had no compulsory military service and therefore could only send a small expeditionary force. Under these conditions, France confronted the brunt of the German offensive and, unfortunately, its army and armaments were archaic. The men still wore terribly visible uniforms, red caps and pants, which made them easy targets for the Germans.

The German troops swiftly went around the French army and moved toward Paris. The situation was critical. Half a million Parisians left the capital and the French government moved to Bordeaux.[188] The French troops, under the high command of Joseph Joffre, held the front on the river Marne, and on September 10 even forced the Germans to fall back.

But then began a very harsh, devastating period of trench warfare, with the use of gas, which by 1915 brought the number of French dead to 400,000 and 600,000 wounded. At the end of 1915 both sides were resigned to a continued war of attrition, but the Germans launched a powerful offensive against Verdun on February 21, 1916. The resistance of Verdun was fierce and by the end of 1916 the Germans were back where they had started. The soldiers on both sides were getting tired, and the only thing the governments could do to maintain morale was to use propaganda. The German press was saying that their troops were about to march on Paris, while the French press exploited the valiant resistance of Verdun. But then, as some pacifist movements were beginning to grow, the United States entered the war, on April 2, 1917. If the French troops were exhausted, Clémenceau, President of the Council *(Président du Conseil)* incarnated the spirit of resistance. He kept claiming that "In internal politics as well as in foreign politics, my formula is the same: '*Je fais la guerre, je fais toujours la guerre*' (I am fighting the war, I am always fighting the war). From February to June the war continued to rage around Verdun with the French troops under Général Pétain's command. In France it was a time of great political instability with rapidly changing governments and with the Socialists asking for the end of the war.[189] In Russia the Revolution began and since Russia was too busy with its revolution, the Germans were able to withdraw troops from the Russian front. In spite of its renewed strength, the German army was also exhausted and it was held back in Champagne. The arrival of one million fresh American troops suddenly gave the French an overwhelming superiority, so Ludendorff saw that the German position was hopeless and resigned. The emperor William II at first refused to end the fighting, but strikes and revolts broke out, and the allies of the Germans were making separate armistices with the French and their allies, so the Kaiser finally abdicated and fled. The Republic was proclaimed in Berlin and the new government accepted an armistice on November 11, 1918. It was celebrated on both sides with great relief and joy. Peace followed with the Treaty of Versailles signed on June 28, 1919. According to this treaty,

France recovered Alsace and Lorraine and Germany had to pay a hefty financial war reparation. Resentment against the conditions of the Versailles treaty grew at once in Germany, and with the economic crisis, Fascism emerged.

In France the price of victory was staggeringly high: almost one and a half million dead, three million wounded and many of them severely maimed. France had lost so many men that its birthrate fell sharply and foreign workers had to be hired to make up for the loss of the three million French workers.[190] French finances had been seriously depleted and prices soared. The only winners to an extent were the farmers, whose farm prices increased, but mechanization was still very rare and farmers still used horses and teams of oxen to do their farm work.

But at least the war was over and the humiliating defeat inflicted by Germany on France in 1870 was avenged. France seemed to have regained some of its hegemony in Europe, but for this situation to last, France had to receive continued help from its allies, Russia had to remain isolated and Germany needed to be kept weak. However, Germany was to come out of the war stronger than France, and it would not be long before it tried again to defeat France and dominate Europe. In the meantime, Fascism was progressing fast and economic depressions and inflation fanned its rise in Italy with Mussolini, in Spain with the "Caudillo" Franco, and in Germany with Hitler and his Nazi party.[191]

France after World War I

The French had put aside their political and social divisions during the war, but as soon as peace was signed the conflicts resumed between Socialists and Communists and the Right and Extreme Right parties. The opposition was made worse by their differences in matter of religion. The Left was traditionally anticlerical, while the Right was in favor of reestablishing relations with the Vatican. In addition the example of the Russian Revolution gave rise to movements of protest among workers who were joining trade unions. The legislative elections of November 1919 brought a coalition of the Right and Center called the National Bloc and the Horizon-Blue Chamber *(La Chambre bleu horizon),* with Raymond Poincaré and Aristide Briand. The *Bloc National* was really a nationalistic and pro-Catholic alliance promoted by the Church and Big Business and represented in the press by the extreme-rightist newspaper *L'Action Française.* However, France's economy was declining, the franc was losing much of its value due to the inflation, unemployment reappeared and

multiple strikes took place at the end of 1919 and in 1920. Public opinion was divided.

There seemed only one solution to the worsening financial situation of
France: make the Germans pay their war debt! So in 1922 Raymond
Poincaré received the specific mandate to make the Germans pay up
because they had so far craftily delayed and postponed their payment.
But the Germans soon proved incapable of paying, even after having
their debt reduced thanks to an American mediation. Raymond Poincaré
fell in 1924 and was replaced by a coalition of Radicals and Socialists
named the *Cartel des Gauches.* The current President of the Republic,
Millerand, who belonged to the *Bloc National,* had to resign, and he was
replaced by a moderate Republican, Gaston Doumergue, while a Radical,
Edouard Herriot, became Premier. Unfortunately the financial situation
of France was getting worse, the franc slid further down and prices soared.
Herriot, when he saw that he could not count on Germany's payment of
its war debt, raised taxes and cut government spending. But it was too
little a remedy. Herriot resigned in April 1925, and so the only savior in
sight was Poincaré, who returned as *Président du Conseil* in July 1926.
Poincaré's efforts following the last measures of Herriot redressed the
situation. French industry started to grow, and by 1930 it would be 40%
above its pre–World War I level, thanks particularly to the development of
the automobile, of petro-chemical and electrical industries. Workers' salaries were low, but they obtained a reduction in work time to only eight
hours per day. Women were also making progress in the work place, in
industry and offices; however, they still did not have the right to vote.
Exports improved too, but in 1929 an ill Poincaré resigned. A series of
Center-Right governments followed and while France was enjoying prosperity in almost a state of euphoria, a terrible crisis was brewing.

A Terrible Crisis

In October 1929, Thursday, October 24, exactly, now known as Black
Thursday, the New York Stock Market crashed and did not recover. In
fact the crisis hit the whole world, with perhaps the exception of Russia.
At first an international crisis, it soon turned into a world economic and
social catastrophe. Unemployment grew and social as well as racial tensions grew. In Germany, the Nazis gained 107 seats in the Reichstag in
1930, then 250 seats. On January 30, 1933, Adolf Hitler was named
Chancellor of Germany by Hindenburg. On March 23, 1933, Hitler obtained full powers. Then on August 2, 1934, when Hindenburg died,

Hitler became both President and Chancellor under the title of *Reichsführer*: He was the absolute master of Germany, in fact a full-fledged dictator supported by the gigantic organization of the Waffen S.S. and Himmler's "Gestapo" (*Geheime Staats Polizei*).

As Hitler was taking power, France's unemployment reached 1.3 million. The French economy was on a downslide and the nation's deficit growing. French governments fell one after another. There were to be forty-two governments in the interwar period, each one lasting no more than six months, and nobody knew how to put an end to the crisis. And then the Stavinsky scandal exploded: It was a financial scandal that ended with Serge Stavinsky's death (suicide or murder) in December 1933. Stavinsky was a plain swindler with protectors in high places. He issued large amounts of bonds with the minimal (not to say nonexistent) warranty of the Bayonne Municipal Pawnshop. The French, exasperated by the economic situation, used the Stavinsky scandal as an outlet for their frustration and anger. The Royalists of the *Action Française* encouraged a group of thugs to create confusion and to beat up Communists and Radicals. There was also the fascist *Croix de Feu* organization, a pseudo-Nazi association that organized anti-government riots. The Left faction of the government fought back, and as these two factions were at odds, France seemed close to a revolution. The worse was fortunately averted thanks to a leftist coalition that led the Popular Front to victory, a coalition of Communists, Radical-Socialists with the backing of the C.G.T. union,[192] in May 1936 with Léon Blum as its leader. Blum came to power under very difficult circumstances because the French had hoped for social progress and wanted more welfare, a more equal distribution of wealth—and they strengthened their demands with strikes. Léon Blum, unfortunately, was not able to realize the deep economic and financial reforms that were expected of him, and in 1936 the government had to devaluate the franc. In March 1937 Blum had to announce that he had to delay the promised and expected reforms. In France Blum was also confronted by the rise of secret organizations such as *La Cagoule,* and the *Comité Secret d'Action Révolutionnaire* (The secret committee of revolutionary action). Outside of France, Blum had to deal with the rise to power of Hitler, Mussolini and the Spanish Red Terror. Too few people supported Blum's policy and many did not want to pay more taxes to pay for the promised social services or to prepare for war. Blum was aware of the perilous international situation and wanted to start a rearmament program, but when he and his Popular Front asked the French to subscribe to national defense loans, many chose to take their money outside of France.

The failure of Blum marked the end of the Popular Front in 1937 and many Frenchmen were heard crying: "Better Hitler than Blum!"

France's Decline at the Eve of World War II

Blum was replaced by Edouard Daladier, who chose Paul Raynaud as his minister of finances, who favored drastic fiscal measures, with new taxes and budgetary economies. In spite of some gains in industrial production, the economic situation of France remained bad, and to make things worse, France was experiencing a steep decline in its demography. From 1921 to 1936 the country had only gained two million inhabitants and in 1936 France still had to count on 2,200,000 foreign workers. There were more deaths than births and the French population was getting older, a dangerous trend for the future of the nation.

1938–1939

From 1938 on Europe began to be more and more at the mercy of Hitler's ambitions. The Führer was conscious that no one could seriously oppose him and that the time was ripe for carrying out his grand design of a powerful and supreme greater Germany. France and Britain wanted peace and people either did not see, or rather did not want to see, the menace of Nazi Germany. In France, people were mostly preoccupied by their social concerns and by their fear of Communism. Furthermore, part of the French people favored an alliance with Hitler and Mussolini. No one even blinked an eye when Hitler assumed the command of the German armed forces (February 4, 1938). Even the frightening moves of Hitler did not stir a patriotic nerve in France. The *Anschluss* of February– March 1938 or occupation of Austria by the Germans was not met by any reaction in Europe. So Hitler felt that he had a green light to pursue his conquests. He next sought to take Czechoslovakia. On September 12, 1938, Hitler, in a particularly violent speech, accused the Czechs of torturing the German minorities on their soil. Czechoslovakia was an ally of France and so when Czechoslovakia mobilized, France followed.

The Grand Illusion of Peace

Chamberlain in the name of England, and Daladier for France, wanted desperately to avoid a war, so they suggested a meeting in Munich with Mussolini and the Fürher. Hitler managed to throw powder in the eyes of the French and British, who accepted his demands. They thought that by giving in to Hitler they had served the cause of peace, but in fact it was at the expense of Czechoslovakia, which was not present at the conference. Nevertheless, when Daladier returned to Paris he was acclaimed as a savior of peace. The French were relieved and repeated "*La Paix! La Paix! C'est la Paix! Nous allons vivre. Nous allons donc vivre encore*" (Peace, Peace, it is peace. We are going to live. We are going to live again). In England Chamberlain, upon his return from Munich, declared: "It is Peace for Our Time" and received a hysterical welcome. They and their countries were soon to pay dearly for this cowardly act and for the two men's blind confidence in Hitler's words. So Hitler had the green light. Now he was looking at Poland and in fact wanted to invade it, and with this in mind he concluded a pact of nonaggression with Russia (August 23, 1939). Hitler's hands were free to attack Poland and it is exactly what he did without warning on September 1, 1939. This time France and England could not back off. On September 3, 1939, France and England declared war on Germany. The dream of peace turned into a horrible nightmare.

The Second World War (1939–1945)

Following the invasion of Poland, the French first remained on the defensive along the Maginot Line that they thought the Germans could never cross. The fact was that the morale of the French army was low, their armament antiquated and they had practically no aviation and few tanks. Unfortunately the famous *Ligne Maginot,* strong as it was, did not extend all the way to the sea, and so the Germans avoided this line of French defense, going around it. Rapidly, the German forces, which were well equipped and enthusiastic, invaded Holland, Belgium and Luxembourg, and in front of their overwhelming superiority French troops kept retreating on roads which were already crowded with retreating civilians who prevented the movement of allied troops. The Germans moved swiftly toward Paris and entered the capital without firing a shot. By June 12, 1940, Maréchal Weygand proposed an armistice to preserve the honor of the army, and by June 16 Paul Reynaud, who wanted to continue the fight, resigned, in fact pushed out by a *coup d'état* headed by Pierre Laval. The President of the Republic then called Maréchal Pétain, who by June 17 announced his intention to ask for an armistice.

The armistice was signed on June 22 in Compiègne, a place chosen by Hitler because it was in Compiègne that the November 11, 1918, Armistice had been signed by the defeated Germans. The conditions of surrender for France were severe. Germany was to occupy the upper three-fourths of France[193] and the two million French prisoners would not be freed. On October 22, 1940, Pétain met Hitler in Montoire and shook hand with him, a symbol of the collaboration of the Vichy government with Germany. Pétain and his cohorts as well as many Frenchmen were not unhappy to bring to an end the war, thinking that it could be the beginning of a great Franco-German alliance. In fact many thought that the brand of German totalitarianism could be beneficial for France. The French, it is true, were on the verge of despair and confused, so they thought that Pétain was right and they sang "*Maréchal, nous voilà!*" (Maréchal, here we are) thinking only a day at a time, hoping to continue to live while blanking out the real situation, blinding themselves to the past, the present and future.[194]

Pétain immediately initiated a government called *L'Etat Français,* in Vichy, with the motto "*Travail, Famille, Patrie*" (Work, family, Fatherland). A government based on moral order and on the basic values of the land.[195]

Général de Gaulle, in the meantime, had fled to England instead of submitting to the new collaborationist regime of Pétain. From London, on June 18, 1940, the Général made a famous broadcast begging the French not to accept the armistice and to resist the Germans, either by joining him in England or by organizing a Resistance in France.[196] De Gaulle's task was not made easy because the Allies took a very long time in recognizing the General's provisional government, and the United States was still naively hoping that Vichy would abandon its collaboration with Germany. In fact, it was not until August 1944 that the USA, Great Britain and Russia recognized de Gaulle's French Committee of National Liberation.

From the Somber Years of Vichy to Victory (1940–1945)

Contrary to the Allies' expectations, the Vichy government, in the illusory hope of preserving a small amount of French sovereignty, collaborated fully with the Germans. It sent French workers to German plants under the label of STO or *Service du Travail Obligatoire* (compulsory work service), it tracked down and arrested Resistance fighters and Jews, and sent them to death camps in Germany. Vichy also sent French units to the Russian front to fight along with the Nazis. Both Pétain and Laval claimed that they collaborated with the Germans in order to pacify them and to save France from more severe treatment at German hands. There was unfortunately a deeper reason for the collaboration: they were quite convinced that the future of France was in a friendly association with Hitler's Germany, integrated within the Fürher's conception of a new Europe. And, hard as it is to admit, there were more French collaborators and Nazis than one would have imagined, people like Brasillac, Doriot, Darnand who created the Milice, a French Gestapo-type police at the service of the Nazis, Céline, Drieu de La Rochelle, etc. . . . The trial of Klaus Barbie and the trial of Papon (1997–1998) have opened many eyes today, uncovering the extent of the collaboration by the French and many ugly acts performed against their own countrymen. Fortunately, on the other hand, many Frenchmen refused to side with Vichy and continued to fight the enemy: they were the Resistance, the Free French, the *Maquisards,* so named because they were hiding in the mountains and in the forests.

Following de Gaulle's call,[197] those soldiers and other Frenchmen who escaped to England gathered around the Général under their symbol, the *Croix de Lorraine* (Cross of Lorraine) at the side of Winston Churchill and his countrymen. Inside France, the brave *Maquisards,* under the leadership of Jean Moulin, harassed the Germans, blew up railroads, killed Germans, gave London important information about German troop movements, about the location of ammunitions depots, and tanks. They blew up bridges, helped Jews to escape and rescued allied airmen who were shot down over France. At the time of the Normandy invasion, the *Maquisards* were extremely helpful attacking and harassing the Germans from behind. Many of these young men and women were unfortunately caught, tortured and put to death. Jean Moulin himself was caught by the infamous Klaus Barbie, rightfully called the Butcher of Lyon.

However, in 1943 the balance of power began to shift. The German war machine was out of steam while the war effort of the Allies increased. The Germans, however, had transformed Europe into a gigantic fortress with defenses, walls and pillboxes all around the French coasts, and indeed it took two full years of intense fighting to break the fortress. While Stalin kept many Nazi divisions busy in Russia, the Anglo-Americans put général Eisenhower in charge of a major landing in Normandy. The invasion took place during the night of June 5–6, 1944, with thousands of ships, and men. In the meantime another landing had taken place in Provence and the tanks of the French général Leclerc were pushing in the direction of Paris, that had risen against the Germans (August 19–25). The Germans could only retreat toward the northeast, but by September 15, 1944, most of France and Belgium were free. As they retreated toward Germany, the Nazis fought desperately, particularly in the Ardennes, the Vosges and in Alsace.[198] But finally, at the beginning of 1945, the Allies were able to undertake the final assault, the French from the west and the Russians from the east. Berlin fell to the Russians on April 19, and Hitler and his henchman Goebbels committed suicide: May 2, 1945, the Germans were at long last brought to their knees, and forced to sign their capitulation in Reims on May 7, 1945.[199]

The Aftermath of World War II[200]

The year 1945 found France and the whole world deeply affected by the war. In five years over fifty million men had perished[201] and large portions of France, Germany, Poland and Russia had been devastated and their economies shattered. Following the Liberation, the French had found their will to live again, but they still needed to purge themselves from the evil acts perpetrated by some Frenchmen during the occupation under Vichy. So immediately after the end of the war, a period of *épuration* (cleansing) took place. Hundreds, even thousands of men and women, members of the *Milice*, officials of Pétain's Legion, informers, traitors, profiteers of all kinds, were summarily executed. Women who had been seen fraternizing with German soldiers had their heads shaved and were spat upon.[202] While some cases were justified, others were often due to personal revenge. It was estimated that up to 10,000 persons were put to death during this period, thousands jailed. Pétain and Laval were condemned to death, but de Gaulle commuted Pétain's sentence to life imprisonment.[203]

Then de Gaulle succeeded in establishing an interim Provisional government, including many members of the Resistance and two Communists. Right away all summary executions, street lynchings were prohibited and the hectic hysteria of revenge was replaced by more orderly judicial procedures. De Gaulle also instituted reforms which had a lasting effect on France: he nationalized coal mines, airlines, the Renault automobile factory, electric and gas works, major insurance companies and many major banks. But France's economy, its industry, its towns had to be rebuilt. De Gaulle's task was enormous, but he thought that, in order to achieve France's recovery, it was first necessary to make a clean cut with the Third Republic. So he called for a referendum *(plébiscite)* and on October 21, 1945, the French, with 96% of them approving, abolished the Third Republic.

The Fourth Republic: 1946–1958

First of all it must be understood that the Fourth Republic inherited most of the troubles of the Third Republic. Nothing much had changed in the constitutional structure of the government, except that women for the first time were allowed to vote. In the elections for the new republic the Communists won 265 of the votes, while the MRP (*Mouvement Républicain Populaire*) trailed with 23% of the votes. The Socialists received 23% of the votes, while the Radicals and Moderates received less than 15%. The three major parties confirmed de Gaulle as head of the government, but on January 20, 1946, he voluntarily relinquished the presidency because he could not accept the stricter controls the government wanted to impose on him. Some believe that he sought a more massive call from the country. With de Gaulle gone, the task of governing and working on the country's recovery fell on the shoulders of the majority parties. The Assembly replaced de Gaulle with the Socialist Félix Gouin. They drafted a new constitution that was immediately voted down by 53% of the voters. So the Assembly dissolved itself and on June 2 a new assembly was elected with a marked gain by the MRP (over 22%) over the Communists (less than 21%) and the Socialists (about 16%). Georges Bidault, head of the MRP *(Popular Republican Movement)* became the leader of the new government. But there followed a period of incessant ministerial instability with twenty-four governments succeeding each other between December 1946 and May 1958. None of these governments lasted more than six months.

Even after its victory France was exhausted. Its economy was stagnant or mixed at best. Destruction had choked every major sector of the economy: roads, railroads, harbors needed to be rebuilt, and there was a great shortage of coal. Inflation was high and food supplies were inadequate because agriculture was slow in recovering from the loss in men and slow in modernizing. France was still terribly dependent on the aid of its allies, and whether it was admitted or not, France had placed herself under the umbrella of the United States, particularly when it accepted the Marshall Plan of economic recovery. Even with the Monnet plan that accepted the financial assistance of the United States, France was slow in modernizing its industry. Labor unrest persisted with major strikes in 1947, 1948 and 1950. Then internal problems were worsened by the situation in the colonial empire. In fact decolonization was gaining momentum with increasing demands for autonomy by North Africa, Madagascar and Indo-China. The Fourth Republic would prove impotent in containing the movement, and would finally collapse in the Algerian snare.

However, the Fourth Republic was not without positive achievement: It organized social security, insurance protection for the family, national and regional planning. It also moved ahead with the modernization of France, even if slowly, and improved the living standard of its citizens. It was criticized to justify its demise.[204]

From the Fourth to the Fifth Republic

Even though governments were falling and rising at a fast clip, progress was made in several important areas. Women received the right to vote and a comprehensive welfare state was established. Demography was on the rise again with up to 800,000 births a year. Between 1946 and 1985 the population grew from about 40 million to 55 million. Surely the guarantees of social services and family allowances were contributing factors to this splendid recovery. France was changing, slowly perhaps, but surely. It was no longer a country of peasants; it was becoming a nation of city dwellers and industrial workers. Thanks to those factors, France was moving toward a new era of economic, technological and industrial boom that was nicknamed *Les Trente Glorieuses* (The Thirty Glorious Ones).

People started to live better, in more comfortable houses, with more modern conveniences (a refrigerator, a washing machine, modern kitchen appliances etc. . . .). People were able to buy automobiles and because of this they were more mobile, took longer vacations, farther away from home. But, naturally, recovery did not proceed without problems. One major problem for France was the growing process of decolonization. France, of course, wanted to retain its colonial empire, but nationalism was growing within native populations, a fact the French government was a bit too slow to understand, and that the French settlers refused to face at first. So France was suddenly engaged in a terrible war in Vietnam (Indo-China). It was to be a long, costly war and in fact a real nightmare, which ended with the fall of Dien Bien Phu in 1955 and the withdrawal of France. Mendès France who orchestrated the Geneva treaty with Vietnam, gave the Tunisians and Moroccans their independence in March 1956. Mendès France, was thereafter the subject of ceaseless anti-Semitic tirades accusing him of having abandoned France's empire. Mendès France did nothing for Algeria because France considered it a part of the metropolitan country. When Jacques Soustelle was appointed Governor-General of Algeria, precisely to maintain Algeria as a part of France, he said: "We must not, at any price, in any way and under any pretext, lose Algeria." Immediately the Algerian nationalists who had formed the FLN (National Liberation Front) began a campaign of terrorism and uprisings that kept escalating. The French government began to pour men in Algeria in the hope of crushing the rebels, but it was in vain, and that sad period has left, to this very day, deep open wounds in France as well as in Algeria. As a matter of fact, the Algerian episode may be considered as one of the tragic events of twentieth-century history and its consequences still continue to haunt France and Algeria. In any case it brought down the Fourth Republic when the French government, afraid of a *coup* by settlers and paratroopers under the command of general Salan, called back de Gaulle, who drafted a new constitution, thus burying the Fourth Republic and giving birth to the Fifth Republic.

The Fifth Republic

The new Constitution of 1958 gave vast powers to the President and to the Premier, while the Assembly's own powers were curtailed. This format corresponded exactly to de Gaulle's ambitions and, indeed, to many Frenchmen's desires. Both thought that a strong government was the only way to rebuild France and to finally bring the Algerian conflict to a close.

In October 1958 de Gaulle offered the Algerian rebels a cease-fire, but the Algerians, then, refused to stop fighting. They imagined that they could stand firm on their claim of independence because, even after pouring large quantities of men in Algeria, France was not even close to a victory. De Gaulle saw no end to the conflict, and after several failed negotiations, he decided that France should grant Algeria its independence. It was done on April 11, 1961. Immediately, a group of supporters of French Algeria, the OAS *or Organisation de l'Armée Secrète* attempted a *coup* against de Gaulle. Negotiations went on anyway, and finally an agreement was signed in Evian, by which France recognized the independence of Algeria. By June 1964 practically all the French troops had left Algeria. This marked the beginning of the end of France's colonial empire. De Gaulle had understood that France could no longer resist the pressures of colonial nationalism. Following Algeria's example, one after another of France's colonies declared their independence.

After the Referendum of April 8, 1962, by which the French people ratified de Gaulle's settlement of the Algerian problem, de Gaulle made it clear that he alone exercised the executive power of the Republic. He subsequently replaced the Premier Debré by Georges Pompidou[205] and started to implement a series of important political and economic reforms. On August 22, 1962, de Gaulle luckily escaped an assassination attempt by the OAS not far from Paris, at the Petit Clamart locality. After this failed attempt against his life, de Gaulle was able to push through a referendum proposing the election of the President of the Republic by universal suffrage. There was strong opposition to this proposal by many politicians, but in the end de Gaulle's referendum was approved.

At the Presidential elections of 1965, de Gaulle had to contend with another candidate on the ballot, Mitterand. But Mitterand was defeated and de Gaulle was reelected to another seven-year term on December 19, 1965. With this vote of confidence, de Gaulle felt that he could try and restore France's tarnished *"grandeur."* His first task was to work on the country's economy and on important issues of foreign policy. However, in 1968, de Gaulle was to face a very difficult period of social and political turmoil. Unrest started on the university campuses and spread, at least partially, to other sectors. This rebellion turned out to represent a deep conflict of generations, and from that time on, many traditional aspects of French society were rejected. Social conventions, family traditions, morality, dress, language even, music etc. . . . were subjected to a complete and major revolution.

The May 1968 Student-Worker Uprising

In May 1968, a student uprising that soon became a student-worker uprising, rocked Gaullist France.[206] Students, more and more frustrated by the poor conditions of universities, lack of contact with distant professors, inadequate classrooms and, above all, the poor prospect of employment after graduation, eagerly followed the call to revolt. Among their leaders was Cohn-Bendit or *Danny le Rouge* (the Red), who invited students and workers to set up barricades in the streets of Paris and to resist French police by throwing stones and molotov cocktails at the CRS. Confrontations became violent and many cars were upturned and burned. The police often reacted violently, however, to the surprise of all. There were only two deaths in the whole affair. Why the uprising? After years of war, occupation and apathy, the youth of France was seized by a remarkable excitement. They were fed up, they were weary of feeling useless, left aside by the older generation. At the same time they were bubbling with impatience to forge a new France, a new world for themselves. Most of their fathers still were anchored in the past, but they were concerned with their future. Their youthful impatience led to the events of May 1968. On May 13, 1968, the workers' unions declared a general strike in sympathy with the students, and over 750,000 students and workers marched through the French capital demanding major changes. The movement then spread to provinces, and before the end of May, France seemed ready for another major revolution. France was paralyzed for awhile: gasoline was scarce, banks were closed, students occupied university buildings, no classes were taught. But after a record short speech of only three minutes on May 20, 1968, de Gaulle managed to quiet down the uprising and to pacify the strikers. Subsequently, half a million people paraded down the Champs Elysées in support of de Gaulle, chanting "De Gaulle does not stand alone!" It must be said that de Gaulle was helped in part by the Communists, who denounced the rebels as false revolutionaries and fascist *provocateurs*. So, almost by miracle, the strikes were over as suddenly as they had appeared. On May 29 the Communist party and the union CGT *(Confédération Génerale du Travail)* launched a powerful demonstration in Paris calling for a Popular Government. On that day de Gaulle was nowhere to be seen, and the reason was that without warning, de Gaulle had left for Baden-Baden in Germany, where General Massu was in command of the French garrisons. To this day nobody can be sure exactly why de Gaulle left France for Germany. The most likely, according to Georges Pompidou and General Massu's testimonies, is that de Gaulle wanted to get away from a situation that he could not correct. He perhaps even thought of going into exile. In any case General Massu apparently convinced de Gaulle to return to Paris. And indeed de Gaulle returned and immediately showed that he was back and ready to govern.

On May 30, 1968, at 4:31 pm, de Gaulle announced the dissolution of the Assembly and called for calm and actions against anarchy. He asserted: "I will not retire! I will not replace my Prime Minister! I am dissolving the National Assembly!" On May 31, 1968, gasoline was flowing again and workers returned to work and the student protest died. In fact the student protest soon came under increasing criticism and the whole affair was finally forgotten. De Gaulle, it seemed, had won another victory. But not really! The May 1968 events had tarnished his image and weakened his authority. De Gaulle, perhaps as a gesture of strength, or perhaps to show his willingness to make changes, replaced his Premier, Georges Pompidou, even though he had coped well during the crisis. As if unaffected by de Gaulle's firing, Pompidou announced that he would be a candidate at the next presidential elections.

Meanwhile, Pompidou was replaced by a pale bureaucrat, Maurice Couve de Murville, who had served de Gaulle as foreign minister since 1958. Edgar Faure was put in charge of reorganizing education. Everyone at this point expected gradual changes as an answer to the demands of the students. But suddenly, without waiting, de Gaulle decided to put his plan of reforms of the Senate and of regional administration to a referendum. It was a tremendous gamble, all the more when de Gaulle announced that he would resign if his projected reforms did not receive the support of the nation. People were stunned and, unfortunately for de Gaulle, 54% of the voters rejected his proposed reforms on April 27, 1969. De Gaulle was disappointed and perhaps even angry, so on April 28, 1969, de Gaulle resigned with these brief laconic words: "I am ceasing to exercise my functions as President of the Republic; this decision takes effect today at noon!" Immediately after these words, the General went home to Colombey-les-deux-Eglises, where he died 18 months later on November 9, 1970, while writing his memoirs.[207]

French Economy after the Second World War and under de Gaulle

When de Gaulle took office, the economy of France was on the brink of collapse and the country was on the verge of financial crisis with rising prices, inflation and decreasing exports. De Gaulle and his then finance minister Antoine Pinay established a policy of austerity, increased taxes, reduced state expenditures and even devaluated the franc. In the long run the reforms brought about an improvement in the economy; France became a major industrial power giving its citizens access to many consumer goods such as automobiles, television, refrigerators, modern bathrooms and kitchens. In addition, the French had longer vacations with pay: three weeks in 1966 and four weeks in 1969. Supermarkets began to replace many small shops and people could buy food, appliances, furniture, hardware and even books under the same gigantic roof. France's face was changing fast and the traditional rural society of yore was growing into a consumer society with all its advantages and pitfalls. While the rich became richer, the poor grew poorer and the abyss between classes widened. One does not have to look further to find in these problems the roots of the May 1968 insurrection.[208]

De Gaulle's Foreign Policy

De Gaulle's first priority was to restore France's former prestige in the world. Unfortunately following World war II, France had fallen under the umbrella of the United States. De Gaulle resented this situation and wanted to become independent from the Americans. To achieve this, de Gaulle closed the NATO bases on French soil and asked that the SHAPE headquarters be moved out of the Loire to Belgium. To further insure France's independence, the President started an independent nuclear force (*Force de Frappe*/Striking Force). It is only recently, in 1996, that President Chirac announced that France would no longer pursue nuclear tests. This announcement came only after years of loud protests by the French South Pacific natives, the Japanese, the New Zealanders, Australians and many other nations. De Gaulle wanted a non-Atlantic Third Force, and with this in mind, he pursued vigorously the development of the Common Market with Germany. Fearing that Britain would favor the United States and thus become a rival to France's leadership in Europe, de Gaulle blocked Britain's entry into the Common Market.

After de Gaulle

Immediately after de Gaulle's resignation presidential elections took place and Georges Pompidou was elected President of the Republic. Pompidou had obtained a comfortable majority and was prepared to continue de Gaulle's program. However, Pompidou, a jovial, intelligent native of Auvergne, was more liberal, less intransigent than de Gaulle, and more diplomatic. As a testimony to this, Pompidou's first measure was to allow Britain's entry in the Common Market. But Pompidou was sick with leukemia which incapacitated him more and more.[209] The Socialist-Communist coalition headed by François Mitterand exploited the situation and won a good number of seats in the Assembly in 1973, mostly by criticizing the President's laissez-faire economic policies. According to the Left, Pompidou was responsible for letting France drift into the same recession, inflation and unemployment that plagued the rest of Europe at the time. Pompidou did not have the time to fight the crisis because he died suddenly of cancer on April 2, 1974.[210]

Immediately two candidates faced each other: The Socialist François Mitterand and his coalition with Communists and, representing the Right, the candidate of the Independent Republicans, Valérie Giscard d'Estaing. With the first round of votes, Mitterand appeared to be the favorite, but the second round went to Giscard d'Estaing, who received 50.8% of the votes. Mitterand nevertheless received 49.19% of the votes, which meant that Giscard had won by a very narrow margin of less than 1% of the votes. Under these conditions the presidency of Giscard d'Estaing was made somewhat uneasy with Mitterand standing close in the wings, so to speak, and the fact that Giscard was not the leader of the largest party in Parliament.[211] Giscard d'Estaing, however, was full of confidence; he promised the French a bright future and an advanced liberal society. With these goals in mind, Giscard introduced important tax reforms, lowered the voting age to 18 and was even open to the demands of ecologists. He also continued de Gaulle's nuclear program and supported the Common

Market while entertaining friendly relations with Germany and the United States. Unfortunately, the President's hopes were shattered by the world recession and a severe OPEC oil crisis, both bringing inflation up (13.4% in 1979) and increased unemployment figures to 1.6 million (1979), representing 10% of the active population. With 900,000 unemployed workers, production and exports declined. In order to solve the crisis, Giscard decided to appoint a new Prime Minister. He thanked Chirac and called Raymond Barre to the task, asking him to deal with France's economy.

Raymond Barre entered the arena with a great deal of energy, but his noble and honest efforts were unable to stop the rising unemployment (1.7 million in 1981) and inflation increased to 12%. Barre tried to stop the country's dependence on crude oil by speeding up the nuclear energy program. In order to control expenses he stopped many state subsidies, but it forced many companies into financial trouble and even into retrenchment. The Barre Plan, as it was called, seemed a necessary remedy, but it did not produce the economic recovery sought. The situation grew worse with an onslaught of social problems, increased juvenile delinquency and a declining birthrate. Over the years, Giscard had become more and more distant, and he was accused by his critics, Mitterand in particular, of being too haughty and authoritarian.[212] At this point a "*bomb*" exploded: the satirical newspaper *Le Canard Enchaîné* (the chained duck) revealed that Giscard d'Estaing had accepted a gift of a diamond from the African emperor Bokassa. Overnight Giscard fell in disfavor. His term ended in 1981, but even with the Bokassa affair weighing on him, he announced that he would seek a second term. He did and even won the first round of votes. But a coalition of Socialists and Communists won the second round by 52% against only 42% for Giscard. So the Socialist François Mitterand,[213] a charming, eloquent Machiavellian man, easily won the presidency. France had suddenly turned to the Left.

François Mitterand:
First Socialist President of the Fifth Republic

François Mitterand took office on May 21, 1981. His election was celebrated with unusual enthusiasm, by drinking champagne and by dancing on the Place de la Bastille in Paris. As he had promised his electors, Mitterand immediately dissolved the National Assembly in order to secure a new majority for the Left and thus be free to create his Socialist France. Among Mitterand's early clever gestures, he visited the tomb of the Unknown Soldier under the Arch of Triumph and then he went to the Panthéon, where he lay roses on several tombs carefully chosen by him for their political significance. On the tomb of Jean Jaures, Mitterand honored the traditional values of Socialism; on the tomb of Victor Schoelcher,[214] he honored antislavery, and on the tomb of Jean Moulin he honored the Résistance.[215] Another clever move was Mitterand's appointment of four Communists as ministers (for transportation, health, professional training and civil service). The move was all the more clever since he already enjoyed an absolute majority in the Assembly. But this was a way to keep the Communists silent and no doubt under his thumb. Interestingly, during Mitterand's presidency, the Communist Party suffered a major decline, to the point of being marginalized. In 1986 the PC (Communist Party) was supported by only one in ten of all voters and by less than one out of five blue-collar workers. On the other hand, Socialists were gaining control of a good portion of the working class that used to be the traditional fief of Communists. Mitterand named a Socialist mayor from Lille to be his Premier, Pierre Mauroy. With all of this in place, the government proceeded to raise the minimum wage and social security benefits. It shortened the work week, adding an additional week of paid vacations (now five), taxed large fortunes, nationalized industries and private banks, abolished the death penalty and decentralized power from Paris to the regions.

In foreign affairs Mitterand tried to find a solution to the Bosnian-Serbian crisis and the Rwanda civil war. He inaugurated the Eurotunnel under the *Manche* (Channel) with Queen Elizabeth of Britain on May 6, 1994. During the first year of Mitterand's presidency everything proceeded at a fast clip, but already in the second year the pace of reforms slowed down. Mitterand's ideals were changing. His government was slowly drifting toward the Center, away from the Left. These changes in economic policy and in political stand damaged Mitterand's popularity and this helped the extreme Right party of Jean-Marie Le Pen, *Le Front National*. This party was gaining votes particularly in large urban centers with an important immigrant population. As a consequence, in the Legislative elections of 1986, the Socialist party suffered a painful setback, bad enough to put Mitterand's government to the test of "*Cohabitation*" (1986–1988) when there was a Socialist president (Mitterand) and a Right-wing prime minister (Jacques Chirac).[216] President Mitterand was no longer able to govern and was reduced to presiding. That is to say that Mitterand no longer had real power, though he retained enough to thwart at times Chirac's Conservative government, for instance, by refusing to sign government decrees. Mitterand, it is true, retained the prestige of the presidential office and, more importantly perhaps, preserved his desire to surface again with real power by winning the next presidential elections.

Mitterand, in 1988, did win a second term with a 54% majority against Jacques Chirac, and obtained the election of an Assembly with a relative Socialist majority, allowing the return of a Socialist government headed by Michel Rocard as Prime Minister. Rocard did not last long, but at first won some victories: Putting down the rebellion in New Caledonia by promising a vote on self-determination in 1998 was a major success. Rocard failed in Mitterand's eyes by moving toward the Centrists. Mitterand replaced him with Edith Cresson, a move that proved to be a serious misjudgment because Cresson, who was called the "Iron Lady" (mimicking Britain's Margaret Thatcher), did not prove more able than Rocard. She was basically inexperienced in politics and she turned many people against her following several unfortunate comments. Cresson's position became all the more untenable when some of her statements echoed too closely Le Pen's Front National discourse.[217] She finally had to resign on April 2, 1992. Pierre Bérégovoy was appointed, but he remained only eleven months in power. First, he was no more apt than Rocard or Cresson, and second, he committed suicide in May 1993 following a dire failure in the April 1993 elections. Bérégovoy was replaced by Edouard Balladur, a neo-gaullist, who soon was under attack for some of his decisions and for not relating well publicly. Balladur began to slip sharply in opinion polls and at the same time the French economy kept declining and unemployment kept rising. Mitterand was in trouble; he fought with his Culture Minister over Eurodisney; the president was in favor of letting Eurodisney in France for economic reasons, while Jacques Lang opposed it as a negation of culture. Nevertheless, Eurodisney opened in 1992 at Marne La Vallée, not far from Paris. Mitterand supported the European Union, but in spite of this, it was approved by the thinnest of margins. Mitterand changed prime ministers several times but without improvement. And so, in April 1993 the Right took 486 seats out of 577 in the National Assembly, thus obtaining the largest majority since 1958. Jacques Chirac, no longer standing in the wings, declared that Mitterand ought to resign. Mitterand, though, had no intention of doing that. He felt that, after all, Cohabitation was possible and that he could continue to handle the awkward situation. But in June 1994 the Socialists lost more ground and had to give up 6 seats out of 22 in the European Parliament. Meanwhile, something odd was happening with Mitterand's personality: He began to withdraw more and more, rarely leaving his residence, at least officially. Then France was made aware that the President had prostate cancer, a fact he tried to hide carefully to his very death.[218]

At the beginning of 1995 presidential campaign, candidate Balladur was challenged by Jacques Chirac who was ready for another bid for the presidency. Chirac started a non stop tour of France, trying to appeal to the small and medium businessmen. He cleverly centered his campaign on areas where the Left had failed, i.e., on unemployment and poverty. He promised profound reforms in these two areas and a total break with the past. In order to beat his Socialist opponent Lionel Jospin, Chirac promised wage increases, more support for education and came back again and again on the Socialists' failures in matters of crime, immigration, poverty and unemployment. Chirac's program was not really a reflected political platform; it was general, vague, but it touched on areas that concerned the French. It was a way to win votes and it worked. Chirac was elected and, once in power, Chirac appointed Alain Juppé as his Prime Minister, an able, competent, ENA-educated technocrat. The two men faced many challenges, the hardest one being to fulfill all the electoral promises. They had to redress the economic and international status of France, they had to respond to the international outcry caused by the continued French nuclear testing in the Pacific, and they had to try to correct the outcry against the government for not delivering the campaign promises. In addition, they were faced by the monetary constraints of the Maastrich Treaty in order to enter the European Union, and that task was made even more difficult because the French were still divided on the issue and skeptical about the outcome. According to a poll published by *Le Monde* on September 4, 1992, the French were 56% against Maastrich and only 44% in favor.

Jacques Chirac's Presidency under the Fifth Republic

Chirac,[219] having achieved his long sought ambition, assumed the presidential office on May 17, 1995, after a campaign on the need to reduce unemployment and making a clear break with the past. His announced program was attractive and imaginative: He would reduce working hours, increase taxes on speculative earnings, take drastic measures against polluting industries and reduce the presidential terms from 7 to 5 years. Promises are great if they can be kept; unfortunately Chirac had to change his focus almost immediately because France had to meet the criteria for entry in the Economic and Monetary Union requested by the Maastricht Treaty. So, instead of going ahead with the electoral promises, Chirac had to reduce the rather substantial budget deficit of France from 6% to 3% of the GDP by January 1999 and maintain the value of the franc. In order to carry out this revised program, Chirac appointed Alain Juppé as his Prime Minister, a well-educated product of the ENA, and at the same time Mayor of Bordeaux. Juppé was a competent civil servant, even if a bit distant and cold. Even with the help of Juppé, Chirac's reforms were slow to come, and he became unpopular as time passed without carrying out his electoral promises. In addition unemployment was still high and another huge problem had to be faced, the huge deficit of the French *Sécurité Sociale* (Social Security). Juppé announced some very strict reforms and he became terribly unpopular. The French were alienated by the Chirac-Juppé program and, meanwhile, Le Pen's party, *Le Front National*, was gaining momentum. Chirac was desperate, so much so that he took the improbable gamble of dissolving the National Assembly,[220] thus calling for new elections and putting his party on the line. What was feared, but not expected—certainly not by Chirac—happened: the French electors veered to the Left, and voted Socialist.

Chirac's move was immediately qualified a "strategic blunder" and people kept asking "why did he do it?", why did he dissolve an Assembly which was comfortably on his side, and why did he dissolve the Assembly at a time when both he and his Prime Minister, Juppé, were so unpopular for not having fulfilled their electoral promises? The most probable answer to those questions is that Chirac feared a catastrophe in the elections which were going to be held a year later. It is not improbable therefore that Chirac wanted to stop the slide and cut short to any worsening of his situation; he wanted to change course radically and move ahead. Some also suggested that he wanted to out distance Le Pen's FN before it attracted to its side more dissatisfied members of the Right. Will we ever know the truth?

After Chirac's Dissolution of the Assembly.
A New Cohabitation with a New Socialist Prime Minister, Lionel Jospin

After the first ballot in the elections which brought back the Socialists, Juppé, who was by then the most unpopular Premier since the 1950's, decided not to run and the elections went, as stated, in favor of the leftist coalition. Lionel Jospin[221] was elected with uncommon enthusiasm and the Socialists won 289 seats, the majority, in the 577-seat National Assembly. Along with the Communists and the Green (Ecologist party) the leftist coalition took 333 seats, while the Center-right coalition took only 243 seats and the National Front 1 seat. It forced Chirac to govern in a state of *Cohabitation* with an opposition party, that is to say, sharing power with a politically hostile government.[222]

At the start Cohabitation went well. Both men smiled at each other and both went a long way to appear in agreement. Chirac made efforts to appear in charge, relaxed and working hand in hand with Jospin. Soon the relations between the President and his Prime Minister became less cozy and they have not recovered; in fact one can say that they are deteriorating slowly, though as peacefully as possible.

Lionel Jospin after his victory was considered the man of the hour and his plans of reforms were applauded. He felt that he had the support of the nation and so, as a hard conscientious worker, Jospin announced that he was going to revise controversial laws on immigration and nationality, and after a fight, he did. Jospin's honeymoon did not last too long; there was the rebellion of the unemployed, the opposition of Communists against Jospin's plan to sell the national airline Air France, and even more serious problems, the two major ones being unemployment and the demands of the Maastrich Treaty. Some 500,000 workers were unemployed[223] and living on benefits of $400 to $550 a month (considered the poverty line in France). Militant jobless workers demonstrated *en masse* in January 1998 unsatisfied by the stopgap measures of the government. Jospin's Communist allies began to drift away and Robert Hue, leader of the Communist party, even called for a referendum on the single European currency, the Euro, claiming that the government should "reorient Europe toward social issues, employment, another way of using money." Jospin was caught between the hammer and the anvil; on the one hand he had to apply constraints imposed by the Euro and on the other hand he had to satisfy the demands of the jobless workers. In order to placate protestors, Jospin promised an across the board increase in benefits for the jobless and needy persons in 1999.[224] Jospin then also promised to cut the workweek to 35 hours by the year 2000 in order to create jobs, a proposal that passed after many debates. Teachers and students followed the unemployed in expressing their discontent. Jospin seemed to be constantly on the *qui-vive* (on the alert), but he managed to control the situation by giving in a little while remaining firm and determined.

Notes

1   From the Greek word *Megas,* meaning big and *Lithos,* meaning stone.

2   A skull of Cro-Magnon man dating from circa 25,000 BC was discovered in the Dordogne area. Men like the Cro-Magnon man probably adorned the Lascaux cave also in Périgord, the cave at Les Eyzies. These cave paintings probably date from 16,000–14,000 BC. *Cro-Magnon* is the name of a site in Dordogne that has given its name to a prehistoric race.

3   From *druide*, a Celtic priest. One of the druidic rituals was the gathering of mistletoe on certain dates with golden sickles.

4   You can see a bronze statue of Vercingétorix, erected in 1865, at Alise-Sainte-Reine, in the Côte d'Or, site of Caesar's final victory over the famous Celtic chief who came to symbolize the brave fighting virtues of the *Gallic spirit.*

5   French is one of the Romance languages (or Neo-Latin languages) which are derived mostly from Vulgar Latin. The point of departure is the spoken tongue and the history of the French language is the history of the various changes through which Latin (Vulgar Latin) passed until it assumed the dignity of a stable national tongue. See Alfred Ewert, *The French Language,* London, 1943, pp. 1–21.

6   "In a sense, the most remarkable thing about Rome was not that it declined and fell, but that it lasted as long as it did, for almost a thousand years. . . . In the West, Roman civilization never really died but survived in many different ways. The language of Rome, like Roman law, has been of paramount importance in shaping the civilization of the Latin countries. Latin is the direct ancestor of the Romance (that is Romanized) languages of southern Europe . . . The Christian society of the Middle Ages also derived a great deal from Rome." Christopher Brinton and Wolff, *A History of Civilization*, I, p. 127.

7   Mérovée, the Frankish king who gave his name to the first dynasty of French kings. Little is known about him. His presumed father, Chlodion (Clodion)-le-chevelu (the hairy), was in 447 the head of the tribe of the Salian Franks situated along the Ijsel (Yssel) river, northern arm of the Rhine delta that flows in the Dutch Ijselmeer lake.

8   Clovis Ier (465–511), king of the Franks (481–511). He became king of the *Francs Saliens* of Tournai upon the death of his father Chilpéric Ier. After beating Syagrius in Soissons in 486, he defeated the Alamans in 496, the Burgondes in 500 and the Wisigoths in 507. Being sole king over Gaul, he received the name of *patrice* from the emperor of the East, he protected Catholicism and by receiving baptism he was the first Catholic barbarian king. History reports that when Clovis was plunged into the baptismal font, the archbishop said to him: "*Courbe la tête, fier*

Sicambre, adore ce que tu as brûlé, brûle ce que tu as adoré" (Bend your head, proud Sicambre, adore what you burned and burn what you used to adore).

9   "The first figure in the building of the Frankish state is the Merovingian king Clovis who reigned from 481 to 511. . . . Perhaps the greatest single reason for the success of Clovis lay in the conversion from the heathen faith to Christianity. . . . The great power of the Catholic clergy in Gaul, and the even greater power of the whole Roman Church, were cast on the Frankish side. Here begins that close co-operation between the French Crown and the Roman Papacy that was to play so important a part in western history" Christopher Brinton and Wolff. *A History of Civilization*. I, p. 177.

10   Charles-Martel is the natural son of Pépin-le-jeune dit d'Herstal (the younger called "from Herstal).

11   Austrasie: Oriental kingdom of Frankish Gaul, a rival of Neustrie, it came to be the cradle of the Carolingian dynasty.

12   Carloman after 747 retired to the Monte Cassino monastery, a famous monastery founded by Saint Benoît in Latium, Italy.

13   Charlemagne, elder son of Pépin-le-Bref, started to reign alone upon his brother Carloman's death in 771.

14   "He (Charlemagne) was tall, active in hunting and in such other activities as suited the new warrior aristocracy. He was temperate in food and drink, but . . . was perhaps rather intemperate in sex relations. . . . Charlemagne was also an intelligent, able, inventive man. . . . " Christopher Brinton and Wolff, *A History of Civilization*, I, p. 183.

15   "The reign of Charles the Great is by any standard one of the most important in the history of Europe. It marks a culminating point in the sub-Roman period. It also provided in fact as well as in theory an inspiration and example to later medieval monarchies. So much of what we take to be typically medieval in institutional life as well as in cultural life in the West can be traced back directly to the empire of Charles the Great." H.R. Loyn and John Percival, *The Reign of Charlemagne. Documents on Carolingian Government and Administration.* St. Martin's Press, NY. 1975, p. 1.

16   Plundering tribes coming from Scandinavia by sea and who named themselves the Vikings. After Charlemagne's death they made deeper incursions in the main rivers of the kingdom. In 886 they put the siege to Paris but were held back by bishop Gozlin. However, Charles-le-Gros (the Fat) chose to pay them a hefty ransom and he gave them the right to plunder Burgundy in exchange for Paris' freedom. In 911, by the treaty of Saint-Clair-sur-Epte, Charles-le-Simple gave to their chief Rollon the country now known as Normandie (Normandy). Rollon accepted to be baptized and he received Charles-le-Simple as suzerain. After that the Normands stopped their invasions, although they continued to travel by sea as far as southern Italy and Sicily, where some settled.

17   This surge of vassal power followed Charlemagne's death and the breakdown of
      his empire. Many lands of the king passed to vassals, and so these vassals fre-
      quently became more powerful than their *suzerain* the king whom they did not
      hesitate to defy.

18   The Capetians: Third race of the kings of France. This dynasty begins with Hughes
      Capet and can be divided into three branches: 1.The direct Capetians from Hughes
      Capet to Charles IV-le-Bel (the Fair) (987–1328); 2. The Capetians-Valois, from
      Philip VI to Henry III (1328–1589); 3. The Capetians-Bourbons from Henry IV to
      Louis Philippe (1589–1848).

19   The Strasburg Oaths can be considered to be the earliest extant piece of French
      prose. They were composed in 842 and they are the oaths taken by Louis the
      German and by the followers of Charles the Bald at Strasburg at the occasion of
      forming an alliance against Lothair. The text is interesting for history but also for
      the history of the French language: *"Pro Deo amur et pro christian poblo et
      nostro commun salvament, d'ist di in avant, in quant Deus savir et podir me
      dunat, si salvarai eo cist meon fradre Karlo et in ajudha et in cadhuna casa,
      si cum om per dreit son fradra salvar dft, in o quid il mi altresi fazet, et ab
      Ludher nul plaid nunquam prindrai qui, meon vol, cist meon fradre Karle in
      damno sit"* (For the love of God and the salvation of the Christian people and our
      common salvation, from this day forward, in so far as God grants me knowledge
      and power, I will succour this my brother Charles in aid and in every thing, as one
      ought by right to run to the help of one's brother, provided that he does the same
      by me, and I will never undertake any engagement with Lothair which, by my
      consent, may be of harm to my brother Charles here present).This old text repre-
      sents an intermediary step between Latin and Old French. In any case, it attests
      the existence and use of a different language from Latin as early as 842.

20   "When Hughes Capet came to the throne of France in 987, there was little to
      distinguish him from the last feeble Carolingians. Yet he was different, if only
      because he was the first of a male line that was to continue uninterrupted for
      almost 350 years. . . . The Capetians procured the election and coronation of
      the king's eldest son during his father's lifetime, and then took him into the gov-
      ernment. When the father died, the son would already be king (establishment of
      the hereditary principle)." Christopher Brinton and Wolff. *A History of Civiliza-
      tion*, I, p. 211.

21   Suger, French monk, crafty diplomat, was at the same time abbot of Saint-Denis
      and adviser to the king (Louis VI le Gros). During the Second Crusade Suger
      became regent of the kingdom. He tried (in vain) to prevent the divorce of Louis
      VII with Aliénor feeling that it might have disastrous consequences (it did! It pre-
      cipitated the Hundred Years War). A scholar in his own right, Suger wrote several
      books among which a *Vie de Louis VI*.

22   Aliénor d'Aquitaine remarried with Henry Plantagenet, who became king of En-
      gland. They are both buried in Fontrevault l'Abbaye in Touraine, an abbey founded
      in 1101 by the monk Robert d'Arbrissel.

23   Son of Louis VII and of his third wife, Adèle de Champagne. He spent much
      energy fighting Henry II and then Richard the Lionhearted, but he joined the

latter during the Third Crusade. He went on to fight John the Landless, who refused to recognize the French king as his suzerain. He took Normandy (1202–1204) and defeated the Plantagenets and his coalition in Bouvines (1214). Philippe also acquired Auvergne and Champagne. He was an excellent administrator of the kingdom, encouraged commerce and the development of towns. He is remembered for the foundation of the Université de Paris.

24 The Plantagenêts: The line of kings of England from 1154 to 1485. On the Plantagenets, see A.F. Scott, *The Plantagenet Age*. NY., 1976.

25 Philippe Auguste defeated there the emperor Otto IV and his allies, on July 27, 1214.

26 The *Albigeois* also called *Cathares* were a Manichean sect that spread throughout the South of France around Albi. Considered heretics by the Pope, the latter ordered a crusade against them in 1209. The crusaders led by Simon IV of Montfort destroyed the towns of Béziers and Carcassonne and in spite of the protection of the count of Toulouse Raimond VI, the Cathars were defeated at Muret in 1213. It was a disastrous war for the South. Louis VIII took part in this war, which ended during the regency of Blanche de Castille, Saint Louis's mother, by the treaty of Paris in 1229. Then the Cathars disappeared after the destruction of their last stronghold of Monségur (1244).

27 Blanche de Castille, Saint Louis' mother, was a remarkable regent of the kingdom. She crushed the revolt of great vassals, put an end to the Albigensian Crusade (1229) and married Louis to Marguerite de Provence (1234). Blanche ruled with a firm hand. She was able to put down a revolt of the *Pastoureaux,* a group of peasants who devastated the country in Louis' absence. Blanche de Castille exterminated the *Pastoureaux*, including their chief, le maître de Hongrie, in 1251.

Louis was no less remarkable; when attacked by the count de la Marche and by the English, Louis defeated them and through the Treaty of Paris in 1258 he recovered Normandie, Anjou, Maine and Poitou. Learning that the Sultan of Egypt had taken Palestine, Louis IX took the Cross and landed in Damiette in 1249 but had to withdraw after losing the battle of Mansourah in 1250, where he was taken prisoner. He paid a ransom in exchange for his freedom and remained in Palestine two years, from 1250 to 1252. He returned to France upon learning of his mother's death. Louis gave his name to the thirteenth century, the first great century of the French Middle Ages.

28 "Saint Louis was deeply pious, almost monastic in his personal life. Louis carried his own high standards over into his role as king. He wore simple clothes, gave alms to beggars, washed the feet of lepers, built hospitals and created the beautiful Sainte Chapelle." Christopher Brinton and Wolffe. *A History of Civilization*, I, p. 217.

29 Marie de Brabant, born in Louvain, 1254–1321.

30 A general massacre of the French in Sicily in 1282, mainly in Palermo.

31   See Georges Bordonove. *La Tragédie des Templiers*. Paris: Pygmalion, 1993; Lizerand, Georges. *Le dossier de l'affaire des Templiers,* in Collection des Classiques de l'Histoire de France au Moyen Age. Paris, 1923; Malcolm Barber. *The Trial of the Templars*. Cambridge: Cambridge University Press, 1978.

32   Louis le Hutin, son of Jeanne de Navarre. He reigned very briefly and because of the confusion of his rule he was nicknamed Le Hutin (the Bothersome, the Quarrelsome). His only positive act was to emancipate the serfs. On a more controversial side, Louis had his wife, Marguerite de Bourgogne, strangled when he suspected her of misconduct. Later he had Philippe le Bel's superintendent of finances hung at Montfaucon.

33   Philippe V le Long, son of Philippe le Bel and of Jeanne de Navarre, became regent of the kingdom, but since his nephew Jean I lived only a few days he was crowned king in 1316. The Estates General ruled in his favor against Jeanne, daughter of Louis le Hutin, by declaring that women could not accede to the Crown of France.

34   He was sacred king on May 29, 1328. All the Peers of France for France and the reign of Louis XI came to pay homage to him.

35   Until then the case of a king with only daughters had not been considered. Almost all the feudal customs admitted the succession of women to fiefs, although only men could fight in war. So in all the kingdoms of Europe women were admitted in successions. Everything looked like the same thing would apply in France. But France legists were of another mind. They claimed that the kingdom was too high a dignity to be left in the hands of a female. No one knows the exact arguments advanced by the French jurists to bar women from the French Crown.

36   The Hundred Years War was a long series of skirmishes which effectively marked the end of the Middle Ages. The reign of Louis XI marked the transition between the Middle Ages and the Renaissance.

37   The only tax Philippe VI was able to institute without the States' consent was *la gabelle*, a very unpopular tax on salt.

38   Edward III was king of England and duke of Gascony. He claimed the French throne on the ground that his claim was more valid than that of Philippe IV of Valois.

39   The only positive achievement of Philippe VI was the purchase of Dauphiné, around Grenoble, which will become the fief of the elder son of the king, hence called *dauphin*.

40   The English longbowmen created chaos among the French knights on their horses and heavy with armor.

41   This Hundred Years War lasted a long time, in fact altogether about 100 years, but it was not a continuous war. On the contrary it was made of a succession of campaigns, of skirmishes interrupted by several years of truce.

42   Etienne Marcel was assassinated because he wanted to open the gates of Paris to the enemies. He was thrown down from the top of a tower.

43   He will help chasing the English from France.

44   The first to take advantage of Charles VI's illness were his uncles, who return to the government and fire the good advisers of Charles V. Each uncle is in fact very powerful, ruling over vast territories. The duke of Anjou rules Anjou, Provence and the Maine. Jean de Berry rules Poitou, Berry and Auvergne; the Bourbons rule over the Marche, Forez and Beaujolais and the most influent was without a doubt Philippe le Hardi, duke of Burgundy. In addition Philippe de Bourgogne opposed Louis d'Orléans, the king's brother, who rules over Orléanais, Périgord and Blésois.

45   After Louis d'Orléans' murder, Jean sans Peur wanted the king to admit that he was right in killing his brother. The king accepted the justification that the murder was done to preserve the safety of the kingdom.

46   The civil war in France was fought between the Bourguignons and the Armagnacs, or between the *Maillotins* and the *Cabochiens*. The name of *Maillotins* was the name given to the insurrected Parisians because they were fighting with *maillets* (masses) taken from the Arsenal in 1381. The *Cabochiens* were the popular faction of the Bourguignons party, named after their chief, Caboche. The fight between the two factions ended only with the Treaty of Arras in 1435.

47   Azincourt was one of France's most catastrophic and bloody defeats of its history.

48   See Jean Favier. *La Guerre de Cent Ans*. Paris: Fayard, 1980.

49   The demeaning settlement of the Treaty of Troyes gave the English a powerful foothold into France that threatened the national sovereignty of the country. The Dauphin fled to Bourges, where he remained until he was forced back into action by Joan of Arc.

50   See Frances Gies. *Joan of Arc: The Legend and the Reality*. New York: Harper & Row, 1981; Régine Pernoud et Marie-Véronique Clin. *Jeanne d'Arc*. Paris: Librairie Arthème Fayard, 1986; Anne Llewellyn Barstow. *Joan of Arc. Heretic, Mystic, Shaman*. Lewiston, NY: E. Mellen Press, 1986.

51   "The miracle of Joan of Arc took place. The wretched, demoralized following of Charles VII was galvanized into action by this visionary peasant girl who reflected the deep patriotism of the French, and who touched a responsive chord at a moment when all seemed lost." Christopher Brinton & Wolffe, A *History of Civilization*, I, p. 226.

52   Where Jean sans Peur was assassinated in 1419.

53   In fact this state of things, resistance of regions to taxation, will remain until the end of the Ancien Régime, to the French Revolution.

54   In fact by the end of the war the French kingdom had the most solidly organized army in Europe.

55   Charles VII had not fulfilled the humiliating clauses of the Treaty of Arras and he
      was impatient to obtain the right to cross the Burgundian lands because he wanted
      to reconquer Calais. But Charles had not made peace with Philippe le Bon.

56   Born in Bourges (1423–1483) Louis XI was king of France from 1461 to 1483.
      He was the son of Charles VII and Marie d'Anjou. He soon started a quarrel with
      his father and, as soon as he became king, Louis XI fired all of his father's advis-
      ers. This started a revolt of the lords of the kingdom against him (Ligue du Bien
      public, 1465). First he gave in but in 1468 he started the fight against Charles le
      Téméraire, who succeeded in catching him prisoner in Péronne. When he was
      liberated Louis XI succeeded to turn the cantons of Switzerland and Lorraine
      against Charles, who ended defeated and killed in 1477. By the Treaty of Arras
      Louis XI obtained the duchy of Burgundy and inherited the counties of Anjou
      (1480) and Provence (1481). After that Louis XI was able to strengthen the royal
      power, reorganize further the army and improve the economy of the kingdom.

57   Louis XI was to be the last Medieval French king. His reign was full of important
      events which eventually reinforce the authority of the king and shape France for
      years to come, preparing it for modern times.

58   The union of Charles VIII with the duchess of Brittany, Anne, will cost France the
      loss of two provinces, Burgundy and Artois, because Charles VIII does not marry
      the Austrian princess to whom he was engaged in 1482!

59   Louis XI near the end of his reign was plagued with some severe skin disease and
      apoplexy. Fearing death, fearing mostly to be poisoned, he locked himself in his
      manor of Plessis-lez-Tours, but he died of a congestion on August 30, 1483.

60   Jacques Coeur was a rich merchant born in Bourges (1395–1456). He was first
      great financier and even financial wizard of Charles VII, was a busy diplomat and
      participated to the reorganization of finances and the army. Accused of extortion
      he was arrested in 1451 but managed to escape. He was later rehabilitated by
      Louis XI. His personal hôtel in Bourges remains a characteristic monument of the
      splendidly rich bourgeois architecture of the fifteenth century.

61   See Frederick F. Cartwright and Michael D. Biddiss. *Disease in History*. New
      York: Dorset Press, 1972; Gwyneth Cravens and John S. Marr. *The Black Death*.
      New York: E.P. Dutton and Co., Inc., 1977.

62   Jean Huss will be judged as heretic by the Constance Concile and burned on the
      pyre in 1415.

63   "No other epoch has laid so much stress as the expiring Middle Ages on the
      thought of death. . . . The endless complaint of the frailty of all earthly glory was
      sung to various melodies. Three motifs may be distinguished. The first is ex-
      pressed by the question: where are now all those who once filled the world with
      their splendour? The second motif swells on the frightful spectacle of human
      beauty gone to decay. The third is the death-dance: death dragging along men of
      all conditions and ages." J. Huizinga. *The Waning of the Middle Ages*, Chapter
      XI, "Vision of Death," pp. 138–139.

64   See for instance the fifteenth-century altar screen depicting the Last Judgement by Rogier Van der Weyden in the Hôtel Dieu in Beaune (Côte d'Or), Burgundy.

65   English translation: "There is no limb nor a form, Which does not smell of putre-faction. Before the soul is outside, The heart which wants to burst in the body Raises and lifts the chest Which nearly touches the backbone. -The face is discol-ored and pale, And the eyes veiled in the head. Speech fails him, For the tongue cleaves The to the palate. The pulse trembles and he pants . . . The bones are disjointed on all sides; There is not a tendon which does not stretch as to burst." J. Huizinga, *The Waning of the Middle Ages*, pp. 148–149 and fn. 9.

66   Son of Louis XI and of Charlotte de Savoie. Born in Amboise (1470–1498). He was king from 1483 to 1498. He married Anne de Bretagne in 1490. Not a very astute diplomat, Charles in order to have free hands in his conquest of the king-dom of Naples gave Roussillon and Cerdagne to Spain, Artois and Franche-Comté to Austria, and after all that his expedition failed!

67   Louis XII, born in Blois (1462–1515), was king of France from 1498 to 1515. He was the son of Charles d'Orléans and Marie de Clèves. He had married Louis XI's daughter Jeanne, but divorced her in order to marry Charles VIII's widow, Anne de Bretagne. When she died, Louis married Marie d'Angleterre but died shortly after. He was nicknamed "*Père du peuple*"(father of the people). The tomb of Louis XII and Anne de Bretagne by Jean Juste is in the Saint-Denis Basilica. It is a masterpiece of the Renaissance.

68   On Templars, see Georges Bordonove. *La Tragédie des Templiers*. Paris: Pygmalion, 1993.

69   Emperor of Germany in 1138.

70   German emperor 1152–1190.

71   Frederic delayed too much and Pope Gregoire IX excomunicated him in 1227. So Frederic left for the crusade and thus is in a curious position: excomunicated but fighting a crusade!

72   Villehardoin, 1150–1213, wrote the *Histoire de la conquête de Constantinople*, one of the most precious documents on the Fourth Crusade. When that crusade was over, Villehardoin remained in the East with the title of *Maréchal de Romanie*. Joinville, 1224–1317, accompanied Saint Louis in Egypt in 1248. His *Mémoires* that he finished to write in 1309 are a precious document on the reign of Saint Louis.

73   It is interesting to note that with Erasmus program and the European Community we are returning to this same principle at the eve of the Third Millennium!

74   See John Fox. *A Literary History of France: The Middle Ages*. New York: Barnes and Noble Books, 1974, pp. 20–57 and 58–104.

75   The oldest French *chanson de geste*, written between 1100 and 1125 according to some scholars, but the debate on its datation remains open. It resembles in

inspiration to the saints' lives. See Gerard J. Brault. *The Song of Roland, an Analytical Edition*. Pennsylvania State University Press, University Park and London, 2 vols, 1978.

76   See John Fox. *A Literary History of France: The Middle Ages*. New York: Barnes & Noble Books, 1974, pp. 134–139.

77   On Troubadours, see John Fox. *The Middle Ages*, pp. 105–121.

78   See John Fox. *The Middle Ages*, pp. 145–167.

79   See John Fox. *The Middle Ages*, pp. 338–342 and 344–351. See Guy Mermier. *Jehan de Paris*. Mellen, 1993.

80   See John Fox, *The Middle Ages*, pp. 293–297.

81   See John Fox. *The Middle Ages*, pp. 271–273 and 302–303.

82   See John Fox. *The Middle Ages*, pp. 274–275 and 303–305.

83   See John Fox. *The Middle Ages*, pp. 305–309.

84   See John Fox. *The Middle Ages*, pp. 309–315.

85   See John Fox. *The Middle Ages*, pp. 225–239.

86   See John Fox. *The Middle Ages*, pp. 240–260. See Guy Mermier. *The Play of Madness*. Lang, 1997.

87   See John Fox. *The Middle Ages*, pp. 261–278.

88   See John Fox. *The Middle Ages*, pp. 216–221.

89   See John Fox. The Middle Ages, pp. 279–292.

90   See John Fox. *The Middle Ages*, pp. 227–232.

91   On French medieval literature see: John Fox. *A Literary History of France: The Middle Ages*. London, New York. 1974; L. Kukenheim et H. Roussel. *Guide de la littérature française du Moyen Age*. Universitaire pers Leiden. Leiden, 1959; Barbara G. Keller. *The Middle Ages Reconsidered*. Peter Lang, Studies in the Humanities no. 11, 1994. On the fifteenth century romance Jean de Paris, see *The Romance of Jehan de Paris*. Guy Mermier, trans., Studies in French Literature vol. 15, The Edwin Mellen Press, 1993. On the romance of Tristran and Yseut, see Guy R. Mermier, ed. Trans., *Béroul: Tristran and Yseut*. Peter Lang, series in Romance Languages and Literature, vol. 50 American University Studies, 1987. On the medieval drama *The Play of Madness (Le Jeu de la Feuillée)*, see Guy Mermier, trans., *Adam d'Arras. The Play of Madness*. Peter Lang. Studies in the Humanities no. 22, 1997. On medieval bestiaries, see Guy R.Mermier, ed., *Le Bestiaire de Pierre de Beauvais*. A.G. Nizet. 1977; Guy R. Mermier, with illustrations by Alexandra Eldridge, *A Medieval Book of Beasts, Pierre de Beauvais' Bestiary*. The Edwin Mellen Press, 1992. For more references, see our bibliography.

92   See John James. *The Traveler's Key to Medieval France. A Guide to the Sa-cred Architecture of Medieval France*. New York: Alfred A. Knopf, 1986.

93   The church of Saintes Maries de la Mer in Camargue is a beautiful example of an early Romanesque church-fortress with the crypt as its heart. Other examples of Romanesque churches are: The church of Marmoutier (Bas-Rhin), Vézelay, the cathedral Saint Pierre-d'Angoulême, the abbey of Tournus in Burgundy, the ca-thedral Saint-Lazare of Autun with its scenes of the Last Judgement on its tympa-num, the church Saint-Lazare of Avallon, the superb pilgrimage church of Sainte-Foy de Conques (Aveyron).

94   See for instance, the magnificent Romanesque frescoes in the church of Saint-Savin-sur-Gartempe.

95   Notre-Dame de Chartres and Notre-Dame de Paris are two splendid Gothic ca-thedrals, but the Gothic cathedral of Reims is also a jewel of the genre. The Gothic sculptures of Chartres, Notre-Dame de Senlis, Amiens and Strasbourg are brilliant examples of the genius of medieval sculptors during the Gothic age.

96   See Jean Delumeau. *La Peur en Occident (XIVe–XVIIIe siècles)*. Paris: fayard, 1978.

97   See *Histoire de France* under the direction of J. Carpentier and F. Lebrun. Paris: Seuil, 1987, pp. 170–205.

98   "The great surge of the Sixteenth century: The keynote of the whole epoch is will power, daring virtù. In absolute purity this quality is best exemplified in Machiavelli's hero, the princely ruffian Cesare Borgia. But the same intensity, the same bound-less hope, the same lust for action are found among the discoverers and the apostles, the scholars and the artists. They are manifest in Vasco de Gama, Columbus, Luther, Calvin, St. Ignatius, as well as in Michelangelo, Leonardo da Vinci and Rabelais. It was in truth a world of giants." Guérard, *France*, p. 123.

99   French theologian (1450–1537), precursor of Calvin. He made the first transla-tion of the Bible into French.

100   French Hellenist (1467–1540).

101   Born in Cognac in 1494, son of Charles of Valois and of Louise of Savoie. He married Louis XII's daughter, Claude de France.

102   French brilliant Hellenist who urged François Ier to build the *Collège de France* in 1530.

103   "François Ier was in many respects a prototype of Louis XIV, with less sustained and self-assured perfection, but with the color, the bravado, the dash of Italian virtù which made the renaissance so much more fascinating than the age of Boileau." Guérard. *France*, p. 130.
       From François Ier's reign dates the redaction in French of all judgments, no-tary acts and registers of birth and death.

104   Indulgences were cash contributions made to the Church to have sins forgiven, thus escaping the traditional penances that could be severe.

105   See Guy Mermier. *Pierre Viret. L'Interim fait par dialogues.* Peter Lang, 1985.

106   Didier Erasmus, learned scientist and humanist, author of the major work *L'Eloge de la folie.* He was to be called "Le Voltaire latin" because of his supreme genius and wit.

107   Michel de Montaigne, French moralist and author of *Les Essais* (1533–1592). Rabelais (1494–1553) was a Benedictine monk and a physician, professor of anatomy, *curé* of Meudon and author of *Gargantua and Pantagruel.* Epicurian philosopher and humanist of genius.

108   The Réforme or Reformation was a religious and political movement that took half of Europe away from the obedience to the Popes. It was Martin Luther who was the movement's main anti-Roman Catholic leader. The movement was later on led by Jean Calvin under François Ier. It grew in numbers under Henri II. The Duke of Guise was responsible for the eight wars of religion that started with the Wassy massacre in 1562 when about sixty Protestants were killed by the men of the Duke de Guise.

109   Indulgences were granted by the Church for sins committed. The Church, in exchange of money or land from the sinners, absolved their sins. For instance, the Church allowed certain persons who would make some contribution to the Church to eat butter during Lent. Martin Luther's main criticism against the Catholic Church was its dispensing indulgences.

110   François Ier first tolerated the Calvinists, but he repressed them later on by having the Vaudois massacred in 1545.

111   Charles IX was the second son of Henri II and Catherine de Médicis. He reigned from 1560 to 1574. He was unable to stop the actions of his mother and of the Guises against the Protestants and let the massacre of Saint-Barthélémy take place. He died greatly disturbed by remorse for the Saint-Barthélémy murders.

112   Henri III, son of Henri II and Catherine de Médicis, was king from 1574 to 1589. He was corrupt, and mostly incapable, who surrounded himself with young men who were called *mignons.*

113   Henri IV was to be a most popular king, like St. Louis earlier, and he was the first of the Bourbon branch of the Capetian dynasty which was to last until the French Revolution.

114   The edict authorized Protestants to hold their Calvinist cult anywhere except at the Court and in Paris. Protestants were granted four universities and some seats in Parliament. When these rights were gradually withdrawn and the edict revoked in 1685, many Protestants left France and that was a great loss of hands and minds for the French nation.

115   Ravaillac was condemned to death and *écartelé* (dismembered, limbs torn by a team of horses) in 1610.

116   Concini, Italian adventurer and a favorite of Marie de Médicis, also known as the
      Maréchal d'Ancre.

117   Maximilien de Béthune, Baron de Rosny, duc de Sully was born in the château de
      Rosny in 1560. A Protestant, he fought with Henry IV and became a minister of
      the king, administering finances wisely and protecting agriculture. In addition,
      Sully improved and built roads and canals. He also improved French artillery. He
      died in 1641.

118   Charles de Luynes, *connétable de France*, born in Pont-Saint-Esprit in Provence
      (1578–1621) became a favorite of Louis XIII and played a major role after Concini's
      murder.

119   Nicolas Vitry, captain of Louis XIII's guards, killed Concini and was rewarded by
      the title of maréchal de France (1581–1644).

120   Richelieu was not liked by Louis XIII, but he surely was the best man to conduct
      the affairs of the state for the king. Richelieu came to power with some top prorities:
      First he wanted to destroy the Huguenots, and second, he wanted to weaken the
      pride and arrogance of the nobles. Cardinal Richelieu carried out his program
      with efficient determination. He set the siege to La Rochelle until the famished
      Protestants capitulated. He never bargained with the Huguenots and they had to
      accept the conditions that Richelieu judged fair for them. Richelieu was often
      harsh against the nobles, but really only against dissident nobility. Richelieu was
      for law and order and wanted the nobility to be faithful subjects of the king. When
      the peasants revolted against too heavy taxes, Richelieu fought them with equal
      harshness. An excellent A first rate economist too, Richelieu encouraged trade
      overseas and established several colonial companies beyond France's borders,
      just like those of Holland and England.
          Military tactician, Richelieu understood that a strong navy was essential and so
      he organized a strong fleet in the Atlantic Ocean as well as in the Mediterranean.
      Richelieu was also an excellent and enlightened economist who saw the benefit of
      establishing colonial companies overseas just like those of England and Holland.
      He also encouraged trade beyond France's borders. Cardinal Richelieu protected
      the Catholic clergy, but he insisted that they act in the service of the state.

121   Giulio Mazarini, prime minister under Louis XIII, kept his position under Louis
      XIV thanks to Anne d'Autriche's friendship. He imposed upon Spain the treaty of
      the Pyrénées (1659) and prepared for Louis XIV the succession of Spain.
          Mazarin was a friend of Richelieu and very knowledgeable of Richelieu's diplo-
      matic negotiations. Anne of Austria was 41 years old when she became Regent
      after Louis XIII's death and she almost immediately fell under the spell of the
      charming and handsome Mazarin, who, in return, lost no opportunity to flatter
      her. In fact Mazarin was a great help to Anne, just as Richelieu had been to Louis
      XIII. Mazarin fought the Fronde revolt shrewdly (the Fronde was a revolt against
      the poor financial politics of Mazarin) and he fought the wars outside France with
      success. Until his death, Mazarin held unquestioned power and was totally in
      charge of the government of France. He was an excellent tutor to the young Louis
      XIV until the latter's coming of age. With Mazarin Catholicism became stronger
      even though Jansenism was gaining ground at the monastery of Port Royal des

Champs near Paris. (Jansénism or doctrines of Jansenius which limited free will, a position held by theologians like Saint Cyran, Arnauld, both from Port Royal, the center of Jansenism under Saint-Cyran, its religious director). The Jesuits fought Jansenism until Louis XIV ordered the order closed in 1709 and the buildings destroyed in 1712.

Thanks to Mazarin's work, Louis XIV was able to assume total power, become the Sun King and bring France to an apex of grandeur intellectually, culturally as well as in arts and politics. As a sign of France's supremacy under Louis XIV, its language became the international tongue, the language of European courts and of all aristocratic and cultivated classes.

122   Mazarin had amassed a huge fortune on the back of the French people.

123   Louis XIV, le Grand (the great) was the son of Louis XIII and of Anne d'Autriche. He first reigned under his mother's regency. In 1661, Louis XIV announced his intention to reign by himself. One of his first acts was to fire Fouquet and to replace him by Colbert as superintendant of finances (1661). (Colbert had discovered some form of embezzlement committed by Fouquet and denounced him to the king who had Fouquet arrested and thrown in jail. Fouquet died in the citadel of Pignerol 19 years later). Under Louis XIV the engineer Vauban was fortifying France's borders and Louvois was reorganizing the army. Louis XIV had many foreign ambitions but his wars, if they brought some glory to France, also emptied its treasury. Louis XIV established the absolute cult of his royal person and pushed centralization to its extremes. His desire of unification was so strong that he could not stand anyone or any group thinking differently from him. So he revoked the Edit de Nantes and persecuted the Jansenists. If his intolerant or excessive political and religious views attracted upon him the animosity of Europe, his taste for the arts and letters inspired many artists, writers and poets: Corneille, Racine, Molière, for the theatre, La Fontaine and Boileau for poetry, Bossuet, Fénelon and Fléchier for eloquence of the pulpit, La Bruyère and La Rochefoucauld for moral satire, Pascal for philosophy, Saint-Simon and Retz for history. Not only did Louis XIV support men of letters, he supported also many artists like Poussin, Le Lorrain, Le Brun, Perrault, Mansard, Puget, Girardon. All in all, Louis XIV inspired the cult of perfection and majesty, as reflected in the palace of his creation, Versailles, eternal reflection of the greatness of French monarchy. (Versailles is situated 18kms from Paris. Its parks and gardens were decorated by Le Nôtre with superb fountains).

124   On Louis XIV: "He was served by a vigorous physique. He was not handsome, of medium height and stocky; he lacked the aristocratic mien of Charles I. The famous Bourbon nose, both aquiline and fleshy, was impressive rather than beautiful. . . . He was a voracious eater in spite of bad teeth and early stomach troubles. Robust rather than agile, he was fond of all physical exercises; he was keen on the hunt and, almost up to the last, a fine horseman. He loved to dance. . . . His appetite for pleasure expressed itself in innumerable love affairs. . . ." Guérard, France, pp. 178–179.

125   Jacques Bénigne Bossuet (1627–1704), famous religious orator and one of the great writers of the Classical period.

126   The Château de Versailles was started in 1668, commissioned by Louis XIV. It was a fantastic, monumental addition to Louis XIII's hunting lodge. The work was started by the architect Louis Le Vau and continued from 1678 by the great architect Jules Hardoin-Mansart while André Le Nôtre redesigned the gardens, adding fountains such as the spectacular Fontaine de Neptune (Neptune's fountain) adjacent to the Dragon fountain. Louis XIV also added in 1687 the Grand Trianon, a small palace mostly to escape from the crowds of courtiers and to be able to have some moments of privacy with Madame de Maintenon. Versailles is a typical example of the rich Baroque style in vogue under Louis XIV's reign.

127   Louis XIV alleged certain rights of his Spanish wife.

128   *Molière (Jean-Baptiste Poquelin) (1622–1673), author of many comedies; Jean Racine (1639–1699), famous author of classical tragedies, although he wrote one comedy, Les Plaideurs; Pierre Corneille (1606–1684), famous author of classical tragedies; Jean de La Fontaine (1621–1695), famous author of Les Fables and of Contes.*

129   Jean-Baptiste Colbert (1619–1683), brilliant statesman under Louis XIV. His influence waned when he started to fight royal expenses. He was replaced by Louvois (1641–1691), who became one of the main ministers of Louis XIV.

130   Louis XV when thirteen years old, in 1723, was declared ready for marriage. He was to marry Anna Maria, Spain's infanta, as a sign of reconciliation between France and Spain. Considering that the infanta was still too young to produce an heir, the Duke of Bourbon, who assumed power after the death of the Duke of Orléans, sent the infanta back to Spain and had the king mary Maria Leszczinska, daughter of the former king of Poland, in 1725. They had two children. Louis XV died in Versailles on May 10, 1774, and was buried in St. Denis.

131   André Hercule, cardinal de Fleury (1653–1743), prelate and minister of Louis XV.

132   The Marquise de Pompadour contributed to the Seven Years' War. On the good side she spent a lot of money supporting artists, poets and writers.

133   The Countess Du Barry (1743–1793) was beheaded during the Revolution, under the Terror in 1793.

134   Ironically, Louis XV was nicknamed "*Le Bien-Aimé*" (Well Loved)!

135   Louis XVI, grandson of Louis XV, son of the Dauphin Louis, the only legitimate son of Louis XV, and the Princess Marie-Josèphe de Saxe, was born in Versailles in 1754. Married to Marie-Antoinette, Louis XVI was considered virtuous and was welcomed with cries of joy when he assumed the throne. Under Louis XVI French finances went from bad to worse and from worse to catastrophic, a situation particularly due to the large contributions of the Court to the Americans. When forced to call a meeting of the Estates-General, the king became hesitant while he decretely supported the émigrés. One day (June 20, 1791) he tried to flee from France with his family, but they were recognized and caught before the border and brought back to Paris. Afterward, they were locked up in the Temple

and judged by the revolutionary Convention. Louis XVI was deposed in 1792 and was convicted of treason, condemned to death and beheaded January 21, 1793. He was buried in St. Denis.

Marie Antoinette was the daughter of the Habsburg emperor Francis I and of Marie-Thérèse. She was born in Vienna. Because of her prodigality and contacts with foreign power she rapidly became unpopular and a suspect. The Revolution imprisoned her in the Temple and after a rapid judgement by the Revolutionary tribunal she was condemned to death and led to the guillotine in 1793.

The guillotine was invented by the French doctor Joseph-Ignace Guillotin, professor of anatomy in Paris. Ironically Doctor Guillotin was guillotined himself under the Terror regime.

136 Louis XVI was clumsy with his body, but skillful with his hands, a good hunter and clever at tinkering with clocks and locks.

137 It is a fact that Louis XVI could not stand to offend people. But that led him often to be hypocritical.

138 For several years the French government remained non-interventionist, but it poured munitions into the colonies. In fact nine-tenths of the arms used by the Americans at the battle of Saratoga came from France. After the American victory in this battle, the French government concluded in 1778 that the insurgents were a good political risk and signed an alliance with them and declared war on Great Britain. The consequences of the American Revolution can hardly be overstated: By over-burdening the French treasury, the American war became a direct cause of the French Revolution.

139 Voltaire, François-Marie Arouet, was a witty, curious and great mind. He was invited many times both by Frederic II and by Catherine II of Russia. He is the author of many varied publications, tragedies, history, tales, criticism, epic po-ems, philosophical treatises etc. . . . He fought religious intolerance and stood for justice. His style was especially limpid, elegant and precise. No one was more human than Voltaire and no one in his time fought more in favor of individual liberty and believed as hard in human progress. In addition Voltaire wrote over 10.000 letters over 60 years.

Montesquieu, Charles De Secondat, Baron de Montesquieu, was born at the château de la Brède in Gironde. Montesquieu is famous for his *Lettres Persanes*, for his book *De la grandeur et de la décadence des Romains* and *L'Esprit des lois*. He was an enlightened precursor of the Revolution.

Diderot, Denis (1713–1784), was a French philosopher and writer, ardent proponent of the eighteenth century philosophical ideas, a critic, a strong person-ality and a powerful thinker. He founded the *Encyclopédie* in 1751 and pub-lished picturesque novels, *Jacques le* Fataliste, *Le neveu de Rameau*. He also wrote plays like *Le fils naturel* and *Le père de famille*. In addition he is the author of a large correspondence and artistic studies.

140 The year 1784 was the height of the Age of Enlightenment (*Siècle des lumières*), the age of *philosophes* that believed in freedom, in personal liberty and feared the evils of intolerance and religion. The Age of Enlightenment was curious about

the world, this world rather than God's world. Reformation in disrupting the unity of Western Christendom in fact helped the weakening of the Church and thus prepared the way for the Enlightenment. Science had broken away from its traditional moorings and prepared the way for great scientific philosophers like Descartes, Galileo, Francis Bacon and Newton. The advancement of science led to more critical freedom and reason was prevailing over revelation. The claim that Christianity was the only true faith was thrown into doubt, but the eighteenth century was not really anti-religious. Simply, religion was no longer the only measure and hope; in other words, religion was secularized, with less talk of hell and damnation. Deism began to be fashionable and in France Voltaire and Rousseau were deists just as Benjamin Franklin and Thomas Jefferson in America. According to deism, God was manifest in all the workings of nature. Deists did not deny the existence of God; they saw God in the wide world and he was perceived as a great watchmaker. The deist God implied universal ethical laws, decency, generosity, and honesty. To achieve these moral values men did not need churches, prayers or saints; all they needed was reason.

141   France was no longer isolated. Its windows and doors were opening widely to all sorts of outside influences and in fact it can be said that if until the Revolution France was French, after the Revolution it became European. The Romantic movement was not French; it had important foreign sources: English with Walter Scott and German with Goethe.

142   Of these 26 million 20 million lived from the land.

143   "The immediate cause of the French Revolution of 1789 was financial. A rapidly mounting deficit, swollen by the expense of the French aid to the American Revolution, drove the monarchy steadily toward bankruptcy. King Louis XVI vainly tried one expedient after another and finally summoned the Estates General, the central French representative assembly that had last met 175 years earlier. Once assembled the deputies of the nation initiated reforms that were to destroy the Old Regime in France." . . . The basic causes of the French Revolution reached deep into the society and economy of France and into the country's political and intellectual history. Behind the financial crisis of the 1780's lay decades, indeed centuries, of fiscal mismanagement. The government had been courting bankruptcy at least since the reign of Louis XIV. The nobles and clergy, jealously guarding the remnants of their medieval privileges, refused to pay a fair share of the tax burden. Resentment against inequitable taxation and inefficient government built up among the unprivileged peasantry, the workers and, above all, the bourgeoisie. The ideas of the Enlightment, advanced by the philosophes, translated bourgeois resentment into a program of active reforms." Christopher Brinton and Wolff, A History of Civilization, vol. II, pp. 95–99.

144   The noble order comprised about 400,000 persons in 1789.

145   Often the French Revolution has been represented as a popular, lower-class uprising but that view is incorrect. In appearance the French Revolution was popular, but deep down the French Revolution was carried out by the bourgeois. The Revolution, therefore, was the collision of a rising aristocracy jealous of its tradi-

tional privileges and a rising bourgeoisie eager to obtain the same status and privileges as the nobility.

146   Persons dependent on wages were suffering because between 1730 and 1780 prices had risen about 65%, whereas wages had risen only 20–22%.

147   Composed of the assemblies in which representants of the whole nation gathered, deputies of the clergy, nobility and the Third Estate. The first meeting of the Estates-General was called by king Philippe le Bel in 1302 to obtain the support of the kingdom against Pope Boniface VIII. The last gathering of the Estates-General took place in 1789. They soon were converted into the National Assembly (Assemblée Nationale Constituante).

148   Public opinion thus began to be a force to be reckoned with. After their death, Voltaire and Rousseau's ideas began to spread throughout France. One basic idea was that liberty was naturally due to the individual. The diffusion of these new ideas was made through novels and plays such as Beaumarchais' *Mariage de Figaro*, Voltaire's tales and Diderot's works. The economic situation exasperated the people, who started to riot and when crushed down by the king's troops led to an unavoidable explosion of violence.

149   Emmanuel Joseph Sieyès (1748–1836), author of a publication on the *Tiers Etat* (1789), was an active politician under the Revolution and remained active in politics. He organized with Bonaparte the famous *coup d'état* of brumaire (an VIII) that dissolved the *Directoire* and made Napoleon *Premier Consul*. Honoré Gabriel Riqueti, Comte de Mirabeau (1749–1791), was in 1789 deputy of the *tiers état* in the Estates General where he was a brilliant and powerful orator. Partisan of a constitutional monarchy, Mirabeau acted on the side of the Assembly and at times on the king's side. This double game made him accused of treason, and he was guillotined.

150   In the provinces there was a sudden wind of panic, of hysteria. There were rumors of brigands destroying crops, killing and raping. Castles were burned, tax collectors and clergy were murdered. But the peasants were not motivated by some sort of great fear; they knew what they were doing and they intended to destroy the manorial regime that had oppressed them for years.

151   The Bastille was practically an empty prison with only five prisoners and not the thousands victims of royal tyranny as it was believed.

152   In the meantime Louis XVI continued to have an inept behavior and people grew more and more suspicious of the queen whom they nicknamed *L'Autrichienne*. So on October 6, 1789, the mob went to Versailles and brought back the king and his family to the Tuileries in Paris. On June 20, 1791, the king escaped from Paris at night hoping to be able to reach loyal forces headquartered at Metz. But they were recognized on the way and brought back in shame to Paris. From that point on no one would trust the king anymore.

153   In order to repress the counter-revolution, anarchy, civil strife, the Convention and the Committee of Public Safety with Robespierre as leader set up what is

known as the Reign of Terror. Terror struck at those who were thought to be enemies of the Republic. The number of persons who lost their lives in the Terror from 1783 to July 1794 was close to 40,000. Thousands of suspects at the same time languished in jail.

154   Maximilien de Robespierre (1758–1794) was born in Arras. He was the instigator of the revolutionary Reign of Terror *(la Terreur)* and executed most of the non-extremists. He also instituted the cult of the Supreme Being *(l'Étre Suprême)* represented by a young and pretty young woman. On 9 thermidor An II (July 27, 1794), Robespierre was overthrown and he died on the guillotine. He was named the *"Incorruptible."*

155   Adopted in October 1793, the Revolutionary calendar was as follows: *Fall*: Vendémiaire, Brumaire and Frimaire. *Winter*: Nivôse, Pluviôse,Ventôse. *Spring*: Germinal, Floréal, Prairial. *Summer*: Messidor, Thermidor, Fructidor. The year began with the Fall equinox (September 22) and was divided into 12 months of 30 days each, with 5 or 6 days added that had to be dedicated to the celebration of Republican feasts.

156   It was the time of *Muscadins* and *Merveilleuses*, men and women dressed in odd, way-out clothes, sometimes overdressed and sometimes underdressed in the extreme.

157   In return, Bonaparte destroyed the thousand-year-old Republic of Venice, which he turned over to Austria.

158   The only positive results of Bonaparte's expedition in Egypt were the introduction in that country of French culture and the discovery of some of the marvels of Egyptian art in France.

159   Fructidor was the twelfth month of the Republican calendar beginning on August 18 or 19. The Republican calendar was instituted by the National Convention on October 24, 1793.

160   Napoleon Bonaparte (1769–1821) was born in Ajaccio, Corsica, on August 15, 1769, second son of Charles Bonaparte and of Laetitia Ramolino. He was educated at the military school of Brienne-le-Château and distinguished himself as an artillery captain in Toulon (1793), as general of brigade during the 1794 campaign in Italy. He was short, dark haired with typical Italian features. He looked better in army uniforms than in civilian clothing. He was moody, temperamental and eloquent mostly when addressing his soldiers. He was sort of a genius military strategist who could inspire confidence when everyone thought the situation was desperate. With all his defects, Napoleon had enough qualities to convince Frenchmen that he was the man they were looking for to help them recover after the revolutionary upheaval.

161   These codes are still in force today.

162   Napoleon, as soon as he was crowned emperor, pursued his visionary plan for France, among other things creating an aristocracy of merit, the Legion of Honor, and encouraging the bright sons of the bourgeoisie to become bankers, industrial-

ists, government officials and businessmen. To this end Napoleon created the
state *lycées*.

163   See Alan Schom, *Napoleon Bonaparte*, Harper Perennial, 1997. Schom writes:
"The autopsy conclusions notwithstanding, there is no doubt that Napoleon was
murdered. Recent scientific analyses of Napoleon's hair have found arsenic levels
from 35 to 640 times that found in the hair of a healthy human being. Facts are
facts" (p. 786). According to Schom, Napoleon was killed by a Frenchman,
Montholon, and concludes: "One final irony: The French emperor, who had successfully escaped death time and again from Prussian, Russian, British, Austrian,
German, Italian, and Spanish artillery, muskets, swords, and bayonets, had been
killed by his closest chosen companion—a Frenchman" (p. 787). In fact Montholon
killed Napoleon because he had promised him a substantial income for him and
his wife. The sooner Napoleon died, the sooner he would be rich and could leave
St. Helena. Schom states however: "The scheme would have worked—if the
Bonaparte clan, in a rare moment of family solidarity, had not blocked his
(Montholon's) access to the loot. . . . " (p.787).

164   Charles X, born in Versailles (1757–1836), king of France (1824–1830), brother
of Louis XVI and of Louis XVIII The 1830 revolution forced him to abdicate.

165   Louis-Philippe Ier (1773–1850), king of France (1830–1848). He had to abdicate
during the 1848 Revolution, and fled to England.

166   After the fall of Louis-Philippe, February 24, 1848, Lamartine was the main
personality of the interim government. This government not only proclaimed the
republic, the universal suffrage, but also abolished slavery in the colonies.

167   One may wonder why Louis-Napoleon was not opposed more strongly, but one
has to consider that the Napoleonic Legend had made inroads in the minds of the
French, who were tired of the bourgeois monarchy. They began to dream of the
past, forgetting the miseries brought upon them by the emperor, and retaining
only the poetry of his reign. All this was reinforced by Victor Hugo's poems,
Thiers' histories. And furthermore the Arch of Triumph in Paris was finished in
1836 and the remains of the emperor were brought back from Saint Helena and
placed in the Invalides, where they still are. All this was enough to remind people
of the great moments of glory of the great emperor.

168   Louis-Napoleon Bonaparte/Napoleon III was the nephew of the great emperor.
His father was Louis Bonaparte, who was king of Holland at his birth.

169   Napoleon III came not as a soldier, but as a politician who knew how to influence
crowds and how to exploit Europe's fear of the June Days and its hopes for order
in France. His coup d'état was accepted by almost seven and a half million votes
against only 646,000 No and 1,500,000 abstentions.

170   Unfortunately within the year of this proclamation of peace, Napoleon III was at
war against Russia, in the Crimean War.

171   Napoleon III's grand plan for France was surely helped by the 1848 discovery of
gold in California. The Gold Rush put at the emperor's disposal great quantities

of the rich metal and it is at this time that the first "Napoleon" gold coins were struck.

172   With the assistance of engineers like Alphand and Belgrand.

173   There was a tactical advantage to the widening of streets: they allowed easy police interventions in case of riots and barricades were less effective when built across large avenues than built in narrow streets.

174   After Paris, Lyon and Marseille and other cities modernized, imitating Paris, with boulevards, public parks.

175   Some have said with some truth that under Napoleon III the Second Empire was more bourgeois than the July monarchy.

176   Money is stable, prices increase but salaries follow and people spend more and live better. The French population that was 35,800,000 in 1851 grew to 38 million in 1868, a figure increased by the reunion to France of Savoie and Nice with 600,000 new citizens.

177   Even the demographic increase is illusory. It comes from the fact that people lived longer, but families had fewer children. In fact both the population and the production of the country become slower than in the neighboring countries.

178   Napoleon III was 52 years old in 1860 and in failing health. So he started to make some concessions to his opposition, but rather than calming his opponents, it gave them more freedom to oppose the emperor.

179   Gambetta left by balloon from square Saint Pierre in Montmartre.

180   The 1870 Franco-Prussian war was short because Bismarck had taken the trouble to isolate France from eventual allies. And in any case, England would not help because it thought that France was in the wrong. Italy wanted to regain Rome, which they did as soon as the French troops left to go fight against Prussia, and the Russians wanted to remove the clause of the 1856 peace that prohibited them to have a navy in the Black Sea. The Austrians detested Napoleon III. So France was left alone against Bismarck who had a much superior army to France.

181   The rebels were called *Communards*.

182   The Third Republic, from its start, seemed built on precarious grounds, and to many people the thought that there had been so many changes in governments since 1789 made them fear that the Third Republic would also be transitory. It was to take a quarter of a century to ensure the survival of the regime.

183   There were 45 governments between 1914 and 1940.

184   The whole affair remains mysterious. Surely Dreyfus was not guilty, but was Esterhazy the only guilty one? Was he part of an anti-Dreyfus, i.e., anti-Semitic conspiracy, or was he a double agent acting for the 2e Bureau and charged to give false information to the Germans? If so, his real role could not be divulged in order to keep the Germans on a false track.

185   In January 1998, the Dreyfus case of 100 years ago sparked a melee in the French Assembly, showing that this notorious case of anti-Semitism remained a vivid issue in France. Recently, the current President of the French Republic, Jacques Chirac, apologized in the name of France to the heirs of Dreyfus and to his defensor Emile Zola for the unjust treatment suffered by both Alfred Dreyfus and Emile Zola, author of the famous article "J'Accuse" published in *L'Aurore* newspaper on January 13, 1898. Chirac called the Dreyfus case "that dark stain, unworthy of our country and our history." The melee in the Assembly was brought about by the current Prime Minister, Lionel Jospin, when trying to answer a parliamentary question about France's role in the African slave trade of the seventeenth and eighteenth centuries. Jospin replied that if the Left was for the abolition of slavery, the Right was not, and he added these inflammatory statements: "Just as the Left was for Dreyfus and the Right was against him"! Immediately cries of "Resign, resign!" were heard.

186   Combes had to resign.

187   "No one power or group of powers caused the war of 1914. Its causes lie deep in the history of the state-system of western civilization, and more particularly, in its history since 1870. The dramatic date of the assassination of Francis-Ferdinand, June 28, 1914, serves as a dividing line between the ultimate, or long–term, factors and the proximate, or short-term factors." Christopher Brinton and Wolffe, *A History of Civilization*, Vol. II, p. 419.

188   The French government would return to Paris in 1915.

189   The Socialists were encouraged by the American President Woodrow Wilson, who wanted to stop the hecatomb of men.

190   In 1921 the population of France was only 39,200,000 inhabitants, i.e., 400,000 less than in 1911.

191   On a 1998 reconsideration of some aspects of World War I, see Appendix 16.

192   Confédération Générale du Travail.

193   France was cut into two parts, the occupied zone under direct German command in the north, including Paris and as far south as the Pyrénées, and a non-occupied zone under the control of the Vichy government, including central France and the Rhone valley. The Italians soon came and occupied the region of the Alps. On November 11, 1942 the Germans occupied the whole of France.

194   Robert Paxton, an American historian, author of the important book on *La France de Vichy: 1940–1944* was recently (February 1998) interviewed by the *Journal Français* (Published in the USA) and asked: "Could France have reacted differently after its defeat?" Paxton replied that many Frenchmen at the time thought that the Vichy régime was unavoidable, but he added that France could have very well continued the fight from its North Africa bases. (*Journal Français*, February 1998, p. 11).

195 "His (Pétain's) aim was to create an autocratic paternal state with an old-world peasant economy. This fitted admirably with Hitler's plan for a New Order in Europe: a rural France could never again cross the path of an industrial Germany. Many Frenchmen rallied to Pétain: probably a minority. France was stunned; the military acknowledged his authority; all opposition was silenced. . . . Many preferred to believe that Pétain was playing a deep game, outwitting Hitler, saving what could be saved out of the wreck, biding time. These were attentistes, the "wait-and-see" people, and they found many sympathizers in America" Guérard, *France*, p. 428.

196 The général de Gaulle is well remembered for his famous declaration: "France has only lost a battle, but has not lost the war!"

197 De Gaulle's clarion call to all true Frenchmen came from London even before the armistice was signed. He said: "A battle is lost, but not the war. France is not alone; she has her fleet, her empire, her great ally, America's inexhaustible resources. The mechanical power which has overwhelmed her will be crushed in its turn by a force immeasurably greater" (June 18, 1940). Guérard, *France*, p. 430.

198 In November the Germans, who still held the north of Alsace and Lorraine, launched a desperate counter-offensive in the terribly harsh battle of the Bulge, but French forces managed to penetrate deep into Germany, occupying Karlsruhe and Stuttgart. The Germans had no other choice but to surrender.

199 Mussolini had been caught, killed and hanged head down at the end of April 1945 and the Japanese capitulated on August 19, 1945, after the atomic bombings of Hiroshima and Nagasaki. The war machine of the Axis (Germany-Italy-Japan) was destroyed. For the first time the world could breathe again and begin to mend its terrible wounds.

200 Maurice Agulhon, *The French Republic, 1879–1992*, Blackwell, 1990, writes, p. 308: "This war (WWII) had lost out its symbolic outcome: it had not aroused the equivalent of the 11 November 1918, simultaneous, unanimous and explosive. . . . The Second World War did not really replace the First in the depths of French consciousness, which is why it has made less of an imprint on French folklore. It must be added that because the 1939–45 war, unlike that of 1914–18, had not brought about the commitment of the entire population. Those mobilized for the campaign 1939–40 were either overshadowed in the collective memory by the extraordinary nature of the Vichy occupation episode, or reduced to the passive role of prisoners of war. One final difference: the victory of 1945 was tinged with anxiety. The vast majority of the French in 1918 had believed themselves to be not only citizens of the strongest military nation in the world, but also inhabitants of a universe which had suffered too much from war to dare to begin again. . . . By contrast, in 1944, with victory on the horizon, even the least informed French person had already had the opportunity to hear distant rumbles about Stalin's vast "Russia" and feel close at hand the generous but invasive United States."

201   The death figures could have been greater except that many wounded were saved
       by the new discovery of penicillin and by blood transfusions.

202   "Today it is referred to as 'wildcat' purging to convey the idea of spontaneous and
       non-regulated purges (the adjective comes from Britain, where a spontaneous
       strike, that is, not controlled by the trade union, is known as a 'wildcat strike'). But
       at the time of which we are speaking the more usual term was borrowed not from
       British political science, but from ordinary crime: the purges were usually de-
       scribed as 'settling old scores.'" Maurice Agulhon. *The French Republic, 1879–
       1992*, p. 313.

203   "On 15 August the jury declared Pétain guilty of dealings with the enemy, a crime
       which carried the death sentence. Condemned to death, but his sentence accom-
       panied by a request for non-execution because of his advanced age, Pétain was
       indeed spared and put into detention in a fortified place, the last being the Ile
       d'Yeu, where he died on 16 July 1951.
           In October it was Pierre Laval's turn. He had been active to the very end; even
       on 12 August 1944 he had tried to persuade Herriot, hastily removed from his
       house arrest, to help him formulate some plan of transition between Vichy and
       what was to follow. Herriot, having refused, had been sent back to Germany, and
       Laval had returned empty-handed to Vichy. . . . In the end he too had given him-
       self up. At his trial, that was short, violent and turbulent, he defended himself as
       best he could but, predictably, received the death sentence. He tried to escape the
       classic firing squad by swallowing poison. The dying man was dragged to the
       place of execution where, tottering, he suffered the ritual rifle fire." Maurice Agulhon,
       The French Republic, 1879–1992, p. 324.

204   "The whole troubled existence of the Fourth Republic, like its dismal end, is indis-
       solubly linked to France's experience of economic growth and the profound mod-
       ernization which resulted. At the threshold of the 1950's, the French economy
       emerged briskly from material shortages that weighed so heavily upon the après-
       guerre period; one by one the bottlenecks eased. The way now seemed clear for
       an expansion that would erase the last traces of the conservatism and
       malthusianisme so often denounced at the time. Nostalgia for the good times
       before the war, waned; the domestic market expanded with the demographic
       revival, and an improvement in living standards moved within reach. In fact, a
       long period of growth and change had begun, the era of the "Trente Glorieuses".
       Jean-Pierre Rioux. *The Fourth Republic, 1944–1958*. Cambridge University Press,
       p. 317. "Retrospectively, one is tempted to credit it (the Fourth Republic) precisely
       for a perseverance in governing little, which left France to develop her energies
       unhindered. Better still, might the lesson of these years not be that the risk of
       shaping the future can, indeed, be taken, and that while failure is never insur-
       mountable, ambition has no price?" Jean-Pierre Rioux, *The Fourth Republic
       1944–1958*, p. 451.

205   Georges Pompidou was born in 1911 in Montboudif, a village of the Cantal
       region in central France, the son of two schoolteachers. He was a brilliant stu-
       dent, entered the *Ecole normale supérieure*, and received an *agrégation* in lit-

erature. At the time of the Libération, de Gaulle needed an intelligent man for his cabinet, so he chose Pompidou and ever since the two men worked well together.

206   On the perception of the May uprising in 1998, see Appendix 17.

207   "And it was at Colombey, on November 9, 1970 that death overtook him, suddenly and swiftly, at the end of the day. At Colombey again, on the 12th, he was buried, according to his wishes, in the cemetery adjoining the church, in the presence only of his intimates, Compagnons de la Libération and villagers. Meanwhile, in Paris, in Notre Dame Cathedral, at the head of a numerous and glittering gathering of monarchs and heads of state, Pompidou attended a funeral ceremony held in absentia." Maurice Agulhon, *The French Republic: 1879–1992*, p. 431.

208   For a contemporary comment (1998) on the May 1968 student rebellion, see our Appendix 12.

209   In fact Pompidou retained for a long time the same presidential powers as de Gaulle allowing him to dominate policy-making as well as the executive branch of the government.

210   "Georges Pompidou died in Paris on April 2, 1974. About his demise, which has to do with biographical chance and could thus for propriety's sake be left aside, history must nevertheless record two details. First, the stoicism of the sick man who, informed of his condition and its fatal prognosis, nevertheless continued to work in his sufferings right to the end, adds a new and more than respectful touch to his portrait. Next, and less venerable in our eyes, the dreason of state which, to the last day and against all the evidence, let it be declared through official channels that the President was well. . . . Like de Gaulle, Pompidou had made his funeral arrangements by separating the intimate ceremony at Orvilliers from the solemn Mass in Notre Dame in Paris. But he had made no arrangements for his political successor." Maurice Agulhon. *The French Republic: 1879–1992*, pp. 438–439.

211   Giscard d'Estaing, even if he did not have the support of the Gaullist party- (he had defeated the party's candidate Chaband-Delmas)- managed to retain the upper hand in Parliament by brandishing occasionally his power of dissolution.

212   Mitterand in 1964 accused Giscard's regime of being without accountability and being "un coup d'état permanent."

213   Mitterand was born in 1916 in Jarnac, a small village of West Central France, in the Charentes department. He was one of eight children and raised a Catholic. As an adolescent Mitterand was a bright student and in love with literature. In 1934 he went and studied law at the Ecole Libre des Sciences Politiques. He was 22 when the Second World War was declared in September 1939. He went to war and was made prisoner and taken to a German camp. Whether he escaped as he said, or was released, Mitterand returned to Paris in March 1942 and worked with a Vichy government agency, his job being to maintain relations with the French prisoners of war. He probably sympathized with Pétain's patriotism and

sense of shame for the defeat of France. According to Mitterand himself, he broke his association with the Vichy régime in 1943 on account of its anti-Semitic actions. It is then that Mitterand claims to have entered the Résistance. Unfortunately he did not get along with de Gaulle, who did not ask him to serve in his 1944 post-war provisional government.

During the Fourth Republic, Mitterand served 11 governments with several ministerial titles. Very independent, even a loner at times, Mitterand stayed away for a long time from disciplined political parties and that is why he chose the UDSR (Union Démocratique des Socialistes de la Résistance), a party which proclaimed itself to be the party for independent-minded persons. It was the collapse of the Fourth Republic and Mitterand's opposition to de Gaulle that propelled him to the political forefront. He vehemently denounced the actions of de Gaulle in the early times of the Fifth Republic. Even though Mitterand was not a member of the two major parties of the Left (SFIO and PCF), Mitterand based his candidacy on his opposition to de Gaulle and presented himself as the only person capable to confront the Right-wing coalition. But in 1971 Mitterand received the control of the Socialist party and immediately, under his guidance, the party allied itself with the Communists. In 1981 Mitterand was elected as the person who could help France to break away from Capitalism. However, in the elections of March 1986, the presidential Socialist party was defeated by the Right-wing alliance, forcing Mitterand into a period of Cohabitation with Jacques Chirac as Prime Minister. In 1988, Mitterand was brought back for a second term during which he pushed for European integration and for ratifying the Maastrich Treaty. But on January 8, 1996, Mitterand died at the end of his second seven-year term after a long struggle with prostate cancer. He was almost eighty years old. Jacques Chirac succeeded him on May 17, 1996.

Mitterand has been called a survivor, a political animal, cunning, devious, equivocal, mysterious, in short an enigma. Surely Mitterand was a very successful Socialist leader, an adaptable "salamander," sometimes traditional and conservative, at other times at ease with the Left and willing to work with it, even courting, by necessity the Communists to the point of being seen as excessively Machiavellian. It is true that many times, Mitterand's words were not followed by corresponding actions; it is also true that his frequently changing course disappointed many of those who had carried him to power in 1981. Blurred as it may be by his many contradictions, by personal and political morally dubious actions, President Mitterand's legacy has, like himself, many aspects of grandeur mixed with less admirable aspects which have resulted in a mixture of admiration, doubts, accusations of lack of moral principles, and sometimes downright contempt. To his death and after his death, Mitterand's clearest image remains one of a brilliant enigma, a splendid red rose (the symbol of Mitterand's Socialist party) with a few faded petals.

214   Victor Schoelcher, born in Paris (1804–1931), deputy of the Martinique and Guadeloupe. He prepared the decree of abolition of slavery (April 27, 1848).

215   This was perhaps, almost surely, a subtle gesture to erase the memory of his own past collaboration with the Vichy government.

216   We shall soon see that ironically history repeats itself in reverse!

217   Cresson is said to have compared the Japanese to a nation of ants and she alledgedly treated the men of another nationality of homosexuals. However, her worse political blunder was to advocate charter flights to return illegal immigrants to their country. True or not, these statements were advanced to explain the fall of Cresson.

218   France learned also that Mitterand had had a daughter (Mazarine) outside of his marriage, a fact that the press and the president kept secret for years.

219   Jacques Chirac was born on November 29, 1932, in Paris. He was educated at the famous Lycée Louis-le-Grand (1950), then attended the Institut d'Etudes Politiques (1953) and the ENA (*Ecole Nationale d'Administration*—1959). He served in the army as an officer (1954–1957) and was wounded during France's colonial war in Algeria. Before being elected President of the Republic, Chirac held several positions in the government: Minister of Agriculture and Rural Development from 1973–1974; Interior Minister in 1974, Prime Minister from 1974 to 1976 and from 1986 to 1988; Mayor of Paris and member of the National Assembly from 1977 to 1995. His main residence is the Presidential Palace of the Elysées. He is married to Bernadette Chodron de Courcel and they have two daughters. Chirac is Catholic. Chirac, of the neo-Gaullist party, was elected President of the Republic on May 7, 1995. He appointed Alain Juppé as his Prime Minister. On June 3, 1997, the Socialist Lionel Jospin replaced Alain Juppé after Chirac's dissolution of the Assembly. Then began a Cohabitation government Right/Left) with Chirac as President and Jospin as Socialist Prime Minister.

220   Probably Chirac's worst *gaffe* (blunder) of his career.

221   Lionel Jospin was born on July 12, 1937, in Meudon, Hauts-de-Seine, near Paris. He is married and the father of two children. He graduated from the Institut d'Etudes Politiques of Paris and was a student at the ENA (Ecole Nationale d'Administration) (1963–1965). He immediately entered politics and was with the administration of Foreign Affairs from 1965 to 1974. From 1970 to 1980, Jospin taught at the Institut universitaire de technologie of the Université de Paris XI in Sceaux. In 1971 he joined the Socialist party and started to participate actively in the party's affairs. He was National Secretary from 1973 to 1975 and reelected in 1987 and again in 1995. In 1988 he became Minister of National Education, Research and Sports until 1991 and again from 1991 to 1992. Among his many political duties, Jospin was also député (deputy to the National Assembly) and President Mitterand's adviser when Mitterand was a candidate in the 1981 presidential elections. In 1997 Jospin was reelected député de Haute Garonne but resigned when Chirac named him Prime Minister on June 2, 1997.

222   For the composition of Lionel Jospin's government, see Appendix 1.

223   A 12.4% jobless rate for France.

224   The unemployed demanded an increase of $250 a month plus a one time bonus of $500.

Chapter 2

Politics

The Political Institutions of France[1]

France has a long tradition of political life. Already during the 1789 Revolution many political clubs were created, fostering political discussions. Also some important political pamphlets and newspapers began to appear. Direct, male-only suffrage was introduced in 1848 under the Second Republic, but it was really only under the Third Republic that political parties were officially established and the trade unions accepted.[2] From then on French citizens felt that it was their duty to participate in the political life of the country. Even if some newspapers circulated previously, it was only under the Third Republic that the press began to assume a major role in the diffusion of political ideas and ideologies. The Dreyfus Affair is an example of the growing role of the press in bringing to the people an awareness of the important political, social and moral issues of the time. The Third Republic reaffirmed the values and principles of the concept of Republic with firm democratic principles. It gave the French people confidence in their schools, in democracy and in the republican values of the nation. The labor movement also helped in developing the citizens' political awareness, thus helping to spread Leftist-Marxist political ideas among workers. Following World War II, the Fourth Republic started with an era of great instability. Parties began to proliferate and most of them failed. The Constitution of the Fifth Republic was written to restore political order and confidence, to put a stop to the constant political changes and disorder.

France's history and French politics are both volatile and moody. These changes in fact reflect a constant search for equilibrium between two forces, the force represented by parliamentary assemblies and the force represented by the power of one man or a single political party.

The current Constitution of the Fifth Republic was adopted on October 4, 1958, with almost 80% of voters in favor. This Constitution is basically the work of de Gaulle, who became the first President of the Fifth Republic. Naturally, the original text has been amended many times since its first application. According to this 1958 Constitution, the power belongs to the French people, that is to say, to the electorate. With the exception of the vote for the Senate, all elections in France are by direct universal suffrage. Since July 1974, all French persons, men and women,[3] can vote if they are 18 years old[4] and if they have not been deprived of their civic rights.[5] The electorate includes over 33 million voters, about 3 million aged between 18 and 21. Contrary to the custom in the United States, where no voting is done on weekends, in France the polls are usually held on Sundays, probably according to the French principle of separation of Church and State, and for the more obvious reason that workers do not have to take time off in order to vote. Requirements for running for office are the same for all elections: candidates must be at least 18 years old to run for municipal councillor, 21 for regional councillor and 23 for deputé (deputy) or President of the Republic. Poll attendance varies according to the nature of the election and, as one may expect, attendance is generally high (70% to 90%) for presidential elections. Parliamentary elections are also well attended, in any case better attended than local elections.

National Elections

In France *Legislative elections* are held to elect the 577 deputies of the National Assembly. They are elected for 5 years by direct universal suffrage with majority votes in two rounds. Majority voting was introduced by de Gaulle in order to combat the political instability due to proportional representation. However, in the 1986 elections, the Socialist government reverted to the proportional system in the hope that smaller political units could be better represented and, naturally also, because it would be to their advantage. The next conservative coalition returned to the majority system in the 1993 elections.

Senatorial Elections

The Senatorial elections for the 321 members of the Senate are chosen by indirect suffrage, that is to say, not directly by the people but by an Electoral College in each department and composed of officials (deputies, councillors, municipal councils representatives). Senators are elected for 9 years with one third of the 321 members replaced in rotation every 3 years.

The Presidential Elections

The presidential elections allow the people to elect their nation's number one representative by majority uninominal voting in two rounds (two Sundays in a row).

European Elections

The European elections elect the 87 French deputies, out of a total of 626, sitting in the European Parliament. They are elected for a five-year term by direct universal suffrage with proportional representation from lists established at the national level. Polls are strictly controlled and cannot publish their findings during the week before the vote. Candidates' expenses are strictly limited to a set ceiling, and funding by outside private contributions is also severely restricted. Funding of political parties by businesses is totally prohibited. On the other hand, the State reimburses part of the expenses of candidates according to a scale based on the results (percentage of votes) obtained by each candidate in the election.

The Presidency

The Presidency is the cornerstone of the French State. What characterizes the French presidency is the nature and extent of the power and influence the President of the Republic has. We must not forget that the strength of the presidency, as we know it today in France, was established by de Gaulle. He felt that someone had to remain "above the battlefield" in order to be able to confront the ups and downs of governments.[6] According to de Gaulle's plan, the President or Head of State was the one who stood impartial above quarrels, and thus was able to repair whenever necessary governmental breakdowns and be an independent arbitrator representing at the same time governmental continuity. The parliamentarians who drafted the new Constitution went along with de Gaulle, but they made sure that he would not become a dictatorial President. With this in mind, they made the President accountable to Parliament. The referendum of September 28, 1958, approved the new concept of the presidency by stating that "the President ensures the functioning and continuity of the country's institutions and acts as an arbiter and guarantor of France's independence and integrity. He is the commander-in-chief of the armed forces, including nuclear force, and he ratifies treaties. He is thus responsible for safeguarding the higher interests of the nation."

The President of the Republic, Head of the Nation

The President of the French Republic is the Chief of the State. Through a referendum, as of October 28, 1962, the French President is elected by direct universal suffrage for a seven-year mandate. Voting takes place on two consecutive Sundays. The candidate who receives at least half of the votes cast is elected on the first turn. However, this situation is so rare that all the elections which have been held to date have taken two elections. On the second turn, electors must choose between the two candidates who obtained the most votes on the first turn. As an illustration, de Gaulle was elected President on December 19, 1965, with 55% of the votes against the Socialist Mitterand, who received only 45% of the votes. Four years later, de Gaulle, whose reform referendum was defeated, resigned on April 28, 1969, and the next president elected with 58% of votes was George Pompidou, who had served de Gaulle for six years as his Prime Minister. After Pompidou's death, two candidates sought the presidency: Valérie Giscard d'Estaing and François Mitterand. Giscard d'Estaing became President with 13,314,000 votes against Mitterand, who received 12,946,000 votes, a very narrow margin indeed.

The President of the French Republic is the true head of the executive branch of government. He is the one who nominates the Prime Minister and who accepts, or not, the slate of government members presented by the Prime Minister. Among his other tasks, the President chairs the Council of Ministers (Conseil des Ministres), promulgates laws and signs the decrees passed by the Council of Ministers. The president can call a referendum on any project of law dealing with the country's administration or with the ratification of a treaty.[7] The president also nominates and appoints individuals to top civilian and military posts. He appoints French ambassadors and accredits foreign ambassadors to France. In addition, the president has the supreme right of granting pardon or reprieve to persons accused of crimes. The French President is also the Chief of the armies and he has the power to dismiss the Parliament and call for new elections in case of serious national crisis.[8] In cases of acute crisis, the president may, in agreement with his prime minister, with the presidents

of the various assemblies, and the Constitutional Council, take all necessary emergency measures, but he has the obligation to inform the nation
through a special message. As an example, de Gaulle used this preroga-
tive during five months in 1961 when he felt that the revolting generals in
Algiers might attempt a *coup* against his government.

To become President of the Republic in France, you must be a French
national, be at least 23 years old and having satisfied the army obligations.[9] The candidate to the presidency must be endorsed by a minimum
of 500 signatures from elected officials from France and/or from overseas territories (DOMs/TOMs).

The president is elected for seven years,[10] called *Septennat*. And after
these seven years, he may run again. Since 1875, only President François
Mitterand has fulfilled two consecutive presidential terms from 1981 to
1995.

When elected President of the Republic, and contrary to many other
officials, the President cannot hold other public or private offices.[11] In the
case of the President's death or resignation, the President of the Senate
becomes interim president until a new president is elected. This election
must take place no later than 35 days after the presidential office has
been officially vacant.[12]

The French Government

The Government of France is formed by the Prime Minister, but it must
be approved by the President. It does not need the approval of the National Assembly, but, when installed, it is responsible to it. A vote with
absolute majority of a motion of censure, if signed by at least one tenth of
the deputies, forces the government to resign. Conversely, the government can put its responsibility on the line on a certain program if it deems
it necessary and/or for the sake of the country.

The government puts into practice the policies of both the President
and his Prime Minister with the assistance of the nation's administration
and armed forces. The role of the Prime Minister is to lead the government, to execute laws and to manage all the State affairs. He represents
the President in Parliament because the President is not allowed in the
Chamber of Deputies, except by strict invitation of the House. In addition, the Prime Minister keeps the Head of State informed about public
opinion. The government, aside from the Prime Minister, is composed of
the Ministers and Secretaries of State.[13]

The Parliament: National Assembly and Senate

The role of Parliament is to vote laws and to control the Government's actions.

The Parliament is made up of two branches: The *National Assembly* and *The Senate,* the upper house of the French parliament. The National Assembly, lower house of the French parliament, is composed of 577 representatives (députés), 555 for metropolitan France and 22 for the overseas departments and territories. The *députés* are elected by direct universal suffrage for five years and Senators are elected for nine years by an electoral college made up of députés, general councillors, and delegates from municipal councils. A third of the Senate is renewed every three years. The minimum age to be elected deputy is 23, and it is 35 to be elected senator.

Parliament meets twice a year. The first session begins on October 2 and lasts 80 days. It is dedicated to the nation's budget. The second session takes place during the months of April, May and June. Extraordinary sessions may be called if necessary. The basic role of Parliament is to vote laws as proposed by the Prime Minister and legislative assembly members. In case of disagreement, the National Assembly has the last word.

Another mission of Parliament is to oversee the Government's actions. The National Assembly alone has the power to upset the government through a motion of censure.

The National Assembly meets in the *Palais Bourbon.* Its role is to be a check on the government while it is France's legislative body. Bills introduced by the government and called *projets de lois* are presented first to a Council of State and discussed by the Cabinet of the Prime Minister before being forwarded to the Houses for debate. The bills introduced by Parliament are called *propositions de loi.* Both *projets* and *propositions de loi* must be adopted by both houses (Assembly and Senate). National Assembly sessions are generally open to the public and their debates are published in the *Journal Officiel* newspaper.

The Senate convenes in the Palais du Luxembourg. Senators are primarily legislators and their main role is to make amendments to the bills that are presented to them. The Senate also has a representational role; it represents the territorial units of the country (municipalities, departments, and regions) and it also represents the French citizens living abroad. The Senate ensures continuity in case of national crisis. When the President of the Republic is incapacitated, leaves office or dies, the President of the

Senate immediately becomes interim head of state until new elections are called. This happened when de Gaulle resigned in 1969 and when Pompidou died in office in 1974. The President of the Senate must be consulted by the President of the Republic before the National Assembly is dissolved.

The Various Government Councils

1. *The Constitutional Council* rules over the regularity of the elections of the President of the Republic, of Parliament and referendums. It makes sure that the laws are in conformity with the Constitution. The Council is made up of nine members, each named for nine years. Three are named by the President of the Republic, three by the President of the National Assembly, and three by the Senate. It convenes in the Palais-Royal in Paris.
2. *The Economic and Social Council* is composed of two hundred members. They can be consulted by the Government about any law or any particular problem within their prerogatives.
3. *The State Council* is made up of civil servants named by the Government. They are quite independent from the Prime Minister and they are called upon to give their advice on all projects of law or decree. They also constitute one of the two Supreme Courts, the other being the Supreme Court of Appeal.
4. *The Cour des Comptes (High Financial Court)* oversees the execution of finance laws and makes sure that public funds are put to good use. Its members are appointed by the Government and cannot be removed.
5. *The Ombudsman (Mediator)* intervenes in matters of conflict about public services. The position of mediator was created February 1, 1973.

The Nation's Administration:
Its Agencies or *Ministères*[14]

All ministerial agencies are placed under the direction of the Prime Minister. He defines their nature, competencies and roles. The Prime Minister is the official link between the Government and the various ministerial agencies. As Head of the Government, the Prime Minister is the hierarchical chief of the Administration. Below the Prime Minister and between him and the various agencies, there is a Cabinet made of personal collaborators. Those are generally chosen among high public servants, frequently top graduates from the ENA *(Ecole Nationale d'Administration),* a prestigious Parisian graduate school that is a traditional pool for top public servants in France. The basic working unit of each agency is the *Bureau,* in turn subdivided into various *Services.*

Manpower

Public service agents are about three million, and two million of them work for national organizations and the State. One million work for local organizations.

The Political and Administrative Territory of the French Republic

The territory of the French Republic is composed of three major units: (1) Continental France and Corsica. (2) Four overseas departments (DOMs): Guadeloupe, Martinique, Guyane, and La Réunion, all representing about 1,300,000 persons. (3) Eight overseas territories (TOMs): Saint-Pierre et Miquelon; the French territory of Afars and Issas; the Comores; the Nouvelles Hébrides, Wallis et Futuna; la Nouvelle Calédonie; la Polynésie française; les Terres Australes et Antartiques Françaises (TAAF): Saint Paul, Crozet, Kerguelen and Terre Adélie, all representing about 812,000 persons. (4) There is a fourth small category called CCTs or Territorial Collectivities: Saint-Pierre et Miquelon, close to Newfoundland and Mayotte in the Comores archipelago, in the Indian Ocean. All, except the TAAFs that are inhabited only by scientists, are represented in the French Parliament. All these territories are quite dispersed on the map and most of them are fairly small with the exception of Guyane and Nouvelle Calédonie, slightly larger than the others.[15]

In most of these *DOMs* and *TOMs*, two great problems remain constant: unemployment, poverty and excessive population growth. France, nevertheless, and contrary to many former colonial powers, has been able to retain these overseas possessions, but there currently are discussions, even treaties, under way that will eventually lead to their independence from France. Still, France has a special interest in these territories, either for historical reasons and for the sake of prestige, but also because they have a political, economic or strategic importance for the Nation. France, therefore, is not eager to part with them and continues to provide them with administrative assistance, and financial aid, insufficient as they may be.

Metropolitan France

Metropolitan France is divided into 95 departments or 101 if we count the overseas departments listed above, and 37,573 communes which vary greatly in size. The *Préfet*, appointed by the Government, is the chief administrator of each department. He is in charge of the interests of the state and he is the head of the executive for the department. In addition, the Préfet is responsible for upholding law and order (except for four cities: Paris, Marseille, Lyon and Lille, where public order is under the responsibility of a Préfet de Police). The *Préfet* also oversees the proper distribution and use of the funds and investments of the State.

Departments and Communes

Ever since the French Revolution, the *Department* is the essential administrative unit in France. Each department is run by a General Council *(Conseil Général)*. The *Conseillers Généraux*, members of the General Council, are elected for six years. They meet at least twice a year to vote the department's budget and to plan the organization of the various services provided by the department to its inhabitants.[16]

The *Communes,* also called *Municipalités,* are the basic unit of French regional administrative organization. They are administered by a Municipal Council *(Conseil Municipal)* elected for six years and by a Mayor *(Maire)*. The Mayor is in charge of the municipal police and he is the executor of all the decisions of the Municipal Council. He represents the State in official events such as weddings.

There are 37,000 municipalities in France, some being very small with fewer than 1000 inhabitants. Presently the government is encouraging municipalities to band together and to form larger urban communities or intercommunal syndicates.

French Regions

In its effort to decentralize the administration of France, Parliament decided in 1982 to create a new territorial unit with more freedom from Paris, the *Regions*. There are 26 regions altogether, 22 in metropolitan France and 4 overseas. Each of these regions encompasses several departments and is basically an economic and a financial development area, the largest being the Paris Region. Each region is responsible for improving within its borders communications (roads, railroads, airports, bridges, etc.), to keep old businesses in the region and to attract new businesses, industries, while interfacing its activities with its neighbors and other main economic areas. The regions are run by regional *Préfets* and by an Economic and Social Council. Each region has a capital, characteristic features, qualities, as well as problems.[17]

The French System of Justice

The Minister of Justice is currently Mme Elisabeth Guigou, a graduate of the ENA.

In France the judicial system is considered an essential attribute of state sovereignty and a basic service in the life of the community.

French judiciary power is independent in principle from the other governmental powers and this independence is asserted more and more by judges who are at liberty to investigate and/or prosecute anyone and even high placed officials in the Government. According to Article 64 of the Constitution, the President of the Republic with the assistance of the High Council of Magistrates *(Conseil Supérieur de la Magistrature)* guarantees the independence of justice.

There is one type of justice for the whole country and everyone has the right to appeal. Everyone has the right to have an attorney and in some cases an attorney is appointed. French justice makes clear distinctions between *civil law,* dealing with quarrels between individuals, *penal law,* which deals with infractions to laws and regulations, *commercial law* which involves litigations concerning professional activities, and *administrative law,* concerning problems arising between individuals and administrative services. In addition, French law makes a clear distinction between *normal appeal* that allows a higher court to reconsider the whole case, and the Supreme Court of Appeal *(Cassation)*, which only reviews the legality of judgments, examines the law, but not the facts. French police may keep under arrest any individual for 48 hours. After that, he must be freed unless charged by a judge. If so, the suspect may be incarcerated in detention pending trial for up to three years.

The *Tribunaux de Grande Instance* (County Courts) judge civil actions and small criminal cases, while the *Tribunaux d'Instance* (Magistrate Courts) deal with more petty matters. Serious offenses and criminal cases are judged by the *Tribunaux Correctionnels* (Court of Summary Jurisdiction), while smaller offenses are handled by the *Tribunaux de Police* (Simple Police Court). Commercial cases are heard by the *Tribunaux de Commerce* (Commerce Court) and labor disputes by the *Conseil des Prud'hommes* (Conciliation Board). Very serious crimes, such as homicides, are judged by the *Cour d'Assise* (Assize Court), whose decisions are without appeal, except to the *Cassation* court (Supreme Court of Appeal) on points of law only. The judge is assisted by two assessors-magistrates and nine jurors.

There are over 8,000 attorneys (Avocats) in France, more than 3,000 in Paris alone. There are 6,500 notaries *(Notaires),* 3000 *Huissiers* (sheriff officers, process servers) and 3700 *Greffiers* (court clerks). The *Notaire* in France is a legal officer who writes legal contracts and acts and guarantees their authenticity. The French *Notaire* is an important institution. His office is recognized by a gold sign hung above the entrance of the building. *Notaires,* called "*maîtres*" by their clients, are very important in French life, as they often act as financial advisers and deal closely with families in drafting wills, inheritance documents, and acting in marriages and death. The *Notaire* also acts in case of purchases or sales of properties. The *Huissier* is a legal officer who is charged with submitting to the public concerned court acts and in some cases to enforce them. The *Greffier* is a public servant working in the tribunal's *Greffe*, located in the Courthouse where the minutes of judgments are kept.

Police

French police is under the jurisdiction of the *Ministère de l'Intérieur*. It is made up of several units: the forces of public Safety, the police attached to the Justice Ministry, *Les Renseignements Généraux*, the information branch of the national police, gathering information and acting as a counter spy agency, the police of the air and of borders *(Police de l'Air et des Frontières)* and the CRS *(Compagnies Républicaines de Sécurité)* which maintains order under the direction of the *Préfet*. Then, under the juridiction of the *Ministère de la Défense Nationale*, there are two police groups, the *Gendarmerie* and the *Gardes Mobiles* which can be transported anywhere in France to keep or reestablish order.

Prisons

There are now 172 prisons in France, two of them for women. The prison population is composed of over 51,000 persons, among whom about 700 women. Most French prisons are overcrowded and some are still ill equipped.

Capital Punishment

France, at the request of President Mitterand, abolished capital punishment in 1981.[18] Recently, at the occasion of the execution of a young white woman (Karla Tucker) in the USA, the polling house *BVA* asked a representative sample of the French population (15 years old and above) some questions pertaining to the death penalty. The majority replied that the death penalty was justified only to punish the most indecent crimes, such as crimes committed against children. When 1,004 persons were asked the reason for their opposition to the death penalty, 34% answered that it was on account of the possibility of killing an innocent person. Thirty percent of the same sample answered that by accepting the death penalty, society behaved exactly like the criminals it condemns. Others (18%) said that death does not dissuade criminals and 13% said that it is still possible that even the toughest criminal can change. A substantial number of persons still feel that the Courts may condemn to death an innocent, and oppose the death penalty.

French Political Parties

1. *The Communist Party (PCF = Parti Communiste Français)*

Created in December 1920 in Tours, the PCF used to be the first party of the Left in France. Nowadays, the Left *(la Gauche)* is also represented by the Socialist Party. For years the PCF and its members supported the Soviets' conception of socialism. It wanted its image to be the defender of peace and workers. Succeeding to Waldeck-Rochet, for many years and until his death in 1997, the head of the PCF was its Secretary General, Georges Marchais, a strong supporter of the Stalinist line of communism.[19] The party began to decline with the fall of the Berlin wall and the subsequent decline of international communism after the disappearance of the Soviet model and the lack of leadership and strategy of Marchais. His position was further weakened when he opposed France's participation in the Persian Gulf war.

In order to attempt to remedy the situation, the PCF elected Robert Hue on January 29, 1994, as its National Secretary. Hue is presently in power and trying to reconstruct the union of the Left by claiming to be the best rampart against the *Front National* (National Front).[20]

The Socialist Party (PS = *Le Parti Socialiste*)

2. Created in 1969 out of the remains of the SFIO (*Section Française de l'Internationale Ouvrière*, a revolutionary workers' party, founded in 1905 by Jean Jaurès), the Socialist Party (PS)[21] grew in 1971 and 1974 thanks to François Mitterand and Michel Rocard. It was Mitterand's genius

to reconcile the Socialists and the Communists in 1972, even if only provisionally. When the Socialists came to power in 1981, they immediately ran into major troubles in spite of their worthy attempts to bring about policies of social solidarity. In fact, they mostly failed to improve the unemployment situation and they found no easy solution to the economic crisis. They were not able to address the citizens' main worries and to bring about the changes in society people expected and which they had promised. Then there were many financial scandals and political intrigues which further discredited the party, the worst scandal being the mismanagement of the transfusion of blood tainted with the *SIDA* (AIDS) virus which contaminated hundreds of hemophiliac patients. Of course, the French in general and the Socialist electorate were very disappointed. In order to improve the party's image, the PS militants in October 1995 elected Lionel Jospin as the PS First Secretary. Jospin could then build a new Socialist political project and, naturally, prepare the party and his own return to power.

Lionel Jospin is currently Prime Minister of France with President Jacques Chirac, in a *Cohabitation* situation.

Until the victory of François Mitterand in May 1981, France had known very few leftist governments. The most noteworthy Socialist government being that of the 1936 Popular Front government. Therefore when on May 10, 1981, Mitterand was elected President of the Republic, it was considered a remarkable victory for the Socialist Party. Mitterand immediately exploited his victory, naming a Socialist government with Pierre Mauroy, dissolving the National Assembly on May 22 and obtaining on June 21 a new Assembly with a strong Socialist majority.

The great change of the Fifth Republic is its electoral bipolarity. Electoral opinions are divided in two main camps: the Right and the Left. Before the Fifth Republic, under the Third and Fourth Republics electoral opinion was often very divided and unclear, with constant shufflings and reshufflings among multiple packs of parties. By occasionally pursuing alliances with the Communist Party, although not drifting further to the Left because of it, the old SFIO became the Socialist Party *(Parti Socialiste),* one of the two main parties of France and the dominant party of the Left. In fact, when the Communist Party became marginalized, the Socialist Party retained completely its credibility as the major party of the Left. Any collaboration of the PS with the PC was for tactical reasons, mostly in times of elections.

De Gaulle, when he arrived to power in 1958, brought about important changes in the French Constitution; in particular he redistributed power away from Parliament and toward government, thus introducing a stronger presidency. The Socialists, who were traditionally attached to a parliamentary form of government, with strong legislative control over the executive, had to adapt and were forced into the bipolarization of political forces. The importance of the President was guaranteed by a majority in Parliament and, therefore, even legislative elections became quasi-presidential elections, forcing the Right and the Left into an electoral power struggle in order to seek the much needed parliamentary majority. François Mitterand, a crafty politician, saw early that he had to espouse presidentialism, that is to say, he had to insist on the importance and dominance of the President in elections, which meant that the Prime Minister became a subordinate of the President. This institution of the Fifth Republic clearly permitted the Socialists to join hands with the Communists. And again it was Mitterand who foresaw the need to adapt rapidly to the new presidential politics, and for the Socialists to present in the election a "Presidential" candidate, that is to say, a person who could seek and get votes far afield.

At present (1998) Lionel Jospin is the Socialist Prime Minister under a *Cohabitation* government with Jacques Chirac, but he is surely considered now a "Presidential" potential candidate to succeed Jacques Chirac. But in December 1998 Chirac made it clear that he was going to seek a second presidential term.[22] According to a *BVA* February 1998 poll, both the President and Prime Minister remained popular in spite of the problems confronting the timetable of the Euro community. While Chirac's popularity remained steady in December 1998, Jospin's popularity was slightly more shaky on account of recent strikes (Air France, the railroads, the Bibliothèque de France) and because of the outcries of the foreign workers without documents *(les sans papiers)* demanding the regularization of their status through hunger strikes. Even if often greatly disturbed by strikes and other manifestations of discontent, the French in general tend to side with the strikers and with the underprivileged, showing that, below their grumblings, they have basically a good heart. After all, the French created *Médecins Sans Frontières* (Doctors without borders)!

The Ecology Party and Génération Ecologie

Created in 1984, the Ecology Party experienced a rapid but ephemeral growth. Until 1989, it hardly obtained 5% of votes; however, it received 10.8% of votes in 1989. But in 1992 this encouraging percentage dropped when a new Green Party appeared, the GE or Génération Ecologie. In 1993 the combined Green and GE candidates received only 7% of the votes. The Green then decided to split away from the GE and it was a disaster: they received only 2.2% of votes in 1994. Fiercely independent, and refusing to belong to the Right or the Left, their only wish was to offer an alternative political force to electors. In France, it is true, the ecology movement has had traditionally very little appeal, but it is regaining some momentum on account of the realization of the evils of pollution that can be severe at times, particularly in Paris and in some other large industrial urban centers.[23]

Génération écologie (GE) was born in May 1990, created by Brice Lalonde. It lived more or less until 1995 when it was discovered to be totally empty of substance, a fact that Lalonde himself recognized when he asked his party to join the UDF *(Union pour la Démocratie Française)*.

L'Union pour la Démocratie Française (UDF)

Founded in February 1978, the UDF is basically composed of two parties: the *Centre des Démocrates Sociaux* (CDS), and the *Parti Républicain* (PR). The UDF was the instrument of President Valérie Giscard d'Estaing when he had to face Chirac and the majority of the conservative Gaullist party (RPR) in the National Assembly. In fact, the name of the party was lifted from Giscard's book, *Démocratie française* (1976). The UDF, aside from representing Giscard's ambition to win for the Right the next presidential elections, represents the liberal Right wing and the Christian Democratic tradition. Its spirit is very similar to that of the RPR.[24]

In April 1998 the UDF expelled from its party Charles Millon on the ground that he allied himself with the FN. The problem represented by the expulsion of Millon from the UDF reflects a wave of moral doubts among the French Right-wing party, mainly doubts over whether or not to cooperate with the National Front in order to win political seats. The expulsion of Millon and of two others for making deals with the FN is a way of showing the UDF's strong disapproval of the FN's anti-immigrants and anti-Semitic policies.

Le Rassemblement pour la République (RPR)

The RPR was founded in 1947 by Général de Gaulle and re-created by Jacques Chirac in 1976. It is a Gaullist party, conservative and Right wing.[25] Philippe Séguin, the new president of the party, has followed in the footsteps of Jacques Chirac.

Le Front National (FN)

The FN was created in December 1972 and led by Jean-Marie Le Pen. The party is considered by many a neo-fascist party, racist, anti-Semitic and fiercely nationalistic. It has attracted a mixture of people exasperated by urban violence, angered by illegal immigration, juvenile delinquency and rampant insecurity. It also attracts people longing for a return to the old traditional values of France. The FN has attracted recently unemployed young men, even some intellectuals and Catholics, electors disappointed by the Right and the Left. The FN's undeniable progress is considered by a vast number of Frenchmen as a real danger for democracy.[26] Mark Hunter, a specialist of French political life who has just published a book, "*Un Américain au Front: Enquête au sein du FN* (Stock) describes the FN's mission as "to purge France from all foreign influence and to assume power." He shows that even if the party has been branded as diabolical, it has been progressing since 1987. Hunter declares openly that the FN is a danger for French democracy. In his book Hunter does not see the FN as succeeding in its ambitions, but he sees it as remaining a pesty minority on French territory. In December 1998, Le Pen replaced his heir apparent Mégret, saying:"I draw my sword and I kill Brutus before he kills me." For the time being, therefore, the bridges seem cut between Mégret and Le Pen, but that does not mean that the FN, even if there is a division in its membership, will alter its political course, or become less racist or totalitarian. While most people agree that the FN must be watched and fought, they also agree that it could not possibly have a significant political future, particularly when its two heads are in conflict. Some people in the RPR are supposed to have said that the party is "interested in all the electors," a statement that some translate as saying "not excluding the FN electors" i.e., a political suicide today. Some also think that opening the doors of the RPR to members of the FN is one way to weaken the FN, a solution few people support. And so while everyone seems to want to destroy the FN, the FN enjoys the free publicity given by its enemies. Fortunately, perhaps the biggest enemy of the FN is the FN itself.[27] The events of spring 1999 seem to prove this theory.

A New Right-Wing Political Party Announced

Former Defense Minister Charles Millon, who was expelled on April 8, 1998, from the center-right UDF (Union for French Democracy) for having alledgedly allied himself with the FN, has declared that he wanted to renew the French political scene by creating a new Right-wing party, simply called *The Right*. But since this declaration no such party has appeared on the scene.

France and International Organizations

France is playing a leading role on the international scene and it is a part of its political vision as envisioned by General de Gaulle. France is one of the permanent members of the United Nations' Security Council, where it holds veto power. It belongs to the Council of Europe and is a member of the European Parliament based in Strasbourg. In addition, France is the home of the UNESCO (United Nations Educational, Scientific and Cultural Organization) and the OECD (Organization for Economic Cooperation and Development).

As one of the founding members of Europe, France played a key role in the construction of a European economy within the larger framework of global economy. The first step was taken in 1951 with the creation of the ECSC (European Coal and Steel Community) and it was followed in 1957 with the creation of the European Economic Community (EEC). In 1992 the Maastricht Treaty was approved, setting up the bases for the European political, economic and monetary union. The EC was renamed EU (European Union), which was completed at the beginning of 1999 with the implementation of the single currency Monetary Union.

France under Jacques Chirac (1995 to Present)

By the end of 1995 the mood of the French people was pessimistic. They saw the situation of France as getting worse in most areas, particularly the economy. Electors went to the polls mostly concerned with social and economic questions, and when they threw their votes to Jacques Chirac, it was mostly on account of his personality, of his promises of changes, particularly breaking social fractures. Chirac appealed to the young and to workers because he had convinced them that, with him at the helm, there would be hope for a much brighter future. In the final analysis, between Chirac and Jospin, Chirac was more trusted and considered more capable of bringing back better days, more social equality and a better economic situation.

Having elected Jacques Chirac, most of the French seriously thought that things were going to improve. So the French people waited for something to happen. But things did not happen, at least were not moving as fast as they expected. So people became anxious, impatient and soon very critical and angry. They wondered when the changes Chirac had promised them would come. The problem for Chirac and his Prime Minister Alain Juppé was that France had to abide by the constraints of the Maastricht Treaty in order to be able to enter into the single currency association of the European Community. Unfortunately, France was facing huge deficits and in order to satisfy the requirement of the European Community it had to reduce these drastically and fast. So, instead of bringing about the changes he had promised, Chirac went for a two-year struggle against public deficits. People felt betrayed and many of them turned in anger against the European goals of France. To make things worse, unemployment was rising sharply and Juppé's decisions to dam the huge deficits of Social Security became very unpopular. The consequence was some spectacular social movements, with a series of important strikes in 1995, 1996 and 1997. There was no revolution, but the movements had a profound impact. It clearly revealed that too many things were not right in French society and that the French were no longer willing to wait.

The Great Change: Installation of a
Cohabitation Government Chirac-Jospin

President Chirac was literally pushed into a tight corner and no longer could persuade the French that he could turn around the situation. So, on a fateful day of 1996, to many's surprise, Chirac, searching for another five-year mandate, decided to thank his Prime Minister Juppé and dissolve the Assembly, calling for anticipated elections. Contrary to Chirac's expectations, apparently, and to his dismay, electors voted to the Left and a Socialist Prime Minister, Lionel Jospin, was chosen to form a new Government. Jospin, strong of the Socialist votes, formed a Government to his liking, with new personalities and faces, many Socialitsts, more women and even a number of Communists. The Right of Chirac was in shock, but the dice had been thrown and the French had voted. A new *Cohabitation* government was instituted.[28] They voted Socialist because neither Chirac nor Juppé had given them soon enough the changes and improvements they expected.[29]

End of 1998–Beginning 1999:
Chirac Halfway through His Term (*Septennat*)

Halfway through his *Septennat*, President Chirac declared that he will seek another mandate after 17 months of *Cohabitation*. But first, why did Chirac dissolve the Assembly, a daring decision that forced him in a government of *Cohabitation* with the Socialists? Probably because Chirac was convinced that he could build a new younger and more modern Right. True, Chirac has successfully managed his *Cohabitation* with Jospin, represented France well abroad, and has successfully backed the Euro. However, many observers wonder if everybody will give Chirac the credit owed to him, and if Jospin won't be interfering in the President's success. In addition, some people also wondered if Chirac's high ratings were not due to his function as President rather than his own qualities. Chirac is perhaps counting on the exhaustion of his Prime Minister, who, in December 1998, was no longer as popular as when he assumed power, and facing political as well as social unrest.[30] However, following the elections for the European Parliament, the surveys indicated that the popularity of both Jospin and Chirac remained stable.

Political Celebrations

President Chirac is a dedicated President, not only active abroad as a distinguished official representative of France and keenly aware of the importance of some significant moments of French history. Not too long ago, in April 1998, President Chirac celebrated the Edict of Nantes that put an end to the Wars of Religion four hundred years ago. Between April 23 and 30, 1598, the French king Henry IV signed the famous *Edit de Nantes* granting Protestants a relative liberty of cult, thus putting an end to 36 years of religious strife in France. Chirac started the celebrations on February 18, 1998, at the UNESCO, saying that the *Edit de Nantes* was a "strong moment in the awakening of France's national conscience" *(un moment fort de l'éveil de notre conscience nationale).* Louis XIV, in 1685, cancelled the Edict, starting a huge exodus of Protestants to neighboring countries and to America. But the spirit of the Edict did not die and, in fact, it eventually made it possible for the first time in Europe to have two religions cohabitating in the same country, thanks to the concept of separation of state and religion. Since then the French Protestants have been ardent supporters of secularism in France.

President Chirac also celebrated the 150th anniversary of the abolition of slavery by France. Slavery was approved in 1642 by King Louis XIII in a decree that allowed France to conduct slave trade along with England, Portugal and Spain and thus slavery reached its peak during the eighteenth century. Chirac's decision to celebrate the abolition of slavery clearly illustrates the French President's dedication to the principles of liberty, justice and civil rights.[31]

Notes

1   On the Symbols of the French Republic, see Appendix 2.

2   Until 1900 France did not have true political parties; at best, groups.

3   Women can vote since 1945.

4   It used to be 21 years old.

5   Conviction of certain crimes lead to the loss of civic rights for a specific length of time set by the courts.

6   De Gaulle knew all too well the ups and down of governments. The Third and Fourth Republics were characterized by chronic governmental instability. The Fourth Republic had 17 prime ministers between 1946 and 1958.

7   In the last ten years the French people have twice been called to vote on a referendum, first on November 6, 1988, on the status of New Caledonia, the final decision given in 1998, and on September 20, 1992, on the ratification of the treaty on the European Union.

8   However, no second dissolution is allowed during the year following the dissolution.

9   This last requirement will no doubt be amended when the compulsory military service is replaced by the so-called "meeting of the citizen."

10   It has been rumored that President Chirac might decide to reduce his term of office to five years. If he does, the elections would coincide with the new millennium.

11   Lionel Jospin wants to have a law adopted preventing elected officials to hold several political offices at the same time. For instance, the preceding Prime Minister Alain Juppé was concurrently mayor of the city of Bordeaux and Prime Minister. This, however, is still a mere wish of Jospin because many French officials who are presently holding several offices are overtly or silently totally opposed to the measure. It is predicted that Jospin's proposal will eventually die a quiet death.

12   See Appendix 3 on some sample articles of the French Constitution of the Fifth Republic concerning the President. *The text is given in French in order to represent accurately the terms of the Constitution.*

13   Naturally when there is a state of Cohabitation, some of the rapports between President and Prime Minister might be somewhat different than when the Prime Minister is the President's choice. This may be at times observed in the Cohabitation government of Chirac-Jospin.

14   We give a list of *Ministères* in Appendix 4. The names of the various *ministères* are in French, but the definition of their role is given in English.

15   The island of Nouvelle Calédonie situated in the southwest Pacific, southwest of
      Vanuatu, has a population of 196,836 inhabitants. Its capital is Nouméa, with a
      population of 76,293 inhabitants.

16   In Appendix 5 we give a list of the French departments preceded by their code
      number. This code number, for instance, identifies the automobiles on their li-
      cense plates. For example, a car with a license "HKL 38" shows that it comes
      from the Isère department in the Alpes–Dauphiné region.

17   See our Appendix 6 giving a list of the regions as political entities, with their basic
      facts, features and statistics (population, unemployment, surface, the number of
      departments that form the region).

18   I am giving here a selection of the articles adopted by the National Assembly and
      the Senate and enacted by the President of the Republic concerning the abolition
      of the death penalty in France (October 9, 1981): 1. The death penalty is abol-
      ished. 8. This law applies to French overseas territories, as well as to the territo-
      rial community of Mayotte. 9. Sentences to the death penalty passed after No-
      vember 1, 1980, shall be automatically converted into sentences to penal servitude
      for life or to life imprisonment according to the nature of the crime
      committed. . . . This shall now be enforceable as a Law of the French State.

19   Georges Marchais was surely a metallurgy worker who climbed rapidly the steps
      first of the CGT trade union and then of the party. It was recently reported that
      Marchais may have had some dubious secrets, such as the fact that he allegedly
      worked for Germany for Messerschmitt during the war, with the STO, but con-
      trary to most STO participants, Marchais had apparently volunteered. (The STO
      was composed of workers taken by the Germans and forced to work in Hitler's
      industries.) As Secretary General, Marchais was so rough and tough that he con-
      tributed to enlarge the number of his enemies, and of those who became disen-
      chanted with the way he ran the party.

20   The PCF head office is 2 Place du Colonel Fabien, 75019, Paris. It is presently
      represented by 23 deputies, 16 senators, 7 European deputies and 2 General
      Council presidents.

21   The PS' Head Office is 10 Rue de Solferino, 75007, Paris.

22   This declaration is not really surprising, as it comes at a time when there are
      increasing tensions between the President and Jospin. In addition the popularity
      of Jospin is declining, while Chirac's is increasing. In other words we are experi-
      encing the unpredictable seesaw of politics.

23   The Head Office of the Ecology party (Greens) is 107 Avenue Parmentier, 75011,
      Paris.

24   The party's headquarters is situated at 12 rue François Ier, 75008, Paris.

25   The RPR headquarters are situated at 123 rue de Lille, 75007, Paris.

26   The headquarters of the FN are 4 rue Vauguyon, 92210, Saint-Cloud. According
      to a poll published on October 23, 1997, in the magazine *L'Evènement du Jeudi*,

the opinion of the French is that they must either ignore the FN (27%) or fight it (46%). In the same opinion survey the French were asked if the ideas of the UDF and RPR were close to the FN ideologies or, on the contrary, removed from them. 48% answered that they were *removed* and 62% answered that they were *very removed*. (On opinion surveys as political tools of French Democracy, see our Appendix 7).

27   The Front National is a big thorn in the heel of France, and the French in majority are against the party of Le Pen. In April 1998 a petition was signed by thousands of concerned citizens and published in the magazine *EDJ (L'Evènement du Jeudi)* of April 2–5, 1998. It requested the prohibition of the FN as a political party. The petition ended saying: "Consequently we request that the Constitution sees that political organizations of this type be banned from the public space."

28   *Cohabitation* is considered by specialists as a temporary "*modus vivendi*," bearable while waiting for another moment of truth. The French don't seem to look at it as a dysfunction of the government, considering that they chose Cohabitation three times between 1986 and 1997 (1986, 1993, 1997). It may be said that Cohabitation has now been institutionalized, even if it exists against the wishes of the founders of the Fifth Republic. In the case of Cohabitation the country is still governed, but with this difference that it is the prime minister and not the President who has the power, with the support of Parliament. Thus the power of the President has become more democratic.

29   More information on *France under Chirac and Jospin* will be found under the following chapters on Economy, Education, Society, etc. . . . .

30   For instance, the Prime Minister has been recently (December 1998) accused by Communists in the Assembly not to be aware enough of what is happening deep down in the country, and not to pay enough attention to the real meaning of the movements of social unrest.

31   In the same mood, Chirac had made an apology to the Dreyfus family for the way France had treated Alfred Dreyfus.

Chapter 3

French Economy

The Situation before World War II

France in the eighteenth century was a strong power, the richest of Europe. As early as the 1800's, however, its economy began to lag behind England and Germany. The colonial wars were costly, and while the country spent large amounts to conquer colonies, it did spend enough in France. Life began to be difficult, particularly when the economic and industrial output started to decline sharply. By 1940, France was totally unprepared and unable to compete with the might of Germany, and as a consequence France lost the war. By 1945, France's industry, economy and all their supporting infrastructures such as roads, railroads, factories, harbors were in shambles, and the capital base was depleted. It appeared that only a miracle could turn around the situation. And fortunately a miracle occurred: *Les Trente Glorieuses.*

The Miraculous Period of Recovery:
1945–1975 "Les Trente Glorieuses"

Against all odds, France began to show definite signs of recovery as early as 1950,[1] and by 1960 the recovery was progressing at an even greater pace, in spite of a series of political and financial crises. The population grew from 40.5 million to 52.6 million up to 1975 and the spectacular growth kept increasing between 1975 and 1990, when the population went from 52.6 million to 56.6 million. At the same time life expectancy rose dramatically, and went from 62 years to 69 years for men, while it went from 67 years to 77 years for women. In fact, this increase has continued to 1998. The face of France was changing radically: from a basically agricultural nation, France became an industrial and commercial nation. People left agriculture for industry and businesses in cities and, as a consequence, the standard of living doubled. The French, with more money to spend, could buy houses and cars. The number of private cars rose from 1 million to 15 million in a few years. Industrial output tripled between 1952 and 1973. No wonder the period was to be called "The Thirty Glorious Years." However, people wondered how this could be. They asked themselves: "Is it the result of the traditional French State Control or is it that, we French, rediscovered some national dynamism and ambition?" Certainly the various governments did try to encourage recovery, but the huge surge of progress came from another source: from the enthusiasm of victory and the elated hopes generated by great leaders like de Gaulle. One must not forget, for example, the crucial role played by Jean Monnet in 1946.[2] He is the one who launched a daring austerity plan giving priority to reconstruction in general, to rebuilding the industry and the means of transportation. We must not forget the Marshall Plan in 1947 that provided France with the necessary finances for the success of the Monnet Plan. There was another element that contributed to the economic turnaround of France, the fact that after World War II the country downgraded its agriculture, thus freeing a large number of hands who went to work in factories and on construction projects. De Gaulle also played a part in this situation. First in 1959 he devalued the franc, giving birth to the new franc (one new franc was equal to 100 old francs). De Gaulle also encouraged trade liberalization with OECD countries, a move that immediately gave positive results because it reinforced the position of France as it entered the EEC competition. What is certain is that the recovery of France was for many years truly spectacular, in spite of many obstacles inherited from the past, such as antiquated business practices and techniques, outdated machinery, antiquated banking systems, as well as heavy bureaucratic methods and business structures and practices. A good example is the French Tobacco monopoly, which is a relic dating back to Louis XIV and Colbert's time. What de Gaulle did after World War II was to act like a Socialist or a Communist, by reinstating a regime of state control and of centralization, what the Général called "*Economie dirigée*" (planned economy under state control). In fact, de Gaulle expressed his belief in *dirigisme* (state control) in a speech, saying that it was necessary for "the collectivity, that is to say the state, to take in hand the great resources of the common riches, and to control certain others without banishing, of course, those powerful instruments of human endeavor." As he promised, de Gaulle, in order to foster postwar reconstruction, nationalized the French electric company (EDF), the gas company (GDF), French aviation (Air France, the transportation system of Paris (RATP), banking, insurance companies and Renault for the automobile industry. This state planning policy bore its fruits, particularly thanks to Jean Monnet, who managed to keep inflation in check and fostered economic growth in both private and public sectors of business, commerce and industry. De Gaulle and Jean Monnet were no doubt the main artisans of the most revolutionary transformation France experienced during its history.

But as always, just as everyone was comfortable, a serious crisis occurred, the 1973–1974 oil embargo crisis.[3] And it occurred under the presidency of an ailing Georges Pompidou. The next two or three years proved to be very difficult indeed. Giscard d'Estaing succeeded Pompidou and almost immediately (1974) had to tackle serious threats of economic recession. With his Prime Minister Jacques Chirac, Giscard took austere economic and financial steps that, alas, did not produce much improvement. Bankruptcies increased and unemployment soared as well as inflation. Chirac resigned, and Raymond Barre replaced him,[4] setting up new radical measures of austerity that proved painful and sometimes even counterproductive, sending unemployment and inflation figures to a record height. Raymond Barre became terribly unpopular, and as a consequence both Giscard and Barre lost the 1981 elections. It was only later when the Socialists had taken over, that the French realized that Barre's policies made sense and were even wise for the country.

After Giscard-Barre, the Socialists decided to do the opposite of Barre's policies, breaking away from the financial austerity program, and starting a program of huge public spending. To do so, the Socialists imposed new taxes on the rich, extended the length of paid holidays and reduced the workweek without cuts in salary. They also nationalized many key industries and banks, exactly the same policy as de Gaulle pursued earlier. For Mitterand, nationalizations were essential in order to recover control of the economy and to be able to fuel economic growth again. The tire manufacturer Michelin was nationalized and so was the automobile manufacturer Peugeot and about forty private banks, thus bringing three quarters of the French credit under state control. Few businesses and industries complained because most of them were in debt and therefore knew that nationalization would make them solvent with state funds. Mitterand did not stop there. He wanted desperately to curb unemployment,[5] and to do so he created new public service jobs. The result was not good and in fact the measure did little else but increased the state deficit. The economy, meanwhile, remained stagnant. Industrial products and commercial goods were not competitive on the world market and inflation increased. To make things worse, state expenses soared with the government attempt to pay the huge debts of the industries it had nationalized, with a devastating effect on the already huge state deficit. Once again, drastic measures were necessary.

So, after long debates, the Socialists decided to return to a tough program of austerity, calling for higher taxes, price controls and wage freezes. Demands for the promised reduction of the workweek from 39 hours to 35 hours were flatly denied. In fact workers had to wait until 1998 to obtain the 35 hours from the Socialist government of Lionel Jospin.

The austerity program of the Socialists came too late and was not able to save the party from defeat in the 1986 elections, even though the tightening of the country's belt was generally good for the overall economy of France. What it did was to reduce the deficit and to slow down inflation, at least bringing it to a more reasonable level. Industry also fared well, as it received a healthy boost from the government subsidies, and unemployment was kept in check.

Early in March 1996, the new Right-wing Chirac government started to undo the nationalization program of the Socialists with a decisive return to privatizations, price freezes, reduction of subsidies to industries, and reduction of some taxes. In other words, Chirac fought the étatisme (state interventionism) of the Socialists by more liberal policies, in fact something quite foreign to the tradition of France.[6] Chirac, however, was aware of the dangers of abolishing étatisme too fast, so he allowed the government to retain control over some key areas, for instance over public works such as the building of the Chunnel under the Manche (Channel between France and England). But many problems remained unsolved: France's exports remained insufficient and France's social charges were the highest of Europe, adding 45% to basic costs. Furthermore France's industry needed to modernize faster in order to produce more efficiently; it needed to invest in new machinery and equipment in order to be able to compete on the world market, particularly with Japan and the United States. Even more urgent for France, it had to breach the gap that existed between pure research and production. Most of the time the French had "the idea," but other countries like the US were able to produce and distribute before France could. The French car industry was lagging behind the Japanese, behind Volkswagen, Fiat and Ford-Europe. Fortunately, there were a few successful sectors like the aerospace industry with the successful production and sales of Airbus and Ariane space rockets. The French nuclear program with the building of electricity-producing reactors helped reduce France's dependency on oil,[7] and technically and strategically made France's defense more independent. But just as these positive results made the French more optimistic the Chornobyl nuclear disaster[8] occurred in April 1986.[9] First it was only slowly and partially publicized, but when the realities and extent of the disaster began to be known, the country was alarmed, to the point that many past supporters of the government nuclear program became worried and fearful. The ecologists throughout the world united against France's nuclear testing, and Chirac, after a few last tests in the Pacific, was forced to stop all French nuclear testing. French production of nuclear electricity remains strong, with 74.5% of France's electricity produced by nuclear reactors. Some electricity is used internally but the rest is sold to other countries of Europe, thus improving the trade balance of the country. The *Electricité de France* company (EDF) that produces electricity for France makes great efforts to reassure the population about the security of the French nuclear plants; nevertheless, since Chernobyl, some French families remain fearful. And the problem of nuclear production will peak around 2015 when most reactors will reach the end of their workable cycle. In May 1999 some good news for the *Greens (ecologists)* surfaced: France is now surrounded by allies who are cautiously backing away from nuclear power and with Germany's announcement that it planned to abandon nuclear power the future of French nuclear power is being seriously pondered. In fact Prime Minister Jospin, who last year closed the world's largest Superphenix reactor, is also talking about a "possible reduction" of the country's dependence on nuclear energy. From 74.5%, nuclear electricity production could be cut down to 60% over the next two decades. Some recent mishaps in nuclear plants and increased leukemia rates around some reactors have further eroded popular confidence in nuclear energy.

It is doubtful at this time that France will act as rashly as Germany, Sweden or Austria, agreeing to phase out nuclear power totally, but French politicians must make key decisions soon as French nuclear plants will need to be either replaced soon or decommissioned.

Franco-European Relations

At the end of 1998, it was clear that most European nations of the Euro community sought to work together in harmony. France, thanks to President Chirac, has displayed a great willingness to cooperate and to adapt, but problems remain, because underneath their desire of becoming Europeans, some people still fear the loss of their national identity. There lies one of the many challenges France and the other Euro nations will have to confront in the year 2000.

France's Relations with Africa

France used to be one of the major European colonial powers, but even though this is past history, it is eager to retain its influence in Africa. Premier Jospin himself has stated that he wanted to keep France's presence in Africa. In December 1997, Jospin set off on an African tour shortly after the departure from Africa of the American Secretary of State, Madeleine Albright. The France of today surely does not want to compete with Africa, but wants to cooperate and assist whenever necessary. In other words, French aid to Africa is not going to stop. As Jospin said in late December 1997 during his tour of Mali, Senegal and Morocco, France wants to replace any trace of paternalism by a spirit of partnership. This new policy includes the reduction of French troops stationed in Africa.

Franco-American Relations

As long as de Gaulle was leading France, Franco-USA relations remained cool or distant. But nowadays the French government wants to maintain cordial relations with the United States. The two countries have recently cooperated in several international conflicts, as in Bosnia and Kosovo. Naturally there are at times differences over solutions or tactics, but the two countries pursue the same overall goal, to keep order and to secure peace in troubled areas.[10] Even though it has been said that France was upset by the new interest of the USA in Africa, the two countries basically have pursued the same peaceful objectives.[11]

French Economy Today
(1998–1999)

France has a current GDP (Gross Domestic Product) equivalent to about $1.5 billion and it ranks among the top five world economic powers, being the world's fourth exporter.[12] It is a fact that France, during the last forty years, has worked hard to be able to be a full-fledged and dynamic member of the European Community. These efforts contributed much to improve all the sectors of French economy and succeeded in raising the standard of living of its citizens. The European construction forced businesses, transport services, banks and industry to become more competitive and to seek new markets abroad. Even agriculture benefited from the EEC requirements, because the French government was encouraged to grant large aid packages to needy rural areas, thus helping to modernize farms and techniques.

In spite of his dislike for government control *(étatisme)* and clearly in favor of a policy of economic liberalism,[13] Chirac allowed the state to intervene in many sectors of France's economic life, in transportation, public works, infrastructures and, by necessity, unemployment.[14]

France's Economic Handicaps

The budget deficit was particularly serious because France's entry in the Euro-Community depended on its reduction and stabilization around 3% of the GDP according to the Maastricht criteria for entry in the EMU (Economic and Monetary Union). The French have long been reluctant to accept the monetary union, although they finally agreed. Their reluctance came from the fact that they did not want to sacrifice their jobs, their happiness and most of all the social programs and services they enjoyed. There was a less obvious reason for their resistance: while they did not mind becoming Europeans, they did not want to lose their French identity. The "Mad Cow" crisis *(La Vache Folle)* that was for a while a menace to the red meat market in France and in neighboring countries added to the anxiety of the French. Finally, with drastic measures, the crisis subsided and in December 1998 French agriculture was doing fairly well.

France's Economic Assets

Fortunately France also has some very promising assets. The major economic asset presently is that inflation is under control. In May 1997, inflation was at its lowest level since the end of the 50's. In addition, France has succeeded in increasing its trade balance thanks to more active exports. In fact, the year 1997 was the best year for exports and France imported less, which gave France a significant positive commercial balance. The improved economic outlook is supported by the good results obtained by the automobile industry (+23%) and particularly by the encouraging gains of Airbus sales (+29%) against the US Boeing, which had to lay off thousands of workers in December 1998. Luxury items exports are also on the increase: perfume, Vuitton bags, Moet Chandon champagne, Hermes scarfs, Hennessy cognac, Michelin tires as well as Evian and Perrier waters.

The now approved (March 1998) reduction of the workweek to 35 hours without cut in pay is supposed to bring down unemployment significantly. Some speak even of the possibility of creating 450,000 new jobs by the year 2000. Working less, therefore giving work to more people, this is how the economic miracle of the 35 hours is presented.[15] It must be said that results will only be seen later, as companies and businesses one by one have to settle the strategy of the reduced workweek with their employees.[16] In a January 1999 speech, Lionel Jospin was optimistic, saying that he expected to see excellent results from the 35 hours during 1999, and adding that it could help create 350,000 to 400,000 jobs by 2001. As the Prime Minister was speaking, the CGT announced that it would sign an agreement of work reduction to 35 hours at the EDF-GDF (*Electricité and Gaz de France*). But, unfortunately for Jospin, not everyone in the country is as optimistic. It is a difficult period for the French Premier because some people tend to perceive in some of his actions a Jospin-presidential candidate.

On the side of France's assets is the perspective of the Euro. According to some economists, the Euro is a tremendous challenge and opportunity for France and its European partners, who will be forced to reorganize and change for the better. In fact, the future (year 2000) is near, and it will surely tell if these optimistic predictions are correct.

Even the 1996 "Mad Cow" episode (cows contaminated by the ESB virus or *Encephalopathie spongiforme bovine*) had some positive consequences for France and its European partners. Consumers started to demand stricter controls on the food they consumed and to know the origin of the meat they bought. In other words, the crisis led to a welcomed move toward food security and consumer protection.[17]

Finally the 1998 predictions for business investments are good, and that would definitively give a boost to economic growth estimated at 2.3% to 2.5% for 1999 with even a probable accelaration during the second semester of that year.

More Progress in Sight

In March 1998 the figures of the French National Institute of Statistics proved optimistic for the French economy, predicting lower unemployment figures (below 12%) starting in June 1998. At the same time, Jospin expected that 250,000 jobs for the young would be created in 1999, bringing down the number of job seekers to its lowest level since 1995.[18] In April 1998, Dominique Strauss-Kahn, the French Minister of Economy, announced more good news; the public deficit of France had been reduced from 3% of the *Produit Intérieur Brut* in 1997 to 2.3% in 1998.[19] Budget predictions for 1999 are even looking at a smaller deficit of 240 billion francs or 2.5% of the PIB. The same predictions advance that by year 2000 the deficit will be further reduced to 2% of the PIB. The government explains that if the reductions in the deficit are slow, it is because it does not want to reduce the deficit at the expense of other important priorities. Among these priorities are the fight against exclusion, improvements in education, research and in lodging. Even with these goals in mind, Jospin does not foresee any tax increases. The Economy minister, Strauss-Kahn, does not want to be recklessly optimistic, but he believes that the current economic situation of France (in 1998) is that of "a sick patient who is about to be cured." Naturally to be totally cured, France must put the lid on unemployment and further reduce inflation. In fact the 1999 budget is predicting a reasonably low inflation of 1.2%.[20]

In conclusion, the present Socialist government of Lionel Jospin must navigate carefully if France does not want to encounter, like the Titanic, some icebergs in its path, namely unemployment and more social unrest. A good sailor so far, Jospin has reduced some major state expenditures, housing, military expenses and he has increased some taxes, while beginning to reduce the Social Security deficit[21] and some social allowances.[22]

The coming of the Euro will have other positive economic impacts for France,[23] such as on investments, and it will allow France to become more adapted to the future, that is to say, to a world ruled by a global information society.[24] In July 2002 all coins and banknotes will be in Euros. Until December 31, 2001, the franc will remain the national currency, but all interbank exchanges will be made in Euros. Meanwhile most prices are going to be indicated in both francs and Euros.

French Economy: Some Important Factors

A fundamental change has occurred in French economy: From being ultra protective, French economy has become more open; in fact one could say that it has never been so open. It has shifted radically from a position of national independence to one of global interdependence, and it has readily adapted to global competition. Now France does not hesitate to transfer some of its plants out of France, to England, for instance, while France has allowed quite a few foreign companies to settle in France, and there are now several French businesses that, while still producing French products, are owned by foreigners. In addition many companies still in French hands are in reality controlled by foreign capital, and these companies represent about one-third of French sales and exports and employ about one-quarter of the work force. France has now accepted the economic realities of globalization and has recognized the possibilities offered by the European Single Market. Nevertheless, France has made it clear to foreigners who want to invest in France that they are welcomed as long that they bring employment and techniques, but that unfair competition is not welcomed. Doubts still linger in many business and industrial circles about the advantage of a totally open economy. For instance, when Toyota decided to settle in northeastern France, in Valenciennes early in 1998, while everybody in the area rejoiced of the windfall of jobs, many others were skeptical, calling the move "a dubious gift." They wondered how long this windfall would remain good for French workers, and argued that these French workers were going to build Japanese cars which in the long run would rob clients from the French automobile industry, and consequently cost jobs. So, it is clear that while the French economy has never been as open as today, there are certain groups who are still calling for a certain level of cautious protectionism.

French Shipping

France is no longer a major maritime power; however, after a sharp slump in 1995, there was a slight 0.6% improvement in 1996, mostly due to container traffic. The harbors of Rouen and Dunkerque have experienced a serious decrease in activity (–20%) and Bordeaux, today, remains the most active harbor, even ahead of Le Havre and Marseille. There is no doubt that, if France wants to remain competitive at sea, it must pursue a very serious policy of investments in shipping and shipbuilding.

The French Railroad System, SNCF

The SNCF has been able to reduce its losses by 959 million francs in 1997 against a huge deficit in 1996 of 15,173 billion francs. The French railroad company now hopes to get totally out of the red in 1999 according to its president Louis Gallois. The SNCF has been split into two companies, the original SNCF and the *Réseau Ferré de France* (French rail network) now in charge of the infrastructures. Through this split alone the SNCF has reduced its debts by billions of francs and traffic has increased by over 5% in 1997

In addition to the (TGV), an acronym for *"train à grande vitesse,"* rolling at speeds of 270–300 km/hr on its special tracks, France joined England in 1995, and built the Eurotunnel, or Chunnel, a fantastic achievement of civil engineering, connecting France and England under the sea with the fast train Eurostar.[25]

The Normandy Bridges

The *Tancarville suspension bridge* was built in 1972, but it still took 45 minutes to go from one side of the Seine estuary of Le Havre on the other side, to Honfleur. So in January 1995 the French government built another bridge, *Le Pont de Normandie* which cuts crossing time to 15 minutes. The cost of construction came to about $460 million.

Roads

France has high quality infrastructures with the longest network of roads and superhighways in Europe. Only two problems: (1) Toll roads (*autoroutes*) are expensive and (2) most of the good roads go from north to south. There are smaller roads going east to west, but they are generally curvy two-lane roads, slowed down by the many small villages they cross. Unfortunately there are no east-west-east superhighways to date in France.

Telecommunications

Some twenty years ago, the French telephone system was at best antiquated. But after World War II, and since the Thirty Glorious Years, France has made giant strides in communication technology. In 1968 only 15% of homes had a telephone, and in 1998, the percentage was over 98%. France has developed before the advent of the Internet a sophisticated system of communication with *Minitel* and smart telephone cards that hold microcomputer chips, and which do away with the old system of coin operated public telephones. Today France Telecom is making great strides with portable phones and with computers and access to the World-Wide Web. Portable phones are so popular that France Telecom is thinking of removing a number of telephone booths in cities.

It is interesting to note that in 1999 the *Minitel* is fast being bypassed by the Internet. While in 1983 the *Minitel* was revolutionary, in 1999 it has become all but archaic. This is another example of the evolution of France and the French as they get close to the Third Millennium.

French Industry

French industry soared during the so-called Thirty Glorious Years, but began to wane during the 1970's. In fact, it lost one and a half million jobs between 1970 and 1990, a good 1/3 of its work force. By 1991 many sectors of industry regained vitality and France was able to resume and expand its exports, thus bringing about a marked improvement of the French foreign trade balance as well as a healthy increase in the competitiveness of French products. The areas that gained special momentum were aerospace, chemical products, automobiles, plastics, electronics, high fashion products, clothing, perfume, and steel to a much lesser degree. In spite of its regained dynamism, France's industry still needs improving, and it particularly must more fully develop its potential in some specific areas, rather than trying to remain competitive in all areas. Naturally, specialization may not be the only solution to improvement, but it is a major way to regain some manufacturing markets abroad.[26]

French industry, however, can look ahead with confidence. It is doing well in major areas such as transportation, telecommunications, leisure organizations, data processing and finance. It is also a leader in research and development of transportation systems, like with the fast train TGV and the airplanes Concorde and Airbus. *La Poste*, the French post office system, is beginning to be a profitable enterprise, particularly since it began to offer financial opportunities, savings and investments.

Automobiles

There is no doubt that globalizing has deeply affected the French automobile industry, which is still living with a certain level of government protectionism. In 1998, French automobile manufacturers were still trying to catch up with sales on the world market, and as an example, Renault has announced the production by the end of 1999 of a car designed specifically for emerging countries. Based on the Renault *Clio* model, the new car will have a stronger suspension in order to be able to ride on dirt roads and rough terrain, and its estimated cost is supposed to be about 25% less than the regular Clio. Similarly, Peugeot has announced that on account of the success of its line of 206 automobiles, it plans to increase its production, and hopes to generate more jobs.

Contrary to automobile manufacturers, the Valeo equipment manufacturer has rejected the protectionist model, opened itself to free trade and competition and, whenever necessary, has moved its plants to places outside of France where production costs are lower, even if confronted by the anger of the French over losses of French jobs.

Employment

While an increasing number of young people continue their studies in order to be better qualified for the job market and to be able to meet the increasing requirement qualifications expected by employers, many of them seek more education simply because they cannot find work. This explains, at least in part, the difficulties met by universities to provide for the ever-increasing student enrollments.

While low-scale jobs remain hard to find, more jobs were available at the executive level. While in 1997 only 37,000 jobs were created for executives, in 1996, 14,800 were created. In 1997 businesses had hired 128,300 executives, a remarkable performance.

Work

Since the beginning of the twentieth century the length of the French workers' workweek has steadily declined, from 40 hours in 1936 and 39 hours in 1982 and now, in 1998, it has been reduced to 35 hours. One must understand, however, that there are still many people who work longer hours, the manual laborers, the tradespeople and those in the liberal professions, who are free from the law. Annual leaves have risen gradually from 12 working days in 1936, to three weeks in 1956, four weeks in 1969, and five weeks in 1982. Part-time work is a solution for many people who otherwise would be unemployed; some women, however, opt for part-time jobs in order to be able to give more time to their families.

France has become sensitive to the working conditions and safety of its workers and working conditions are regularly monitored in plants and businesses by management as well as by unions.

French Salaries

A review of the salary situation since 1996 shows that French salaries have lost up to 1.3% of their purchasing power due to the increase of social taxes and retirement contributions, and higher salaries are the worse affected with a loss of 3% for executive-level individuals. In the public sector, France employs almost 2 million civil servants including teachers and professors. The average salary is 15,000 francs a month after taxes and contributions. Naturally this 15,000 francs figure is only an approximate average because many earnings are more than 18,000 francs a month, while about 10% of individuals still earn less than 8,000 francs a month.[27] The salaries of French workers are affected by two social taxes, the CSG (*Contribution Sociale Généralisée*—General social contribution) and the CRDS (*Contribution au Remboursement de la Dette Sociale*—Contribution to the repayment of the social debt). Both taxes represent 21.1% of the average gross salary. Men and women still do not always earn equal salary for the same job (minus 20% on the average) in spite of the fact that much progress has been achieved in this area.

Trade Unions (Syndicats)

Trade unions are strong in France and fight for the French workers' right to negotiations. Unions in France operate quite differently from US unions.

They tend to seek labor-management dialogue rather than long strikes and confrontations. But unions do not hesitate to call for a strike when they see that the government and management are not responsive to their demands. Not long ago the unions for the truck drivers called a strike against the penalty points for speeding, and to support their demand of retirement at 55. The strike was supported all over France, paralyzed the country for days, and the unions won. One thing that is worth noting, in spite of the gross inconvenience often caused by strikers, the French public was in general quite supportive of the strikers.

The major French trade union is the CGT (*Confédération Générale du Travail*—general work confederation), the CFTC (*Confédération Française des Travailleurs Chrétiens* and the CGT-FO (*Confédération Générale du Travail-Force Ouvrière*—general work confederation-workers' force), CFDT (*Confédération Française Démocratique du Travail*—French democratic workers confederation). Since 1993 French teachers have been supported by the FEN (*Fédération de l'Education Nationale*—National education federation) and by the FSU (*Fédération Syndicale Unitaire*—United trade union federation), a subdivision of the FEN. White-collar workers, when they join a union, are members of the CFE-CGC (*Confédération française de l'encadrement*—Confédération générale des Cadres*—French confederation of executives).

On the employers' side, the *Conseil National du Patronat Français* (CNPF—French national employers council) represents most big businesses. Smaller companies tend to organize around the *Confédération des Petites et Moyennes Entreprises* (CGPME—General confederation of small and medium-size businesses). The farmers' union is the FNSEA (*Fédération Nationale des Syndicats d'Exploitants Agricoles*—National federation of farmers unions).

In France the major unions are legal representatives of the employees, and employers are under the obligation to recognize the union representatives.

Under these conditions, one would think that union membership would be high in France, chiefly when one considers the number of workers who follow strikes and eventually benefit from them, but that is not the case. Union membership in France is relatively low and the reason for this is mostly historical: Unions were led by a core of militants organizing demonstrations and strikes, and less interested in bargaining reasonably with management. This historical revolutionary basis has stuck to the unions' image that has little appeal to the majority of the French work force interested first and foremost in its specific individual interests. Another reason for the little appeal of unions is that in many cases employers accept collective bargaining equally with union and non-union workers. Workers therefore see little advantage to belonging to a union when they feel covered just as union workers by the agreement extended by their employer. In fact the major social advances obtained by workers have been obtained more by collective bargaining agreements worked out by union and non-union workers than by unions alone.

Strikes are a fundamental right under the French Constitution, and they are generally organized by a union. The CGT is often a leader, organizing large demonstrations. Long strikes are rare, basically because, with a fairly low membership, unions are not rich and rarely can provide pay assistance to strikers.

French Consumers

In 1998 French consumers spent more than in past years, particularly on basic items such as cars, homes and appliances. Home construction rose by almost 20% in March 1998 and spending on automobiles rose by about 4%. People believe that with falling unemployment and lower interest rates and mortgages, it is a good time to buy or build. Other sectors also benefit from the current optimism. Concerns for health and personal appearance have increased the sales of mineral waters *(Perrier, Badoit, Evian, Vichy)* and other high-quality health foods. Consumption of low-fat dairy products has soared and the consumption of regular table wine has decreased by half since the 1950's, while the consumption of expensive quality wines has increased slightly. But it is a fact that the French drink much less wine today than before WWII, and the same thing can be said for bread.

Housing

Today about 60% of the French own their residence, with an increasing prevalence of one-family homes. In addition many people now own second vacation homes in the country *(résidences secondaires)*, in the mountains or at the seashore. During the past 15 years much progress has been done improving the overall comfort of houses. People have decent modern kitchens with a refrigerator, a dishwasher and microwave oven and they enjoy decent bathrooms, electronic leisure equipment such as TV's, cassettes, CD players, and computers. This does not mean that these modern comforts are accessible to all. There remain, unfortunately, a large number of unemployed workers, foreign manual laborers and poor people who must continue to live in marginal conditions in large inhuman apartment buildings or in worse conditions. Alas, such miserable places often breed social unrest, drug use and what goes with it, insecurity and violence.[28]

French Finances, Banking and Taxes

Since the Second World War *French Finance* has undergone dramatic changes. First the responsibility of financing was shifted from the governments to the banks and, second, the government has given more importance to the *Bourse* (Stock Market) in the hope of encouraging more Frenchmen to save in long-term options such as the *SICAV*.

When the French government nationalized companies and industries, particularly under Mitterand's presidency, it acquired huge debts. The State-controlled companies had debts amounting to about 500 to 600 billion francs. The French government, for instance, had to settle a debt of 206 billion francs for the SNCF, 45 billion francs for the nuclear central *Superphenix*. In addition, among many others, it had to rescue the retirement insurance company GAN in debt of 20 billion francs, a loss due to very bad property loans and heavy insurance indemnities. The French bank *Le Crédit Lyonnais* has been riddled with huge debts too. It had to be financially rescued three times with a financial loss of at least 50 billion francs. Naturally, the cost of rescuing these companies has been an enormous burden on the national budget and French taxpayers. Social Security had a huge deficit, dating from 1989, that still lingers over the budget of Chirac and Jospin; however, the debt that amounted to 37.7 billion francs in 1997 is supposed to have been reduced by 12 billion francs by the end of 1998. This optimistic view is supported by a return to a solid level of economic growth, by a decrease of unemployment, by a rise of 2.7% in salaries and by a very low inflation rate of 1% or less.

The *banking sector* in France is dominated by three deposit banks, the *Banque Nationale de Paris (BNP)*, the *Société Générale* and the *Crédit Lyonnais*, and two merchant banks, *Paribas* and *Indosuez*. Next to those are mutualist and cooperative banks and loan-oriented banks such as the *Crédit Agricole*. Now the *Crédit Lyonnais*, the *Crédit Agricole* and the BNP are the three largest banks, but next to them the competition of the financial Post Office network, *La Poste,* has been added. Curiously the *Crédit Agricole* has been much more successful than the other banks, and is in fact the most profitable of all, and that in spite of the rapid drop in the number of farmers, decreasing farm incomes and desertion of the countryside. But with the decline of agriculture, the *Crédit*

Agricole is now forced to diversify and this may eventually put it in the same situation as the other banks.

In France *taxes* are relatively high in comparison with the average taxes of the rest of Europe. Social taxes and contributions account for these higher taxes. In France taxes are 19.3% of the PIB (Gross interior product), a higher percentage than in all other 15 members of the European Union (Germany: 15.4%; Spain: 12.3%; UK: 6.3%; and USA: 7.0%. The only European country where taxes are higher is the Netherlands with 18.4%.

Agriculture

Approximately 85% of France is taken up by arable and wooded land, representing 116 million acres. Although the medium-sized family farm is the most typical, there remain some rare one-family farms, particularly in central France and in mountain areas. Elsewhere, in the north of France, the farms have increased in size with 37,000 farms. The French government does not encourage small landholdings, as they tend to be divided and subdivided through inheritances.[29]

In 1914 nearly half of the population of France lived on the land. After the Second World War, this situation changed drastically, as there was an important migration of rural workers to towns where jobs were more available, and wages more attractive.

Agricultural Production and Exports

France is still Europe's leading agricultural producer. In 1985 France produced 54.3 million metric tons of grain, 28.3 million tons of sugar beets, 7 million tons of potatoes, 8.8 million gallons of milk, 1.9 billion gallons of wine and 1,343 tons of cheese. France's 340 varieties of cheeses make it the world's second producer after the US. Stock raising is also on the increase in France. In 1986 France produced 1,675,000 tons of beef and 394,000 tons of veal. The production of pork, lamb, goat and horsemeat is insufficient to meet domestic needs, so large quantities must be imported. The Mad Cow crisis did affect the health of the meat trade, but it seems that things are back to normal in 1999, in spite of some Mad Cow disease cases still occasionally reported in France.

The French vineyards cover 2.6 million acres, and a total of 323 million gallons of wine are exported, along with 26.6 million of pure alcohol (figures for 1986).

French agricultural exports were estimated at 70.04 billion francs in 1986. Protectionism has slowed the growth of international markets however, France retains the second rank in world agricultural trade. Since the introduction of the Common Agricultural Policy in 1962, France has been obliged to harmonize its own agricultural policy with the decisions of the other EEC members in regard to prices, agricultural output and subsidies to farmers.

At the end of the Second World War, 36% of persons worked in agriculture. In 1990, this percentage has decreased to 7%. This huge drop represents the massive exodus from the country to urban centers that took place during the *Trente Glorieuses* industrial boom.

French Farmers and the European Common Market Exigencies

Not long ago, in 1998, the Breton farmers were angry about the competition they met about their cauliflowers, so they dumped tons of cauliflowers on roads and railroad tracks. Then it was the turn of the French strawberries producers to be angry because they only produce 80,000 tons of strawberry, while the Spanish growers produce 370,000 tons and sell them at a much lower price than the French. The result was an agricultural war. The irate French growers poured several tons of Spanish strawberries in front of the Spanish consulate and burned 500 trays of the red delicacy. If the Common Market agricultural policy is to work, France must further harmonize its agricultural policy with that of other EEC members in regard to prices, production and subsidies.

National Defense

Under Jacques Chirac, French defense is being thoroughly transformed in order to prepare for a European defense. The traditional conscription system is to be totally abandoned, to be replaced by an all-professional French army, while reducing the size of French armed forces by 150,000 men. The number of soldiers stationed in Africa will also be reduced from 8,000 men to 5,000. The National Service is to be replaced by a few days of "meeting of citizens"*(rendez-vous citoyen)*.[30] In addition the military budget which in 1996 represented 2.33% of the French GDP or 12.3% of the State budget, will be drastically cut from about 5 billion francs to 230 million in 1998. The big fear in France is that the reduction of its defense budget will lead to a greater dependence on the USA. Those who do not approve of Chirac's measures bring out the fact that the reform of French defense will cut 60,000 jobs by the year 2000 in the French armament industry. Recently, there have been talks of a joint French-English defense effort supported by President Chirac and Tony Blair, Prime Minister of England.

Tourism, An Important Economic Asset of France

Tourism is very important for the economy of France and, fortunately, France is a favorite destination in Europe for tourists and businessmen. Tourists do not go only to Paris; they go to the Riviera, to the Atlantic coast beaches, to the mountains to ski in winter[31] and they enjoy the seven national parks of France and the still quaint villages all over the country. France, on the average, welcomes over 60 million tourists each year. This represents well over 12 billion francs in earnings for the hotels, resorts, airlines, superhighway tolls, etc. . . . . Vacationers not only fly, drive or take the train, they also go on cruises on the many canals of the country or take hot-air balloon rides, in Burgundy, for instance. In addition many Dutch and Germans, in particular, spend their vacations in summer houses they bought, taking advantage of the decline in real estate prices due to the exodus of the French from the countryside.

Tourism is also a great asset to France because of the natural richness and diversity of its landscapes and the country's reputation for its cultural activities, and for its fine foods and wines.

France's Economic Quality of Life

Even though they often complain, the French, on the whole, have an excellent economic quality of life, especially when compared with the situation of some of their other European partners. Luxembourg is an exception; it is supposed to have an average 60% higher level than the other OCDE countries of the European Union. There are problems in large urban centers, of course, but there still remains in France towns and places that offer an excellent quality of life, cultural opportunities and few crimes.

Someone who came to France just after WWII and just returned at the eve of the year 2000 would be struck by the incredible metamorphosis of some French cities. Surely, deep in the countryside, there still remain some isolated villages that have not changed much, but such places are disappearing fast while many provincial towns have acquired an economic and cultural dynamism only second to that of Paris and very large urban centers like Lyon, Marseille. For example, Grenoble, in the Rhône-Alpes region, is at the top of the list as an attractive modern town, with an excellent quality of life and a dynamic cultural environment. Grenoble's university vocation, including its important scientific community, its state of the art scientific and engineering plants, is one of its main assets. The campus of the University of Grenoble houses 45,000 students. Grenoble, it is true, has some of the drawbacks of provincial towns—it can be quite deserted on Sundays and it has experienced some security problems, but nothing comparable to some other larger urban centers, like Strasbourg, for instance. Outside of Grenoble, there are many other towns that are well prepared, we think, to meet the challenges of the year 2000, and that have also a good quality of life and a dynamic economy—Caen, Toulouse, Montpellier, Besançon, Nantes, to mention just a few.

French Economy at the End of 1998
and at the Beginning of 1999

The year 1998 was good for French economy.[32] The PIB (gross interior product) grew by 3%, but by the end of the year some economists wondered if this growth would continue even if it is the hope of Dominique Strauss-Kahn, Minister of Economy and Finances. In the fall of 1998, Bercy, the home of the Economy and Finance Ministry, predicted a growth of 2.7%, while others advanced a lower figure of only 2%. We now know that the growth expected by mid-1999 should not exceed 2.3–2.5%. Why this pessimism, when unemployment has decreased, when exports have increased by about 12%? Simply because the internal economic engine is not yet strong enough to pull the whole economy of France. So between the optimism of Bercy and the pessimistic predictions of others, the French government of Jospin must try to preserve through 1999 the good performance of 1998, not an easy task.

Notes

1   "Rebuilding began as early as 1946 and progressed throughout the Fourth Republic, but political uncertainties—France had 15 cabinets between 1947 and 1954—persistent balance pf payments problems, and continuing inflation served to restrain progress." W. Allen Spivey, *Economic Policies in France 1976–1981*, 1982, p. 1.

2   Jean Monnet, French economist, born in Cognac in 1888, author of the modernization plan of French economy (1945). He kept inflation in check through price and wage controls and he saw that the nationalized EDF could produce nuclear energy.

3   The 1973–1974 oil embargo affected France even more severely than other nations with sharp increases in energy prices. In fact the oil prices quadrupled and France was badly hit particularly because it was importing about 75% of her energy supplies. To be precise, France in 1973 was the third largest importer of oil and gas. B. Belassa in "L'Economie française sous la cinquième république 1958–1978," *Revue économique* 30 (1979), p. 955, states that the impact of energy prices on France was equal to a 3% tax on the country national income.

4   Raymond Barre became prime minister of France in August 1976. He was a distinguished economist with great experience in government. He came decided to bring major changes to the economic policies of the country, but his task proved to be harder than anticipated.

5   The unemployment rate in 1975 was 3.9% and 6% in 1979 and 6.8% in December 1980.

6   As mentioned earlier, state control in France has been the rule since the seventeenth century with Louis XIV's finance minister Jean-Baptiste Colbert. And de Gaulle after World War II returned to some extent to *étatisme* (state control).

7   Nuclear-produced electricity was particularly helpful during the severe oil crisis.

8   The site of the world's worst reactor meltdown and release of nuclear radiation was called Chernobyl, but it was renamed Chornobyl.

9   It is interesting to note that the old and damaged Chernobyl nuclear plant is supposed to be decommissioned and closed by year 2000.

10   An example of occasional tensions between France and the USA is the latest disagreement they expressed about the latest Gulf crisis with Saddam Hussein. The two countries demonstrated two different approaches, or styles: the USA and England used air strikes against the Iraqi leader, while France, along with other countries, were in favor of a more diplomatic and moderate reaction to Iraq's lack of cooperation with the UN weapons inspectors. The attitude of France

is not new; it considers the USA as an ally, but in the tradition of French diplomacy, it refuses to align itself simply in principle, automatically.

11　A delagation of US congressmen visited France in January 1998 and, although they admitted having some differences with the French, they came away from meetings with President Chirac and the French Defense Minister Alain Richard with a good feeling of good understanding between the two nations. Benjamin Gilman, the US chairman of the House Foreign Affairs Committee, declared on January 20, 1998, after meeting with Chirac: "France has been a firm and longstanding ally of the United States. We are very proud of our relationship and our meeting here helped to solidify the relationship." On "Franco-American relations through history" in brief, see our Appendix 11.

12　These figures do not intend to be exactly accurate for 1998, as they are extrapolations based on an economic report of 1994; however, they provide a good basis for a reasonable estimate of the present situation.

13　Today, with Chirac as president, France is clearly committed to a policy of economic liberalism. Several former state industries have been privatized such as the French tobacco industry *(Seita)*, the aluminium Péchiney company and the steel industry Usinor-Sacilor.

14　In France the State is the foremost employer in the country. Its civil service employs more than two million persons and over one million in the educational system alone.

15　It must be said that the business sector took a strong stand against the idea of 35 hours of work without decrease in pay, but as we know the measure passed.

16　The decision of the Socialist government to reduce the workweek from 39 hours to 35 without cut in pay is supposed to take effect in the year 2000. Companies with 20 employees or more have to apply the measure by 2000, but smaller businesses are granted two extra years to comply, i.e., until year 2002. As an example, new negotiations on the 35 hours have just begun in mid-December 1998 at the SNCF, when only 44,000 railroad workers out of 174,000 are currently working under the 35 hours program. Implementation of such a plan all over France will no doubt bring the biggest change in labor laws and practice since 1936, when the Popular Front introduced paid vacations and a 40-hour week. Martine Aubry, Ministre de l'Emploi, wants to be flexible, but she wants the year 2000 to be the "transition year" to the 35 hours, indicating that there should not be any undue delays.

17　Unfortunately it has been reported that the Mad Cow disease has not totally disappeared from France, and in some regions of France the number of cases has increased in 1998. However, this disease is really quite limited and contained in France compared to neighboring countries, Great Britain in particular.

18　It is true that some pessimist souls claim that the increase in jobs is mostly due to part-time employment.

19   According to Dominique Strauss-Kahn, France's percentage of growth should remain moderate, at about 2.8%, but it may be possible to increase this percentage in the future.

20   The French National Assembly debated in mid-December 1998 the 1999 budget that contains a budgetary deficit of over 200 billion francs. On the positive side, Prime Minister Jospin is granting the poorest persons a 3% increase in solidarity allocations retroactive to January 1998.

21   In order to decrease the deficit of the Sécurité Sociale, the government has replaced the contributions paid on salaries or wages by a *Contribution Sociale Généralisée*, a flat tax based on all types of incomes.

22   The decrease in parental allowances will occur whenever parents show an income exceeding a certain level.

23   "The French will have a 'pivotal position in the euro zone's financial sphere,' says Svenja Nehls-Obégi, senior economist at Deutsche Bank's Paris office," *Business Week,* February 15, 1999, p. 52. In an article titled *"The French Flex Their Muscles,"* *Business Week,* February 15, 1999, p. 50, the authors, Gail Edmondson, Stephen Baker, Heidi Dawley and Thane Peterson write: "The creation of the euro zone robs the French of a great advantage: protected financial markets that channeled capital into domestic institutions and instruments. But French banks bring special expertise to the euro zone battlefield. France has long excelled in finance, with an elite cadre of technicians trained to manage money for the dirigiste state.". . . "France has many of the raw materials it needs to become a heavy-weight in the new euro zone. With a few more strategic deals, it could live up to its unrealized potential" (p. 52).

24   The Europeans, including the French, seem to be waiting with optimism the arrival of the Euro, and the Euro is coming fast. The committee of the Euro has tentatively decided to provide shopkeepers and businesses with bills and coins in Euro by the end of 2001 so that they can be prepared to give change to their customers starting January 1, 2002. This plan, however, still needs the agreement of the Central European Bank (BCE).

25   The "Chunnel" is 32.2 miles long under the Manche (English Channel) and it is 131 feet beneath the sea.

26   Refer to the excellent book of Erik Izraelewicz, *Ce monde qui nous attend. Les peurs françaises et l'économie.* Grasset, 266 pages. Izraelewicz tells us in his book that the chances of success for France in this world are strong, but he suggests that France must give up its culture of immobility. For those who find Economy arcane, there is a new book out explaining in simple terms some of the major economic words and systems (growth, exchange rates, financial markets, etc. . . .): *L'économie expliquée à ma fille* by André Fourçans, Editions du seuil.

27   For example, a 31-year-old postman receives an average net salary of less than 8,000 francs a month, a take-home pay which is further reduced by taxes and

retirement and health contributions. A woman director of school, 44 years old, earns about 10,000 francs a month before taxes. For a sample of average monthly salaries as of October 1, 1997 see our Appendix 9.

28   For further details on housing conditions in France, see our Appendix 10.

29   The French government has been active in taking measures in view of spurring agricultural reforms. It tried to incite elderly farmers to retire, while helping young people to find urban jobs, instead of trying to remain farmers on too small farmlands. It also helped those who wanted to remain as farmers to learn more modern methods, and it tried to consolidate very small farms into larger more productive units. In spite of these efforts, most farms in France are still worked by a single farm-owner and his family. Mechanization has greatly decreased the need for manual labor.

30   The French Senate adopted March 7, 1998, by 215 votes against 96 the project of reform changing the military service to a 5-day citizens meeting, thus instituting an all-volunteer army.

31   France has a large skiing area with over 80,000 miles of ski runs. Most people know the attraction of the Alps for skiing since the Winter Olympics of Grenoble in the 1960's and of Alberville in 1992.

32   The French regional newspaper *La Provence* reported excellent economic news for France in its editorial of Saturday, February 27, 1999, p. 20, stating that 1998 has been the best year for France in economic growth. France's yearly growth has reached 3.2%, that is, the strongest growth rate since 1989. The only shadow being the slowing down of industry due to the crisis in Asia. In addition, the daily newspaper *La Provence* reports that in 1998, 400,000 jobs were created, bringing down unemployment to 11.5%. There were 4,000 fewer persons without a job in January 1999 than in December 1998. All in all the present figures of unemployed are at 2,895,900. Households have spent more in 1998 and prices have decreased to 0.2% in December 1998. The *Bourse* (French Stock Market) also has had its best year in 10 years with a gain of 31.47%.

Chapter 4

French Society

Population

Up to the seventeenth century, France was a leader in Europe in matters of population. In fact, France had the largest population in Europe, larger than Italy and England at the eve of the Revolution. In the nineteenth century, French population stagnated, although this stagnation was partly compensated by the arrival of immigrants. At the eve of World War II, England and Italy had caught up with France. During the 1930's there were hardly 600,000 births a year, but right after the Liberation, in the 1940's, there were 869,000 births and 874,000 in 1964. But after 1964 the birthrate began to decline and settled around 750,000 with a further decrease in 1996 with 734,000 births. During the 1930's women had an average of 2.1 children and right after WWII the rate went up to 3.0: it was what we call the Baby Boom years. In the 1970's the rate declined to less than 2 children per woman (1.8 in 1978). From 1983 on through 1996, the rate never increased beyond 1.6 to 1.8. The National Institute of Demographic Studies (INED) is predicting a possible increase to 2.1 in 1999 with no forseeable further increase.

In March–April 1999, France counted 60,082,000 inhabitants and according to the INSEE *(Institut National de la Statistique et des Etudes Economiques)*, the French population has increased by 0.38% since the 1990 census.[1] The number of births is up by 1% and the number of marriages was also up by 10%. In 1996, 279,000 weddings were celebrated, a 10% increase in relation to 1995, and the largest increase since the 1970's. This increase, however, may be only temporary and mainly due to a change in the fiscal status of couples living together. By the end of 1996, fiscal advantages granted to unwed parents were drastically cut. This may therefore account for some additional weddings in 1996; people married to recover social advantages. In 1996 France acquired 238,000 persons, out of which 198,000 were due to the natural balance of births and deaths, and 40,000 were due to immigration. In 1996, 734,000 children were born, that is to say, 6000 more than in 1995. French women gave birth to an average 1.72 child per woman, an index that is slightly below the required number to keep population at the same level. One fact remains certain: French women have their babies later in life and on the average after 27 years old. About deaths, it seems that people die older, on the average by 74 for men and 82 for women. As an example we can mention the famous case of Mme Jeanne Calment, who died after celebrating her 122nd birthday on February 21, 1997. This aging of the French population raises significant economic and social problems, particularly as it is reducing the number of working persons paying taxes and financing the social programs.

France has an average population of 105 inhabitants per square kilometer and as such it is among the less densely populated countries of Western Europe. Germany has 228 inhabitants per square kilometer while the UK has 239 inhabitants per square kilometer. In France, population is very unevenly distributed, with a dense population in the great urban and industrial agglomerations and along the coasts. The center of France is by far the least populated area with 50 inhabitants per square kilometer. or less, while Paris and its region has 18.9% of France's population.

France is not a nation of emigrants and only 1.5 million French citizens live abroad, but France is a nation if immigration. Many of the newcomers immigrated from France's Mediterranean neighbors, Spain, Portugal, Italy and chiefly citizens from the Maghreb countries of North Africa, from sub-Saharan Africa, the Middle East and Southeast Asia colonies, Turkey, Poland and former Yugoslavia.[2]

The National Institute of Demographic Studies claims that without immigration France would count at least 10 million fewer inhabitants. However, France remains unevenly populated. The most populated areas are Paris and the Ile-de-France, with approximatively 887 inhabitants per square kilometer, while the Lozère department in central France counts only 25 inhabitants per square kilometer. Paris is by far the largest urban center with over 10,740,000 inhabitants, i.e. 18.9% of the total population of France, far ahead of other large urban centers like Lyon, Marseille, Lille and Bordeaux. Paris' average population density is 890 inhabitants per square kilometer. Approximatively 75% of the French population live in towns of 2,000 or more inhabitants, and more than 50% of the French live in metropolitan areas. But aside these populated centers, there is a part of France that is becoming a desert, the France of countrysides (la France profonde). It keeps losing inhabitants, constantly and rapidly. The lack of jobs is the cause of this rampant depopulation. Villages are not only losing their inhabitants, but they are in many instances abandoned. The regions worse hit are Corsica, the Alpes, Auvergne, Limousin, Brittany, Franche-Comté, Haute-Marne, Manche and Lower Normandy as well as a diagonal going from the Ardennes in the northeast down to the Pyrénées in the southwest. No one today thinks that there is a way of stopping the trend unless jobs are created, and that does not seem to be a possibility in the foreseeable future. What is happening, however, is the invasion of rich foreigners, from the UK, from Germany and from the Netherlands, who come and settle in this vacuum created by the exodus of French farmers. This may not be the best solution, but it is "a" solution for these areas that would otherwise have become total wastelands.

In March 1997, the active population of France was 25.6 million (14.1 million men and 11.5 million women). More and more women in the 25 to 49 year old range enter the job market, but there are fewer younger women in the 15-to 24 year old range; this group either has difficulty finding jobs or tends to pursue studies longer.

Education

Education is the number one preoccupation of French parents and of the French people in general. The high expectations of the French public are reflected in the importance of the French education budget managed by the Ministry of Education. It represents roughly 8% to 9% of the country's GDP, that is to say, over 292 billion francs ($53 billion), i.e., 17.7% of the overall state budget, or about $2,000 per inhabitants or $7000 per student. In fact the education budget of France is the largest state budget that has to take care of over 1.1 million staff positions, 890,000 teachers representing more than half of all state employees or about 3.6% of the total working population of France. In 1994 there were nearly 14 million young people (nearly a quarter of the total population of France) enrolled in educational programs.

The French educational system is mainly State-supported and depends on the Ministry of National Education to carry out the required programs. A junior minister assists the Minister of Education, representing specific sectors such as vocational training, and the Ministry of Agriculture plays also a role in the administration of the agricultural schools.

Brief History of French Education
Before the Revolution, parochial schools had the monopoly of education, and the goal of the Jesuits, who were the main Catholic teaching order,

was to form Christian children. The French Revolution changed the purpose of educators, who then wanted to educate the whole population without any religious motive. So they changed the law and they made school compulsory, and instead of teaching religious values, taught Republican moral values. With Napoleon things changed again. The emperor attached great importance to education, and particularly important to him was the formation of an enlightened elite that could serve him well. With this goal in mind, Napoleon created the *lycées*.

During the latter years of the nineteenth century (1879) the anticlerical Republicans saw education exclusively as secular. Jules Ferry was the founder of secular education in 1881. However, even today when the number of churchgoers is relatively low, Catholic schools remain important because they are often viewed as more rigorous while controlling their students' behavior more effectively.

Nowadays, since WWII in any case, the primary mission of schools, Lycées and universities is to form intelligent citizens, to develop and maintain national unity and to help integrate in French societies the sons and daughters of foreign parents who immigrated to France. The Minister of Edication is responsible for maintaining quality education for all, equal access to schools, non-discrimination and a secular neutral environment. In France, public education is free except for some university fees. The State defines and establishes programs, degrees, public examinations and guarantees that they are open to all.

The Different Levels of the French Educational System

Preschools: The "Maternelles":
The *Maternelle schools* are for children aged 2 to 5 or 6, and correspond somewhat to the US Nursery schools. In France the *écoles maternelles* have existed since the last quarter of the nineteenth century and they are much more than child care centers and, in fact much more than kindergartens. They are regarded as beginning educational establishments. Naturally, at this level attendance is not compulsory; however, enrollment is very high, as they are considered effective tools of personality and learning development and also of social integration. The building and upkeep of these schools are the responsibility of towns and cities, but the Ministry of National Education hires the teachers.

Primary Schools (Ecoles Primaires)
The *Ecoles primaires* are for children 5 to 10 years old. Most children enter primary school at the age of six. Like preschools, primary schools

are the responsibility of the *communes* (towns/cities), this since 1833, and, contrary to preschools, attendance in primary schools is compulsory; teaching is secular and free.[3] Teachers of *écoles primaires* are recruited by competitive examination by the Ministry of Education. In private schools under state contract, teachers' salaries and costs of upkeep and operations are borne in part by the State and in part by the *communes*. Nowadays (1997–1998) there are more and more children 2 years old enrolled in pre-elementary classes and just as many 3 to 5 years old in the *écoles maternelles*. It is interesting to note that in primary schools, one teacher teaches all subjects. Such is not the case later on.

Primary school runs 5 years. The first three years are called preparatory *(cours préparatoire)* and dedicated to basic skills. The two final years are called "*cours moyen*" and dedicated to perfecting the basic or fundamental skills.

French elementary school children have the longest workweek in Europe with 27 contact hours, 6 hours per day, Monday through Saturday, except for Wednesdays. The present Jospin government and the Minister of Education, justly concerned by the hectic pace imposed to children and their parents, are seeking to lighten the load as much as possible. But while many French parents agree, just as many do not want to see the education of their children diluted. French children are expected to read by the age of 6.

Middle Schools
Middle schools or *Collèges* are for young students 11 to 14 years old. They correspond to the Middle or Junior High school in the USA (grades 5–8). There are 7,000 *collèges* in France, educating over 3 million students. *Collège* studies last four years. Since 1975 all children may enter *collège* without consideration of their level of achievement. Selection comes soon, however. The operation of *collèges* is the responsibility of each *département* (district), but the State hires, trains and pays the teachers. The State also provides all the teaching material required, such as books, computers, etc. . . . There are also private *collèges*, but the State pays and supervises the teachers. Each *collège* teacher is responsible for one or several subjects, but not for all subjects. Students have therefore several teachers to cover their curriculum. In the first year, students learn one foreign language and usually in the third year they begin a second foreign language.

When they are 16, students who wish to end their studies may leave school if they wish. However, this is exceptional, as about 94% of students not only finish collège, but continue their studies and compete for the *Certificat d'aptitude professionelle (CAP)* or for the *Brevet d'enseignement professionel (BEP),* or switch and enter a *lycée.* Students with a weak performance are no longer moved to pre-professional or pre-apprenticeship classes; they remain in collège and can take advantage of the various support systems offered such as special sections.

Secondary Schools or Lycées

Most French students (78%) enroll in public *lycées* that are for those 15–18 years old. *Lycées* are equivalent to US High Schools and they are under the control of the Ministry of Education. There are two types of *lycées,* the *professional lycées* and the *regular or non-technical lycées.*

Professional lycées provide students with vocational training for jobs in the various services (secretarial, accounting, hotel jobs, mechanics, electronics, civil engineering) and the *regular lycées* lead to the *Baccalauréat* examination that is now earned by over 75% of students.[4]

Some people have been concerned by the heavy study load carried by *lycées* students, but most French parents, worried by the future of their children, and afraid that they will not be able to find a decent job, are demanding more work rather than less. The current Minister of Education, Claude Allègre, wants to align school time with the 35-hour week of workers. His recommendation for 26 hours of formal lessons does not please French parents who see in this reform the possibility of degradation of the educational system and the danger of teaching only what the students want to learn.[5]

Lycées are built and maintained by the regions, but the State pays the staff and the teachers, and oversees the educational structure, the methods used, the matters taught of all the *lycées* in France, which provides a reasonable state of uniformity throughout the country.

Education and Health

Each French public school and the lycées have a health service that provides vaccinations and specific health screanings for eyes, ears, teeth, as well as psychological problems.

Higher Education

Higher education includes all the programs that are open only to those who have completed the *lycée* and passed the *Baccalauréat examination* that is roughly equivalent to the US first university year. In France higher education is divided between *universities* and *Grandes Ecoles.* Anybody with the *Baccalauréat* is intitled to attend a university, but that is not true for the *Grandes Ecoles,* where recruitment is a highly selective entrance examination.

The vast majority of students are enrolled in universities, and only very few prepare for the *Grandes Ecoles* examinations because the selection is so competitive that the chances of admission are extremely slim even after two years or more of demanding preparatory courses. University studies are currently organized in three cycles.[6] The first cycle (first two years) leads to the DEUG *(diplôme d'études universitaires générales)* [Bac+2]; the second cycle also lasts two years and leads to the *licence* (equivalent to the US B.A. or B.S. degrees) [Bac+3] and to the *maîtrise* (equivalent to five years of US higher education [Bac+4]. The third cycle leads to specialized degrees (equivalent to the US master's degree), DESS *(diplôme d'études supérieures spécialisées)* or DEA *(diplôme approfondies d'études)* followed by the Doctorat (equivalent to the US Ph.D.).

The administrative organization of universities was seriously modified following the May 1968 student riots. Now universities are composed of several units or UFRs *(unités de formation et de recherche)* headed by a director. The president of the university is chosen for 5 years; he or she manages finances and the general administrative running of the various faculties. Each university is autonomous in principle; however, most of the resources come from the State, and therefore all staff members are state employees *(fonctionnaires).* Boards elected by the university staff and students participate in the university administration.

Aside from regular universities, there are technical universities called *IUT (instituts universitaires de technologie)* which lead to a two-year degree in technological or civil engineering subjects and to employment. At present, over 75,000 students attend IUTs.

Proposed Reforms and New Priorities for Education

Claude Allègre,[7] the French Prime Minister of National Education under the Chirac-Jospin government, wants to reform university studies by modifying their structure in two cycles instead of three cycles. The proposal submitted by Jacques Attali to Allègre recommends two levels of qualification: First students would study for a *licence* in three years, and beyond, students would work for a *maîtrise,* two years dedicated to professional training and six months to a *stage* (practical training) followed by one year of research. Or they could opt for a doctorate in three years with the writing of a thesis.

Attali's intention is to regroup universities, *Grandes Ecoles* and research centers in order to make passage from one to the other easier.

However, he hastens to say that he does not want to take away from the *Grandes Ecoles* their specificity, that is to say, *"le viviers privilégié de l'élite technicienne"* (the privileged preserve of France's technical elite).

Among the new priorities of the government (democratization, diversity, upgrading technology and lightening programs), the reduction of work time for students is high on the list. Claude Allègre wants to introduce *"les 35 heures pour les lycéens"* (the 35 hours for high-school students) because he wants students to learn less in order to learn better. It is true that the proposal is supported by students who are tired of too much work, of programs that are too heavy and of too long hours in school. The proposal would reduce schoolwork to 30 or 25 hours, not including the hours of work at home. There is currently much stress in schools, with the competition to earn the best grade and the best rank in class because from these grades and ranks depends success at the *Baccalauréat*. And French parents want schools to give their children the best chance to pass this examination.

One of the priorities expressed by President Chirac was to eradicate illiteracy in France. He would like every child coming out the primary cycle (CE2) to have mastered all the basic knowledge including the ability to read well. At present, the percentage of children who have some reading or writing handicap has been reported as oscillating between 15% to 20%. Total illiteracy is quasi inexistent in France, but there is a problem in the domain of understanding the message, with about 8% of children and some adults who still have some difficulty understanding a normal sentence. Ségolène Royal, delegate Minister of schooling, has set up a new set of priorities for schools and *collèges* in France, with the goal of making the young students better citizens. With this in mind, the Minister wants to improve civic education by making it compulsory and an integral part of the curriculum.

The Minister of Education wants to change the way the CNRS *(Centre National de la Recherche Scientifique)* functions. This area of national education, as its name indicates, is a research think tank and most members do not teach at all. Allègre thinks that the CNRS must adapt to the needs of the new millennium and abandon its ivory tower attitude and participate more in the teaching of the research it does. Allègre has repeated many times that the knowledge acquired in laboratories must be transmitted to the young and to the industry. In other words the Minister of Education wants the CNRS to be a dynamic source of innovation open on the real world instead of remaining, as it is now, self-centered and practically closed to the "real" world.[8]

The Grandes Ecoles

The *Grandes Ecoles* were set up in the eighteenth century to prepare an elite for high-level administrative posts. They are powerful institutions stressing the sacrosanct value of competitive examinations, of high intellectual standards and achievement. In principle, the competitive examinations give contenders an equal chance, and again in principle, these schools are open to all, without tuition fees. This being said, if there are many candidates, only a few are chosen. It is one of the reasons why these institutions have occasionally been criticized for perpetuating a caste spirit and for creating an elite corps of "*mandarins*" (an intelligentsia).

There are today about 200,000 students hoping to enter the various *Grandes Ecoles* and studying for highly competitive examinations leading to a very limited number of places. Students generally prepare for these entrance examinations in post-Baccalauréat classes offered in some of the top lycées of France. The choice of *Grandes Ecoles* is limited to the following: (1) *Polytechnique*, run by the Ministry of Defense with a general as its director. It is the top engineering school of the nation. Students wear uniforms and graduate after 2 years with a commission that they can resign if they want to enter public service or private business, and most of them do that. Graduates, men and an increasing number of women, often are called to top government jobs. (2) The *Ecole Normale Supérieure* is a special school for the intellectual elite. The school admits very few students after a gruelling entrance examination. The ENS has produced an impressive number of literary and political figures such as Sartre and Pompidou. The candidates who fail to enter the ENS generally pass the university Agrégation examination, a teaching degree for top lycées and universities. (3) The *Ecole Nationale d'Administration* (ENA) was founded in 1945 to recruit high civil servants for all branches of the government. Like the ENS, the ENA has produced a large number of important political figures. (4) The *Hautes Etudes Commerciales* (HEC) is another Grande Ecole leading for important managing positions in business. (5) *Centrale* and (6) Les *Mines* are both highly respected engineering schools, and *the Ecole Supérieure de Sciences Economiques et Commerciales* (ESSEC) is a top business school also leading generally to high-level positions.

Le Collège de France

The *Collège de France* was founded in 1530 by François Ier, who wanted to create a scholarly institution independent from the Sorbonne. The *Collège de France* has this peculiarity that it does not issue diplomas and its professors do not really have students. The public does not have to register for classes and just attends lectures. The only prerequisite for professors is that they talk about a topic that they are currently researching. There is no curriculum.

The *Collège de France* is nevertheless a prestigious institution that has had many famous intellectuals and prize laureates as its professors, distinguished individuals like Roland Barthes, Claude Lévi-Strauss, Emile Benveniste, Michel Foucault. The Collège does not cater only to the humanities, but to the sciences also, and it tries to keep a reasonable balance among the various disciplines.

French Universities

French universities are very unequal in size and are distributed unequally within the country. The city of Paris houses about one sixth of France's students, but there are smaller universities in the main urban centers such as Lille, Toulouse, Lyon, Grenoble, Aix-en-Provence, Nice, Bordeaux, Montpellier and Nancy.

L'Université de Paris XII and Its Satellites

The first university was founded in the twelfth century and was confirmed by Papal Bull 1215. In 1793, it was suppressed by the French Revolution, but was reestablished in 1808.

The University of Paris today is a satellite system made up of thirteen universities. After the May 1968 student uprising, Minister of Education Edgard Faure undertook major reforms aimed at modernizing the educational system of French higher education. The current structure was set up in 1970. Universities were allowed to develop their own courses and to plan their own buildings. The University of Paris was subdivided into twelve campuses with their own specialties:

Paris I: Panthéon-Sorbonne, is dedicated to languages, humanities, politics, economics and law.

Paris II: Panthéon-Assas, is dedicated to economics, law, social sciences, politics and history.

Paris III: Sorbonne-Nouvelle, is dedicated to contemporary languages, literatures, and civilizations.

Paris IV: Paris-Sorbonne, is dedicated to civilization, languages, literature and arts.

Paris V: René Descartes, in the sixth arrondissement, is dedicated to medicine, dentistry, pharmacy, psychology, biomedical science, human sciences, law, social sciences, technology, and physical education.

Paris VI: Pierre et Marie Curie, is dedicated to fields of exact and applied sciences, medicine, biological and natural sciences.

Paris VII: Université Denis Diderot, Jussieu, in the fifth arrondissement, is dedicated to exact sciences, biology, medicine, social sciences and arts.

(There is no Paris VIII).

Paris IX: Paris-Dauphine, in the sixteenth arrondissement, is dedicated to applied mathematics, information technology, economics and management.

Paris X: Paris-Nanterre, is dedicated to arts, humanities, law, economics, technology, sports and physical education.

Paris XI: Paris-Sud, is a scientific university.

Paris XII: Paris-Val-de-Marne, is dedicated to physical sciences, chemistry, biology, medicine, arts and letters, social sciences, communication, town planning and economics.

Paris XIII: Paris-Nord, is dedicated to the humanities, arts, sciences, law and medicine.

Each campus has its own library or libraries.

Other research centers exist in the Paris Academy outside those associated with the various campuses of the universities of Paris. The main research centers are: *L'Ecole Pratique des Hautes Etudes, L'Ecole des Hautes Etudes en Sciences Sociales, Le Musée d'Histoire naturelle, L'Institut national d'Agronomie, L'Institut de Physique du Globe, L'Ecole nationale supérieure de Chimie, L'Ecole nationale des Chartes and L'Institut d'Etudes politiques de Paris.*

The Bibliothèque Nationale and the New Bibliothèque de France

The *Bibliothèque Nationale*, rue Richelieu in Paris, has been from its creation in 1926[9] and until 1998 the showcase of French culture and the repository of human knowledge. The contents of the Bibliothèque Nationale were moved in 1998 to the new *Bibliothèque de France* built under the direction of François Mitterand on an 18-acre site on the eastern side of the city.[10]

Science and Technology

French science and scientific research are in an excellent position in Europe and the world. French scientists are particularly known for their development of basic knowledge in chemistry, physics, electronics, life sciences, biology, mathematics, applied technology, earth sciences, and agronomy. The achievements of French scientists, particularly in basic research, have earned them a prominent place and several of them have been distinguished with the Nobel Prize.

France is also particularly strong in the field of electronuclear research and production, with a great deal of experience. It has also demonstrated the reliability and security of its nuclear plants.

The French are also prominent researchers in human and social sciences. They pursue their research in universities and in institutions of higher learning and research, such as the *Ecole pratique des hautes études, the Ecole des hautes études en sciences sociales* and the National Center for Scientific Research, *CNRS* (Centre National de la Recherche Scientifique). Recently, the French "New Historians," including Emmanuael Leroy-Ladurie, Georges Duby, Jean Favier, Roger Chartier, François Furet, have been praised for rethinking and modernizing history, the methodology of its research, and greatly improving the tools of historians. The study of sociology and anthropology has greatly benefitted from the brilliant work of Claude Lévi-Strauss.

Religion

Despite its lay Republican traditions, France can be considered a largely Catholic country, but on the eve of the Third Millennium, the religious profile of France is changing, with the new social liberties, with the changes in morality and under the pressure of the foreign population. France, since the baptism of Clovis in A.D. 496, has been known as the elder daughter of the Catholic Church. For 1,300 years Catholicism was the official religion of the nation. With the advent of the Revolution in 1789, Catholicism was banned and lost its official status in 1830, although churches continued to be funded by the state until the Declaration of Separation of Church and State in 1905. In spite of declining participation in the Catholic faith, France, 70% to 80% of the French, remains Catholic by tradition.[11] This means that the French Catholic, at least half of those who claim the faith, attend church at least for important occasions, such as marriages, baptisms and funerals. The number of priests is currently in decline, corresponding to a decline in religious vocations and to a certain number of priests either leaving the priesthood for another profession, or getting married. In 1998 there were only 24,800 priests in France with many churches closed or opened only occasionally. In the countryside, one priest frequently has to serve several parishes.[12]

At the beginning of this chapter, we noted that the religious profile of France was in mutation. One reason for this is that the second religion of

France, just behind Catholicism, is the religion of Islam with over 3 million followers. This large figure is due to the important number of legal (and some illegal) immigrants that France has received particularly since the end of the Algerian conflict. Moslem communities now outnumber Protestants (950,000),[13] Jews (750,000), Buddhists (400,000) and members of the Greek Orthodox Church (200,000).

Religion in certain areas of France is still an important aspect of life. In Brittany, the northeast, Lorraine, and Alsace there is still a strong religious participation.

In addition to regular Churches, there are also in France, like elsewhere, a number of religious sects, including Satanists that worry the French government, particularly since the desecrations of cemeteries in Carpentras and Toulon and the 1996 suicides of 16 members of the Solar Temple (OTS) in the Vercors.

On the other hand, there is among the young and some adults a renewed fervor for pilgrimages to Santiago de Compostela, to Chartres particularly, but not exclusively. There is a rejection of materialism that brings back the faith to many. Professor Jean-François Mattei of Marseille declares that he has been surprised by the renewed interest of his students for metaphysical questions: "*Les Trente Glorieuses,*" he writes, "*que l'on devrait plutôt appeler les trente trompeuses, avaient trop mis l'accent sur l'économie, la consommation de gadgets, la vie de plaisir. Quand l'homme se trouve privé de repères, il finit par replonger en lui-même*" (The Thirty Glorious Years, that ought to be called the Thirty Misleading Years, had insisted too much on economy, consumerism, gadgets, and life of pleasure. When man is deprived of direction, he finally turns inwards) [*Le Figaro*, Mercredi 29 janvier 1997, p. 10].

What seems to be true is that the decline in religious observance may be slowing down somewhat.

The Family

The French family plays a very important role in French society. France has a family policy that morally and legally guards its existence. The family, in fact, is at the top of the French system of values.

Marriage, People Living Together, Single Parents and Divorce

Marriage has become more fragile, but it remains an important institution. In France around 250,000 weddings are celebrated each year, but people marry later, the average being 25 to 28 years. Unfortunately, an average of one out of three marriages ends in divorce and live-in arrangements are increasingly common. Also married couples tend to have small families with only 5% with four or more children.

In 1990, there were 1.7 million *unmarried couples living together* and 12 million married couples. Eighty seven percent of Catholic couples had a Church ceremony after the mandatory civil wedding in front of the town's mayor.

Between 1976 and 1986, the number of couples living together has doubled, and by 1990 their number was close to two million, although statistics are not always accurate. Many people delay marriage for practical economic reasons, unemployment being a major one, and the need of more education is another.[14] Even the birth of a child does not necessarily lead to a marriage. Thus the number of births outside marriage has been on the increase. As an example, in 1980 there were 10% of births out of wedlock, while in 1995 the percentage had jumped to 38%. Among the 1.2 million single-parent families, 86% consist of women who raise their children alone. This situation is viewed today as normal and single-parent families are no longer social outcasts. In fact their existence is being recognized as a new family model by the state.[15]

Children

While recognizing that being a parent is not easy, most French people, married or unmarried, consider that having children contributes a great part for their personal happiness, and the majority feels that having children or having had children is the most important element of their success in life. If it is true that the French have few children today (1.7 per woman), less of them are anti-children, and more men and women who did not want children before are beginning to want children. All admit that children are not the condition of happiness, but, rather, a terrain on which happiness can grow.[16]

Divorce was allowed in France by the French Revolution, then banned under clerical pressure and restored in 1884. In 1976 divorce by mutual consent was legalized. Increasingly, it is the wife who asks for divorce and she is almost certain to be awarded the custody of the child or children. Couples not only divorce more, they also divorce sooner after marriage, with an average of 4 to 5 years after their wedding. In Paris alone, one marriage in two ends in divorce. Some 120,000 divorces are pronounced in France each year, a steep increase from 40,000 only in 1970.[17]

Retirement

A 1997 poll shows that the French in general are in favor of retirement at 55. Not long ago, after a tough strike, French truckers have obtained satisfaction. The trend started when many businesses started to encourage pre-retirement at 52, 55 and 57 and even at 50. With people living longer, the number of active people contributing to society is decreasing. From 3 to 1 twenty years ago, it has become 2 to 1 and it won't be long before it becomes a 1 to 1 relation. A young worker today gives 17% of his salary to maintain retirements at their level, but if the trend continues, in 2010 the same worker would have to contribute 26% of his salary. While the French want to retire at 55, Germany has brought the retirement age back to 65, and England, Denmark and Norway to 67. According to the *Figaro* (March 3, 1997, p.2) many people in France are afraid of the consequences of the retirement at 55. In fact, many people consider that it is a dangerous dream and hardly a source of new jobs for others. As a matter of fact, Marc Nexon writes in *Le Point* (No. 1384, March 27, 1999, pp. 32–33) that Jospin is walking on a minefield with the problem of retirement. According to the article the disappearance of the Baby-Boom generation from the active population by 2005 will seriously and even dangerously increase the retirement budget of France. As a consequence responsible persons in the government are beginning to think that the only solution is to raise the age of retirement possibly beyond 65! This is a solution no one wants, neither the French workers nor their unions.

Seniors

In France, like in many other developed countries, the increasing aging population is a worry to the State, but also to the family. The trend began in the nineteenth century, but it was temporarily stopped by the Baby Boom era of post-WWII. It is predicted that by year 2020, those over 60 will compose one quarter of the population. This is a demographic, social and economic problem because, as the population ages, the number of young people decreases. If the population continues to grow, it is due to the longer life expectancy, with 80.9 years as an average for women and 72.7 for men. The economic consequences are undeniable, as retirement and health care costs are increasing financial burdens on the State Social Security system and other support systems, while there are fewer young workers contributing to finance them.

There are other problems connected with old age, one being the impact on the family who has to take care of the older relative, or who must finance his or her placement in an institution. The other problem is solitude of many older people who do not have a family taking care of them. In spite of the numerous clubs called *"du 3e âge"* (third age) who provide distractions, travel, companionship to old people who would otherwise be left to themselves, there are many suicides among the aging population. In fact, half of the suicides in France affect the over-55 population, and solitude is the primary factor.

The Poor

Every winter we hear of many poor, homeless persons dying of cold or malnutrition, and this is a situation that the French government is eager to solve. In March 1998, Martine Aubry, Labor and Solidarity Minister of the Jospin government, announced a 20 billion dollar program of assistance to the poor in France, to the unemployed and homeless. This program is aimed at about 10 million persons living in precarious conditions, and often without Social Security or other benefits. Hard as it might be to believe, 10% of French households live below the official poverty level, and 6 million persons are totally dependent on government welfare. Martine Aubry's plan is one of several government measures destined to battle exclusion. But Minister Aubry is a realist, and she knows that the measures can only work if at the same time efforts are made to reduce dependence on benefits, and if more jobless workers find jobs.

However, at the end of 1998 many responsible officials warned that the social contributions of the country need to be kept at a reasonable level and that the country could not continue to give without something in return. Not long ago the associations of unemployed persons demanded an increase of 1,500 francs of the minimum assistance provided to the unemployed. Jospin agreed to an increase of only 3% of the RMI (the specific government assistance to help reinsertion in the work force), to the 1.6 million unemployed. But the prime minister said at the same time that the French government, in its desire to help, could not extend itself *ad infinitum*. He reminded people that the country already contributes to several assistance programs such as the allocation to single parents, the allocation to widows and widowers, the allocation for old age, the allocation for invalids and to handicapped adults, all paid to approximatively 1.9 million persons. Jospin, though wanting very much to reduce the distress of the poorest people, wants to find more realistic solutions than simply handing out money. If the trend continues, France risks becoming even more a country of assisted people rather than an active society.[18]

Important Measures to Protect Children and the Family

France has very clear legislation to protect families and children. At the normal level there is the family allowances *(allocations familiales)*, a bonus families receive for producing children, but there are many other measures taken to prevent cruelty against children. For example, Ségolène Royal, Delegate Minister to education, has announced measures to fight modern slavery among children. She says that she will seek children, mostly girls, who are employed illegally, and in the name of the French law of compulsory education, will free these children from the clutches of the bosses who exploit them.

Death and Funeral Rites

In France most people are buried in a cemetery and cremation, though advancing somewhat, is not yet widespread. Even if a person has rarely or never been to church, the majority of persons receive a religious burial. Funerals used to be handled by the towns' *Pompes Funèbres* (the official funeral parlor), but increasingly the French *Pompes Funèbres* are becoming private.

The Condition of Women

The condition of women has greatly changed and radically improved since WWII. More and more women are independent, participate actively in the economic activity of the country, although their salaries still trail behind men's salaries. In France, many women take part in the political life of the nation, but their representation in the National Assembly is still low (6% while representing 53% of the electoral body) in comparison with other European countries.[19]

French women had to wait until the arrival of de Gaulle for their "liberation," that is to say, to obtain the right to vote in 1945. There was a feminist movement in France, but it was by and large much less revolutionary than the movement in the USA. Today, we could say with Elisabeth Badinter[20] that France is beyond the feminist era. And it is true that French women have "almost" won the war against discrimination; however it is equally true that equality is not always present in practice. Nevertheless, discrimination is illegal, and women working out of their home is the norm, even when they have children and more women today can hold jobs that were previously reserved for men only. But inequality still lingers, as Sheila Perry brilliantly suggests in her chapter on women in her *Aspects of Contemporary France*, p. 149:[21] "There is still a place for women's activism in France. It is premature to reduce feminism to mere vigilance, as Elisabeth Badinter would have French women do. An

examination of women's condition in France "shows that women's eman-
cipation has been regulated and kept within limits compatible with sexual
identity, that is to say in line with their unequal status."[22]

Stress

Some 57% of the French declare that they are stressed by their work.
About 30% of women and 20% of men are being treated for anxiety or
depression at an estimated cost of 800 billion francs not reimbursed by
Social Security. Stress is not a recognized professional illness in France
and therefore is not considered as a direct cause for stopping work. Nevertheless, the French are perhaps the highest consumers of anti-depres-
sant medicine.

Authority Contested

At all levels of French society, authority is frequently contested by the
young and by some adults. In fact authority has been replaced by another
social value, *autonomy*. Before WWII and even up to the 70's, the father
was the *"pater familias,"* i.e., the symbol of authority in the family. This
is no longer the case for most families in the 1990's. Parents' authority
has waned, and in some families totally vanished. The young have obtained their legal majority at 18, and so they can do what they want when
they reach this age without the consent of their parents. They can live
with a boy, with a girl, marry, divorce, choose the profession that they
want, etc. . . . Even at work, in businesses, the relations between bosses
and employees have changed. Everyone is much more relaxed, more
informal, and the bottom line is that the sacrosanct hierarchy is no longer
respected. Naturally, one cannot exaggerate this, and in many cases there
still remains a certain level of reasonable politeness or cordiality among
employees and bosses. Authority, in France, is not fought head on, except in case of work conflicts; it is rather no longer considered a value. In
addition, in a number of workplaces today, authority and responsibilities
tend to be shared between the managers and workers. In many businesses employees can choose their work schedule and even work more
hours on certain days in order to have a free day during the week. We
could say that flexibility is replacing authority.

Insecurity

All over France and more acutely in large urban centers and surroundings
suburbs *(banlieues)* people complain of being haunted by a feeling of

insecurity. They fear aggression, theft, rape, and insult. Many people, particularly older people, say that they don't feel safe going out at night and feel insecure even at home. About 8 out 10 Frenchmen are worried by the rising tide of violence and demand action from the government, and they want more than simply additional policemen. Aggressions against bus drivers, stoned buses, passengers insulted or beaten in the subway occur practically daily in some regions. Sometimes bands of youths burn cars, like in Strasbourg on New Year's Eve 1998 when sixty cars were torched simply for pleasure. Most people attribute this violence to unemployment and to the decline of parental responsibility, while some point the finger at immigration.

Health

After a considerable effort at modernization following WWII, France currently has high medical standards, and the country rates high in medical and biomedical research.

With the assistance of Social Security,[23] the French take good care of their health, visit their doctor frequently and purchase a lot of medicines at their local *pharmacie* (drugstore). With Social Security footing most of medical expenses,[24] the French are less reluctant than most Americans, for instance, to consult a doctor who frequently makes home visits,[25] and to ask for a prescription, and doctors, at least until recently, used to prescribe substantially more medicines than their American colleagues. No wonder that since 1950 the expenses of Social Security have skyrocketted, particularly with the aging of the population and the increased costs of advanced medical technology. The French government now wants to bring down the number of prescriptions a doctor can give a single patient, but it encounters a great deal of resistance from the medical corps, who does not want to see its professional privileges removed.[26]

SIDA (AIDS): About 20,000 persons are suffering from AIDS in France, with 9,000 alone in Paris. In addition 110,000 persons are supposed to be infected with the HIV virus that is the cause of AIDS. This terrible illness represents a death rate of 14 men and 3 women per 100,000 persons, but thanks to recent new treatments the number of deaths attributed to AIDS is on the decrease. In 1995 there were 3,846 reported deaths due to AIDS, and in 1996 already, the number of reported deaths had declined to 2,885. This improvement is due in part to the increasing number of persons who seek treatment, as hospitals report a 10% decrease in admissions for *VIH* (HIV) viral infection.

Life Expectancy/Longevity

In France, life expectancy increases because of better and better health care, and in 1998 men died on the average at the age of 74, while women died on the average at 81.9.

Dying before 65 is considered a premature death nowadays; however, it occurs more frequently in France than in the UK. This is attributed in part to some of the specific habits of the French, to smoking, eating and drinking; however, we have all heard of the *French paradox*, that sees French people eating fat and drinking wine living as long as those who just drink tea or water. Other major factors of death in France are suicides, road accidents, heart attacks and breast cancer, which is the number one factor of premature death in French women.

The French and Their Cult of Health

The well-known American cult for youth, health, fitness and slimness has arrived in France. The French now want to be in shape, and they do anything possible to keep their health and to improve the beauty of their body. For many French people, to be slim, in shape, healthy and attractive is as important as being rich and powerful. Many surely think that they are all interconnected. So, they jog, they walk, they run, ski, bicycle, climb mountains, play tennis, squash and go to "lean" resorts, just like in the United States. In short, France is in the middle of a "body boom."

The French, who were great smokers, are beginning to smoke less and as a consequence the sales of cigarettes dipped by 9.3% since January 1996. But cigars suddenly have become the rage.

After the Mad Cow Disease

Since the great scare of the Mad Cow Disease (ESB or *Encéphalopathie Spongiforme Bovine*), French people are now much more careful with what they buy, eat or drink and they demand more information about products. They want to know the date, composition and origin of the food they purchase. They also worry a great deal about the water they drink, which explains the explosion in sales of mineral waters in France. In 1996 alone, the French drank 7 billion liters of mineral water.

The French government is doing its best to keep its population physically and mentally healthy. In February 1998, for instance, it kicked off a suicide prevention plan since there were more suicides (12 000 yearly) in France than road accident deaths.

Another growing health problem that worries health officials in France is the increasing obesity among adults and even among children.[27] Obesity is often due to too much watching TV while eating snacks and fried foods. The number of young obese in France has increased by 17% in ten years and about 10% of young adolescents are considered overweight today.

The French Paradox

Most Americans cannot understand why all the French do not die of heart attacks with their eating habits. They eat butter, rich cheeses, creamy sauces, fatty meats and pâtés; however, they have the lowest rate of heart disease in Europe, and live longer, standing just after the Japanese in that regard. Researchers have called this mysterious phenomenon "*the French paradox.*" Some scientists attribute this paradox to red wine. But France is not equally healthy, according to a report of the *Washington Post* and edited by Robin Herman.[28] According to this report the French of northern France suffer the same rate of heart disease as the Germans, but the rate drops significantly in the southern provinces. Men in Toulouse, apparently, live almost five years longer than other men in the Nord-Pas-de-Calais region. The disparity is attributed to their different diets. Northern French people eat more meat and use butter, while the southern French favor olive oil and eat more fresh produce. In the north people drink beer and spirits, while in the south they drink red wine with their meals.

How long will this French paradox last? A 1999 issue of the *British Medical Journal* and several other scientists express the fear that the French might be losing this wonderful protection from heart attacks because their eating and drinking habits are changing. Wine consumption has dropped to half of former levels, and snacking and eating fast food are on the increase. Perhaps in a few decades the French will have caught up with the coronary death rate of Americans, but this sad state of things will be fortunately delayed as long as the French continue to eat smaller portions than Americans do, as long as they eat twice as many nuts as Americans, as long as they drink one or two glasses of red wine slowly with their meals and as long as they eat two or three times more grain fiber than Americans or Britons.

Concerns About the Environment and Pollution

Pollution of the air, of water and of the earth is a serious concern in France. The main cause of pollution of the air is no doubt the cars, the trucks, the buses and motorcycles. Paris suffers the worst, naturally, considering that the number of vehicles in the French capital has increased five times in fifteen years. That is enough to explain why there are dangerous increases in cases of asthma, bronchitis and death from carbonic gas, nitrogen dioxyde, ozone and other types of pollutants. When there is no wind in Paris, the atmosphere turns yellow and people cough. In order to remedy the problem, the government has decreed that on days of peak pollution circulation will be reduced: only the license plates with even or odd numbers will be allowed, not both. In other words, ideally, one out of two automobiles will be allowed to run in Paris, with some exceptions, official vehicles and cars carrying at least three persons. In addition the government has announced a new type of non-polluting taxis about to be released in Paris. These taxis will use liquified petroleum gas. This GPL gas is a mixture of Butane and Propane, thus producing little carbon, and releasing no benzene, no sulphur and no lead into the atmosphere. Naturally, the planned ten taxis of this kind are not going to make much difference, but it is a beginning. Peugeot, a pioneer in the technical production of these less polluting automobiles, agrees that much improvement is still needed. The GPL is expensive (2.08 francs a liter compared to diesel at 1.28 francs) and the tank holding the GPL is large, reducing the taxi's trunk space considerably. In addition the non-polluting taxis will not be cheap, about 10,000 to 15,000 francs more than regular automobiles.

France, fortunately, has a long history of fighting pollution. Since January 1971 it has created a Ministry for the protection of nature and the environment. This governmental office passes laws establishing green areas, parks and protecting water supplies, controlling the treatment of sewage and household wastes.[29] Groundwater has not escaped pollution, particularly where there is intensive agriculture. The French government is currently trying to educate farmers not to use uncontrollably liquid pork manure or some types of polluting fertilizers. France also closely monitors its seacoasts and beaches through the seacoast conservation agency, and each year dangerous points are announced to warn bathers of problems.

France takes an active part in national and international actions to protect the environment and the ozone layer, and it has recently joined England in ratifying a treaty banning nuclear tests (after staging a series of widely criticized test blasts in the South Pacific in 1995 and 1996).

Family Budget, Purchasing Power and Household Consumption

The living standards of the French have increased steeply since 1950, and they increased their wealth more over the past 40 years than during the entire preceding years and century. What happened was a noticeable increase in wages and in social benefits. The establishment in 1950 of the SMIC *(salaire minimum interprofessionnel de croissance)* or minimum wage has provided assistance to many unskilled workers, mainly young people, women and small-business employees.

The improvement in the standard of living has encouraged consumer spending. More than 75% of families now own at least one automobile and above 85% of households own a TV set, a refrigerator, a washing machine, telephone, a computer.

French families spend today relatively less money for food and clothing, but slightly more for housing, transportation, leisure and health. Table wine consumption has dropped by half since 1950, but the consumption of quality wines has doubled. Consumption of low-fat products is on the increase, but on special feast days, Sundays and holidays, French families still eat very well and enjoy fine traditional cuisine. True, the fact that more women are at work explains the trend toward quick meals with frozen foods weekdays.

Consequences of Reduced and Adjusted Work Hours

The length of the legal workweek has been steadily declining in France, and from an average of 48 hours, it dropped to 40 hours in 1936 and to 39 hours in 1982. In 1998 the French government passed a law reducing the workweek to 35 hours. In addition many businesses have agreements with their employees allowing them to adjust their schedules according to the needs of their families. Some people work longer 4 days a week, while others take a day off mid-week (mostly women who want to be with their children on their day off school). The trend, therefore, is a better dialogue in labor-management, and that further explains the erosion of the influence of trade unions, as we have seen earlier.

Leisure Activities and Holidays

With less work time and therefore more free time, the French dedicate a good portion of their leisure time to various activities, cultural activities, cinema, theater, concerts, tourism, gardening, watching television,[30] reading[31] and sports activities.

Longer paid vacations as well as rising standards of living have fueled *travel* and attracted more and more people on French beaches and mountains, and abroad.[32] In France over 60% of the population leave for vacations *every* year, many going abroad, but many also going to their *"résidence secondaire"* (holiday house) in the mountains, along the

Mediterranean or Atlantic, Brittany or Corsica. Nowadays, many senior citizens travel a great deal in organized groups thanks to the special tours specially tailored to their tastes and needs. The SNCF *Carte Vermeille* helps seniors to travel on the train, buses and metro at reduced rates. Also many organizations, like the EDF *(Electricité de France),* organize comprehensive tours in France and abroad for their own members and retirees. They also own hotels in various parts of the country where they provide vacations at very attractive prices.

France makes an effort to encourage city dwellers to experience the great outdoors, farm living, hiking, fishing, horseback riding, while staying in rural lodgings *(Gîtes de France).* There are now 40,000 rural *gîtes* available throughout France. The "*vacances à la ferme*" (holidays on a farm) are also attracting more and more families with children. Some country farms are opened like B&Bs and advertise to urban people "*le tourisme vert*" (green tourism). They offer families the opportunity to breathe fresh air and for their children the opportunity to interact first-hand with farm animals they may have never seen before.[33]

Television in France is very popular and on the average the French watch at least three hours of TV a day. Televisions-sets that used to be found only in living rooms, have begun to appear in dining rooms and bedrooms.

People in France still go to the movies, even though TV has somewhat hurt cinema attendance, but certainly much less than in the US. The French still crowd theaters in big cities like Paris, particularly to watch blockbuster films such as *Titanic.* Parisian cinemas registered 26.5 million entries in 1997, hardly less than in 1993 (26.6 million).

Attendance at *plays* is strong in France, and not only in Paris, chiefly because provincial towns and regions have opened or reopened theaters, attracting audiences to light comedies, classical plays and contemporary works.

Since WWII, the French have discovered a new passion for *music*, thanks to the many concerts offered in Paris, and to their CDs at home. *Museum* attendance has always been high in France and it is increasing as museums modernize. With tourists, museum attendance reached 16 million visitors in 1993. French museums are for the French the incarnation of France's cult of culture. Great museums are not only found in Paris, but in most large provincial towns. For instance in Grenoble, Saint-Etienne, Antibes, Nice, Bordeaux, Montpellier, Albi, etc. . . . They are dedicated to painting, science, technology and history, not to mention the myriads of specialized small museums such as "*le musée du béret,*" "*le musée du tire-bouchon*" (béret museum, corkscrew museum). A new generation of museum curators is redifining the meaning and role of museums, trying to make them not only places to look at art or things, but places where the public can learn. In 1977, the Centre Georges Pompidou was opened to preserve modern art and, better yet, to make it accessible to the widest public possible. In January 1987 the *Musée d'Orsay* was inaugurated, housed in the former famous railroad station built for the French 1900 World Fair. There the public can admire works by Courbet, Manet, Monet, Gauguin, etc. and photographs, objects and drawing. Since 1985 many of Picasso's masterpieces are exposed in the *Musée Picasso* located in a lovely seventeenth century house, the *Hôtel Salé* in Paris.[34]

The Press and Publishing

Television has hurt a few newspapers perhaps, but on the whole the French are avid newspaper readers. On the average they read at least one newspaper a day and magazines as well as specialized periodicals dedicated to sports, automobile, cooking, gardening, beauty, finance and people.

France counts about 94 daily newspapers. The largest Paris daily papers are *Le Parisien, Le Figaro, Le Monde, France Soir, L' Humanité*, a Communist newspaper, *La Croix*, a Catholic paper appearing in the afternoon, and *Libération*. Among the newspapers of the regional press, we can mention *Le Dauphiné Libéré* from the Grenoble region, *Le Progrès* from Lyon, *La République des Pyrénées* in the southwest, *La Provence* in Provence, etc. . . . There is also *Le Canard Enchaîné* (chained duck newspaper), an important political satirical humorous weekly specialty is the uncovering of abuses, scandals, and corruption of public officials. It has a very large readership of about 2.5 million and sells 550,000 copies weekly.[35]

The French are also the biggest magazine readers at least in Europe and probably in the world. *Le Nouvel Observateur, L'Express, Le Point, l'Evènement du Jeudi (recently renamed L'Evènement)*, and *Paris Match* are among the best read magazines. Specialized magazines on hunting, finance, knitting, gardening, automobiles, photography, sports, etc. . . . abound, and on account of the French's increased leisure time, they are doing well.

We must mention here the news services that provide the news to the newspapers, radio, TV and magazines, the *Agence France Presse* (AFP), founded in 1944. It has customers all over the world with a huge staff of reporters and photographers. Each day it transmits the news of the world in several languages. It is as important as the *Reuter Agency.*

France is well known for its major *publishing houses* such as Gallimard, Larousse, etc. . . . In fact publishing in France is a very important cultural industry. There are over 800 publishing houses publishing novels, textbooks, comic books, detective novels as well as scientific and practical books of the "how to" type.

The French love to play and *gamble.* On the average they spend yearly 118 billion francs gambling in casinos,[36] lotteries, on horses and playing lotto. This, by the way, represents 10 times the budget of the Ministry of Culture and on the average 2,000 francs per person.

On Sundays around 4:00 pm, millions of Frenchmen live two or three intense minutes, the *Tiercé*, a horse race during which to win bettors must designate the first three winning horses. Famous for betting is the club called PMU (*Pari Mutuel Urbain).*

Sports

The French are avid participants in all kinds of *sports,* playing or watching. Individual sports are on the rise because many French people want to remain healthy and physically fit. Tennis, water sports, skiing, jogging, squash are very popular. The French claim that these sports are good *"pour la ligne"* (to remain trim and thin) and for the nervous system. *Collective sports* within clubs or associations also attract a large section of the population. Soccer *"le foot"* is no doubt the most popular sport, all the more after the victory of the French in the new *Stade de France* in 1998. The enthusiasm of the French for soccer is followed closely by football, tennis, judo, golf and sailing. The French love for bicycle racing is visible each weekend on French roads, where local teams ride, and particularly each year in summer with the famous *Tour de France* bicycle race of about 3,000 miles.[37] Other big sports attract thousands of enthusiast supporters at events like the Roland-Garros tennis championship, the European and World cups soccer matches as well as the rugby Five-Nation Cup.

The French also love automobile racing, and the 24-hour Le Mans race which began in 1924 is an international event that draws the world's finest drivers and large crowds of spectators.

A word must be said about the Olympic Games that were revived in 1896 by a Frenchman, Pierre de Coubertin, in the hope of promoting better understanding between nations of the world. Since then the Olympic Games have been held in France several times, in Chamonix in 1924, in Grenoble in 1968 and in Albertville in 1992.

Festivals

When the French don't travel abroad, they frequently attend one or several of the many *Festivals* organized in France. These festivals are organized by the local cultural committees of regions or towns, like the summer festival of music in Aix-en-Provence or the famous summer theater festival of Avignon attended by thousands. Festivals enjoy great popularity in France because they allow the French people of various regions to reclaim their cultural identity that modern life has eroded. The distinguishing local features, costumes, feasts, have become historical folklore, but festivals help remind people of past traditions. The city of Nîmes, for instance, has a fiesta with bullfights. It is the event of the year that takes place in the ancient Roman amphitheater, but to connect the feast with modern times, it includes modern music, jazz, rock, reggae and rap. In Brittany, Quimper has also a fascinating festival. For a whole week in July, the Bretons gather and relive a way of life that has irrevocably vanished. Women put on their beautiful and quaint headresses, they display their embroidery and people tell Celtic tales of yore. There are concerts too and, as a proof that the Breton spirit, individuality and language are not dead, they sing, tell stories and say mass in Breton on Sundays. In Brittany too, there is, every seven years, the famous religious "*pardon Breton*" (religious Brittany pilgrimage) in the small quaint village of Locronan. In Nice, on the Mediterranean coast, there is the famous Carnaval festival before Lent, with religious and mostly pagan overtones. It is the occasion of parading beautiful floats carrying beautiful flowers and young ladies. In Menton, close to the Italian border, there is also the festival of flowers and lemons *(citrons)* which attracts many French and foreign tourists during the winter.

French Celebrated Holidays

The French celebrate many holidays throughout the year, some of them are religious holidays, others historic, national or local.

Among the country's most celebrated holidays are the following:

New Year's Day or *Le Jour de l'An*, a legal holiday since 1810. Families and friends celebrate the New Year with a midnight supper, kissing under the mistletoe and occasionally exchanging small gifts, mostly chocolate.

On January 6, the French celebrate the *Epiphany*, or "*fête des rois*" by eating a pie or "*galette*"containing a small charm hidden in it. The person who bites on it and finds it becomes a king or queen and has to choose either a king or a queen. Epiphany, however, is not considered a legal holiday.

On February 2 *Candlemas (La Chandeleur)* is celebrated. This is a Catholic holiday. People prepare crêpes while holding a coin, thus assuring happiness and wealth until the following year. The name *Candlemas* comes from the celebration by practicing Catholics who after mass walk in procession bearing blessed candles.

Shrove Tuesday or *Mardi Gras* is celebrated on the Tuesday preceding Lent. It is not a legal holiday. The celebration includes eating crêpes or waffles before the 40-day period of penance (Lent). There is also a parade of floats with the appearance of *Carnaval* (Carnival) that is supposed to represent Evil. At the end of the day *Carnaval* is burned.

Easter (Pâques) is a religious holiday as well as a recognized legal holiday. The celebrations take place on Easter Sunday and Easter Monday.

May Day, Le Premier Mai, is a celebrated legal holiday. On this day there are many parades of workmen in the streets. People give each other little sprigs *(bouquets)* of *muguet* (Lilies of the valley).

On May 8 *Liberation Day* is celebrated. It is a legal holiday marking the end of World War II. Wreaths are placed on the tombs of the unknown soldier in Paris, under the Arc de Triomphe, and at the base of the *monuments aux Morts* (monuments to the dead soldiers of both world wars) throughout France.

Pentecost (La Pentecôte) Sunday and *Monday* are legal holidays observed on the seventh Sunday and the following Monday after Easter.

On the last Sunday of May, the French celebrate *La Fête des Mères (Mother's Day)*. While *La Fête des Pères (Father's Day)* is celebrated on the third Sunday in June. Both are not legal holidays.

La Fête Nationale, Bastille Day, is celebrated on July 14. It is a national and legal holiday. The celebrations include military parades, down the Champs Elysées in Paris, and fireworks displays at nightfall followed by dancing in the streets. Fireworks and dancing take place in most towns and villages too.

Assumption Day, L'Assomption, is a legal holiday celebrated on August 15.

October 30: a new celebration: *Halloween.* Recently the American celebration of Halloween has known a great success in France with huge sales of pumpkins, parades of children in disguise and with painted faces.

All Saints Day, La Toussaint, is celebrated on November 1. It is a legal holiday. People place flowers, mostly chrysanthemums, on the graves of their loved ones.

November 11 is *Armistice Day (Le Onze Novembre)*. It has been a legal holiday since 1921 and commemorates the Armistice putting an end to World War I.

Christmas, Noël, is a legal holiday celebrated on December 25. People decorate their Christmas tree *(sapin),*[38] and after the midnight mass they eat a special feast called *Le Réveillon.* Children place their shoes in front of the fireplace hoping that Santa Claus *(Le Père Noël)* will bring them gifts, which they'll discover in the morning.

On all legal holidays workers are granted a day off with pay.

French Culture

France for centuries has seen itself and has been perceived from abroad as a country of culture. And it is true that culture is an integral and historical part of France's image. Foreigners and the French themselves acknowledge this fact by rushing to the cultural centers of the country, to the *Louvre* museum, to the *Pompidou* center, to the Opéra, to the *Comédie Française.* France as a nation has an active cultural policy strongly supported by the French government.[39] This national patronage goes back to the Renaissance and even earlier, with the creation of the *Académie Française* in 1635, or the opening of the *Louvre* Palace in 1793. The French government has remained since these times a patron of the arts and the Ministers of Culture under the Fifth Republic have not only continued this patronage, but tried to make French culture more democratic. On the eve of the twenty-first century, this cultural policy is being actively pursued. *L'Etat Français* (The French State), represented both by the Minister of Culture and the Minister of National Education, has increased the budget supporting France's cultural heritage, the museums, theaters, archives, cinemas, etc. . . . In addition many local authorities in the provinces and cities contribute their share to the support of French culture through their local museum, their *Maison de la Culture*, ballet schools and even centers for comic strips. Although there is not the same private patronage tradition as in the USA, some French associations and private businesses also contribute to culture, supporting cinema, opera, restoring public buildings or rebuilding ancient prehistoric dwellings. Some also fund special art exhibits such as those that are held in the *Musée d'Orsay* or the *Grand Palais* in Paris.

The Ministry of Culture also funds conservation, restoration of some of its 38,000 historical monuments, and archaeological projects. It cleans the façades of churches, cathedrals and other monuments darkened by pollution, it restores stained-glass windows, renovates organs, cleans statues, bridges, roofs. The Ministry of Culture also preserves parts of the French heritage by classifying landscapes and buildings as historical monuments or treasures. France has also a long tradition of careful preservation of national documents, archives, including now films, radio and television broadcasts and computer documents.

For the French, culture is history and history is culture.[40] They are fascinated by their past and celebrate it continuously through all sorts of celebrations, concerts, lectures, exhibits, bicentennials, centennials, etc. . . . But culture is not only the past; it is also the present and the future. The State promotes current and future creativity by funding artists and supporting creative efforts in the arts, literature, music, architecture, dance, cinema and theater.[41] Recently, France spearheaded cultural meetings dedicated to the francophone world. For instance, the Limoges *Festival international des Francophonies* has become a yearly event as well as the *Francofolies* of La Rochelle for music. Non-francophone cultures are not ignored and there are many places and organizations available where one can learn about other cultures, such as the House of Latin America, the Institute of the Arab World, the festival of the Three Continents showing films from Africa, Asia and South America. The *Maison des Cultures du Monde* regularly invites foreign musicians to perform. And as the Third Millennium draws near with the perspective of a Cultural Europe, the French tradition of reciprocal contact and exchanges increases. There are already many student exhanges between France and many other countries. And within Europe, students from the European Community can attend universities in their own country or in a country of their choice, within the community under the Erasmus or other common programs.

President Chirac is reported to have a project at heart, the building of a *Musée de l'Homme, des Arts et des Civilisation* (Museum for Mankind, Art and Civilization). He is said to want this cultural building built near the Eiffel Tower, quai Branly, in Paris. According to the French President, this museum ought to demonstrate that there are no hierarchies between the cultures of the developed world and of primitive cultures. If approved, this project ought to start in 2002. Its cost is presently estimated at 1 billion francs.

Even if it is only a dream, Chirac's vision represents the importance culture has in France, and it also reveals the French belief that art is a sacred value in itself, that it has no color and that any hierarchical comparisons are false.

French culture abroad is kept alive by the numerous branches of the *Alliance Française* and by the offices of the *Services culturels* (cultural services) attached to French Consulates and Embassies.

Cultural Celebrations and Events

Aside from the regularly scheduled festivals, France has around the year a large number of cultural celebrations. Among those, the *Fête de la Musique* (Feast of music), *La fête du Cinéma* (Feast of cinema), the *Cannes Festival du Cinéma*, the Deauville film festival dedicated to American movies, the exact equivalent to the Sarasota French film festival in Florida.

Literature is also celebrated in October with a feast called *Temps des Livres* (time for books) and a large Paris book fair called *Salon du Livre*.

Once a year, France opens the doors of its official monuments to the public, including the Elysée Palace galleries, the Institut de France, the home of the Prime Minister, L'Hôtel Matignon, or Palais Bourbon. At such times, the French public has free access to buildings and treasures that are otherwise private or closed to visitors.

The French Language

The French language is one of the Romance languages and derives from the vernacular Latin spoken by Roman soldiers in Gaul, *Vulgar Latin*, but it also includes many Celtic and Germanic words. French is a common second language in the world and it is one of the five official languages used by the United Nations. French is spoken in Belgium, Switzerland, and in many countries of Africa, Asia, in the West Indies, the Indian Ocean and the Pacific. French serves as the common language among the many indigenous languages and dialects spoken in those countries.

Until recently, French was traditionally accepted as the accepted international language spoken by 160 million people and present on no less than five continents. However, after WWII, English gradually became the number one international language and now French is at best the number two international language, and it is very much challenged by other languages such as Spanish, Japanese and Chinese, at least in the business world. This decrease in importance of the French language[42] is a serious concern to the French government, all the more that no nation in the world fights as hard as France to preserve in language its quality and international use.

The French *Académie française*, in existence since 1635, has always had as a goal the preservation of the French language, of its grammatical and semantic purity.[43] The *Académie* and the French Ministry of Culture have fought relentlessly to dam the invasion of *Franglais*[44] in the French language.[45] In spite of these efforts, the reality shows that French has been invaded by foreign words and expressions, particularly in the technical language, in the language of young people and under the influence of the television and the press. One must be realistic and accept the fact that in the long run usage only will decide if foreign words or expressions stay or if they fade away as passing fads. In fact the French language, which is an evolution from Vulgar Latin, is still in constant evolution. French since the Classical Period has been constantly enriched, enlarged and therefore "corrupted" by foreign additions and borrowings. After WWII, French was hit by a tidal wave of English terms and the French themselves are constantly modifying their own language, their own grammar and syntax. For instance, the past tense called *"passé simple"* (preterit) is practically moribund. Syntax is simplified, clipped. Negatives tend to disappear: For instance, you'll hear some people say *"je sais pas"* instead of the grammatically correct *"je ne sais pas"* (I don't know). TV is surely an influence in the deterioration of grammar, vocabulary and syntax. With TV, the image is everything and words are less important. Computers themselves do not improve the situation. Levels of language tend to disappear and more and more in conversation words are replaced by mere grunts and grammar is oversimplified if not forgotten. One says, for instance: *"tu viens?"* instead of saying *"est-ce que tu viens?"* One other contributing factor to the decadence/evolution of the French language is that people, particularly the young, watch TV instead of reading. Children and adolescents more and more listen to music, play arcade games and spend hours watching TV shows that unfortunately tend to promote sex and violence, etc. . . . The decline in readers of poetry, novels and classical literature is disquieting, but many adults still read and French bookstores are well attended. As for the young, optimists argue that if the young read less, they now travel more, listen to the news of the world, and if they don't read Molière, they are at least fond of science fiction novels.

Regional Minority Languages, Dialects and Patois

In 1539 the decree of *Villers-Cotterêts* imposed the use of the French language in all official acts. The goal of this decree was to replace Latin, but the consequence was the replacement of all regional or minority languages of France by French. In 1768 a new decree was enacted demanding the *francisation* (gallicizing) of the island of Corsica.

Dialects

Aside from the French language, derived from the Medieval *Francien* dialect, several dialects still remain more or less alive in some regions of France. *In the west*, the dialects of Saintonge, Poitou, Anjou and Brittany. *In the north*, Picard, Walloon and Normand. *In the east*, Champenois, Lorrain, Franc-Comtois, Alsacian. *In the south*, Occitan, Provençal, Catalan and other sub-dialects, including the Basque language or *Euskara*, and the *Lingua Corsa* of Corsica.

If the French language (opposed to other dialects of the country) has become the official language of France, it is because of the politics of centralization of the French kings and governments who, for several centuries, wanted to unify the various civilizations of France by giving them a single language. In France today the French speak *French*, but the old civilizations still exist: Bretons, Basques, Occitans. And that is why there is today a reawakening of regional consciousness. For instance, many Bretons feel that they are Bretons first before being French, and those who feel strongly about their roots want to be able to keep their identity and their tongue which represents it best. The same can be said of the Basques or of the Occitans whose militants have been quite vocal in their demands.

Alsace has a unique history because it is situated on the west bank of the Rhine, close to the Vosges and Jura mountains, a border crossroads since the Roman occupation in 58 B.C. and to several occupations by the Germans. Alsatians who were born before 1870 and were alive until 1945 changed nationality four times. Alsace was incorporated into Germany in 1870, then returned to France in 1919, reconquered by Germany in 1940 and liberated and returned to France in 1945. These events explain in great part why the movement for regional autonomy is less active in Alsace than in Occitania, the Basque country, Brittany and Corsica. The Alsatians have come close to losing their real sense of identity, and with their turbulent history they could well be asking if their unique culture is French or German. All Alsace wants at this point is to be allowed to grow along the Rhine that has become the "vertebral column" of Europe. Alsace only wants to be accepted with its specific differences and dual languages, French, and Alsacian, its Germanic dialect.

Brittany is surely one of the most original regions of France. It is divided into *Armor*, the seacoast, and *Argoat*, the forest. Its windswept peninsula extends far into the Atlantic Ocean in the west and south and into La Manche (English Channel) in the north. Three of France's six fishing ports are located in Brittany, Concarneau, Lorient and Douardenez. Brittany's historical and linguistic divisions are *Breizh-Izel* or lower Brittany and *Breizh-Uhel* or upper Brittany.

Brezhoneg, the Celtic Breton dialect, that is very similar to Welsh, is mostly spoken in lower Brittany, while upper Brittany speaks mostly French with a local dialect of French called *"gallo."* Upper Brittany was much more receptive to the French influence, while lower Brittany remained through the ages much more sheltered from French influences and thus was able to retain its unique language and culture. There exists a mild autonomist nationalist movement that tries to revive Breton culture and to keep alive the Breton language. Only very few advocate anymore separation from France.

The Basques have long been established in the Pyrénées region since 2000 B.C. The Romans called the tribes that did not welcome their colonization the *Vascones*. To this day, the Basque people retain a strong sense of their own identity, with their language that continues to puzzle linguists, as no one is sure of its origins. The Basques also retain their identity through a typical sport called *La Pelote*

Flanders *(La Flandre)*, Flemish-speaking France, or *Westhoek,* is a very small area of northeastern France. Its language is a small minority language with 25% of the population of 400,000 speaking Flemish.

Occitania is the largest and most complex of the linguistics minorities of France. It occupies one third of France and includes about 13 million people. The reason for the complexity of this region is that it is not, and has never been, a single political entity. It is composed of a number of smaller traditional provinces and political entities linked together by one language and one culture. The language is the *Langue d'Oc*, the first of the Romance languages to develop a literature, the great poetry and songs of the Medieval *Troubadours*. Occitan civilization during the medieval period was without a doubt the most advanced of all Western Christendom. The language is similar to Spanish, Catalan, French, Portuguese, Italian and Rumanian, a descendant from Latin, one of the Romance languages.

Occitan, however, is not a single tongue of Occitania; it is divided into several local dialects.

By the end of the fifteenth century, the French language had begun to replace Occitan, and Occitan dialects practically disappeared in written form. François Ier's decree of *Villers-Cotterêts* required that all administrative and religious documents be written in French. While the Occitan language continued to be spoken, it began to be more and more a *"pa-*

tois" spoken by older people. In the nineteenth century, there was a temporary revival thanks to the poet Paul Mistral and his poets of the *Félibrige*, but the Third Republic threatened the language once more. This was particularly done under the influence of Jules Ferry, who wanted to eradicate all the *patois* of the country, and enforce the speaking and writing of French in all the schools of France.

Corsica, *La Corse,* also known as the *"Ile de beauté"* (isle of beauty), from the Greek *"kalliste"* meaning beautiful, is situated 80 kilometers west of the coast of Italy and 180 kilometers from the French Riviera. It is also 12 kilometers north of Sardinia.

In Corsica the French language and French culture are compulsory because the French regard Corsica as one of their departments, but the Corsican language and its culture remains revered by the Corsicans.

There have been recently in Corsica many ugly scenes of violence, attempted murders, murders, blowing up of government buildings, etc., by a minority of Corsican nationalists struggling for independence. At this point the French government is not giving in to them and is trying to restore peace on the island. Corsicans are proud of their Corsican identity, of their roots and of their language, but fortunately most of them so far want to live peacefully with France.

Gastronomy

France has the reputation of being a country of great gastronomy, and at the eve of the Third Millennium, this remains in great part true. Many businessmen and politicians still eat lunch in the wonderful restaurants of Paris and of the provinces, and many families still eat at home the traditional 2-hour luncheon with hors d'oeuvre (entrée), salad, main dish (meat, fish) vegetables, cheese and dessert. However, modernity has brought some major changes to French daily life. And while some families still enjoy traditional eating habits, many more are in a hurry and resort to fast foods, and snacks during the workweek. While lunch used to last two hours, now more and more people spend only half an hour, particularly in Paris and other big cities where they must allow time for transportation. It is unfortunately true, the French are not spared by the standardization of eating habits, and that can be in part explained by the fact that many women work, and their absence from home during the day upsets the rhythm of family life. In addition, in many towns the children eat at their school *cantine* (cafeteria). Even if the French don't like *MacDo*

(MacDonald's), they settle for a hamburger, mineral water and expresso coffee rather than ordering what most of them still love, *Le Steak-frites* (Steak and French fries). When asked, the French say that "There is no time for a long lunch" and "Restaurants take too long and cost too much money." Now it is the evening meal that counts the most.

The French, however, have kept a last gastronomic bastion, the Sunday lunch, shared with the family and friends. No hamburger then, but a good solid traditional meal with meat, fish, vegetables, cheese, salad and dessert, of course with good wines. Surely the French family today eats less potatoes and much less bread than before WWII, and *la viande de cheval* (horsemeat) has almost disappeared along with the quaint *Boucheries Chevalines* recognized by the horse head above the store.

The French are more interested nowadays in quality foods, organically grown products and controlled meats and fish. They also are fond of the raw foods Japanese style and often eat in Chinese, Vietnamese or Japanese restaurants. There is also a conflict of generations in eating habits. Those 60 years old and older like traditional dishes, while the young eat fast in order to go watch TV or to go and play.

France remains a country of *cheeses* and cheese regularly appears at meals; however, the consumption of lowfat *Yaourt* (yoghurt) is on the increase. The French still remain the biggest consumers of cheese with 23.2 kilograms per person per year.

In April 1999 the press reported a serious problem with French cheeses made from raw milk. It would seem that the French are getting more sensitive than they ever were before to the problems of health and safety. Now many don't want to eat the delicious Camembert from Normandy made with raw milk, i.e., with bacteria (non-pasteurized), and everyone knows that it is the raw milk that gives the cheese its special delicious taste. French gourmets fear that France will soon join the English and the Americans in prohibiting the sale of unpasteurized cheese.

As for *wine*, the French drink less of it since WWII. They used to drink 120 liters per person per year on the average, and now they drink less that 80 liters and even down to 30 liters, depending from the areas surveyed. When they do not drink wine or beer, they prefer mineral water or pop drinks like Coca-Cola. When they drink wine, they do not drink much table wine *(vin ordinaire)* and prefer to drink less but better quality wines. Health seems to explain the decrease in wine drinking, and the younger generation drinks even much less wine than adults. They drink juice, beer, pop or bottled mineral water. The young in fact look at wine as the drink of the over 60 years old generation.

Cultural Outlook of France since 1945

The Second World War ended in May 1945 after the capitulation of Germany. It was followed by a time of extraordinary euphoria, but the mood was far more subdued than the explosions of joy of 1918. The gloominess latent under the thin surface of victorious smiles came from the fact that the French felt that they had lost their place as a great world power. They also realized that they would have never won the war without the input of the Allies, and they felt small next the two giant blocks of America and the Soviet Union. Even though the French were proud of their resistance to the enemy, they remained under the trauma of their defeat and foreign occupation. The final victory of 1945 was not enough to save the French national honor. At the time of the *Libération*, France's economy was at its lowest ebb. The discovery of the extermination camps of the Nazis and the atomic bombs on Japan brought an additional cloud of gloom over the country.

Literary life surely felt the impact of this mood. Many writers, poets had died during the war, Paul Nizan, Jean Prévost, Saint Exupéry and, unfortunately, many other intellectuals had collaborated with Vichy and the Germans. Drieu de La Rochelle, the director of the famous *Nouvelle Revue Française*, for instance, collaborated with the enemy, and Robert Brasillach, Léon Daudet, J. Bainville and Charles Maurras too, were closely linked with the *Action Française,* a daily monarchist, antidemocratic and fiercely nationalist political newspaper (1908–1944). When not accused of links with Vichy or the Germans, some writers like Jean Giono were accused of overt pacifism, while Louis Ferdinand Céline was accused of anti-Semitism.

During the Second World War some writers were mostly forgotten, Romain Rolland, Alain, Jules Romains, for instance. Others like André Gide, Paul Giraudoux, Antoine de Saint Exupéry and André Malraux reflected on the great changes in values brought about by the war. Other writers had gone into exile: André Breton took refuge in New York, Benjamin Péret in Mexico, Jean Bernanos in Brazil, and Saint John Perse went to America, never to return.

Those writers who fought in the Resistance were thrown into the limelight, André Malraux, René Char, Louis Aragon, Paul Eluard, Albert Camus, François Mauriac and Jean Paulhan. These writers thought that they had a moral responsibility, a literary and philosophical mission. They felt that they were the leaders who would help humanity recover its lost values and rebuild a better world. Literature thus became socially, morally and politically engaged (engagée). For Jean-Paul Sartre, for instance, literature had a socio-political function and, under his influence, the literary values became political ones.

French literature before World War II had seen great literary figures in poetry, theater and the novel. They are too many to mention them all, but the following cannot be passed by:

Guillaume Apollinaire, who died during WWI, Alfred Jarry, Georges Courteline, Anatole France, Maurice Barrès, Charles Péguy, Paul Claudel, Marcel Proust, André Gide, Paul Valéry, the new Surrealist poets like André Breton, Robert Desnos, Paul Eluard, Louis Aragon, Max Jacob, Jules Supervielle. During the period 1919–1939 some great names dominated the theater, like Jean Giraudoux. During the same period, the novel was brilliantly represented by writers like François Mauriac, Georges Bernanos, Henry de Montherlant, Jean Giono and Colette. With the Second World War over, many new literary schools flourished. In poetry with Jacques Prévert, René Char, Saint-John Perse. The theater was dominated by Jean Anouilh and Montherlant, while Existential philosophy and literature dominated the literary world with the writings of Jean-Paul Sartre, Simone de Beauvoir and Albert Camus. Then, as we approach our times, a new poetry was born and a new novel, Le Nouveau Roman with Robbe-Grillet, Michel Butor, Nathalie Sarraute and Madeleine Duras. We must also mention the new vitality of francophone literatures, from Québec, Africa, Morocco, Algeria, the West Indies.

Art had also its great artists between the two world wars and after 1945. Among the great painters of pre-WWII we can mention, after the great Impressionists, Cézanne and Van Gogh, and Cubic and modern artists Miro, Modigliani, Max Ernst, Picasso, Bonnard, Matisse, Braque, Dufy, Chagall, Giacometti, Léger and Rouault etc. . . . In the world of Music the nineteenth century saw many great French composers like Hector Berlioz, Charles Gounod, George Bizet and Claude Debussy, the founder of modern music.

The seventh art should not be forgotten either, as France has produced many legendary film directors like Truffault, Godard, Malle and Rohmer, Lelouch and Besson and an equal number of stars from Catherine Deneuve, Jean-Paul Belmondo, Isabelle Adjani to the ever present Gérard Depardieu, etc. . . .

Some Aspects of French Behavior

The French in Public

When you look carefully at the French as they relate to others in public, you cannot help noticing that in general they appear colder, more severe than Americans. They tend, for instance, not to smile at each other, except when they are with close friends. They surely do not smile when walking alone in the street. Their public face is generally serious, but this must not be construed as an unfriendly behavior. Simply they do not smile without a cause. Parents teach their children not to smile at strangers and girls particularly will normally keep a blank face even if a man smiles at them, except of course if they know the individual. So if you are a stranger smiling at a French person, you will usually get back an empty or cold stare.

The French, contrary to the Anglo-Saxons, the English in particular, move a lot when they talk and this behavior is even more exaggerated in the south of France, where people are in general more jovial, at least more expansive in their expressions and body language. They move their arms, shrug their shoulders, point, frown and laugh. In other words the French tend to accompany their conversation and moods by gestures. When people meet they invariably shake hands, even if they meet for the third time that day, and, if they know each other, they embrace or kiss, twice, and frequently three times, right cheek, left cheek, right cheek. It is called *"la bise"* or *"faire la bise"* in French. No, they don't express their friendship by kissing on the mouth.

While the French tend to be more effusive than the Anglo-Saxons, they take up much less personal space than Americans. Americans, even in public, are more relaxed than the French. They sit, cross, uncross their legs, slouch or spread their legs. In other words, Americans seek not the ideal posture, but they want to be comfortable. The French take up less room, they are more "condensed," more straight in public and official situations at least. However, some change in business relations has taken place already; there is much less formality between men and women, and much less formality between bosses and workers. There is respect but the *"tu"* form is more frequently used than the *"vous"* among many workers and executives. But it would be still dangerous for a foreigner not knowing the rules to use the *"tu"* form right away. This area of *"vous"-"tu"* is still very unclear, and when in doubt, *"vous"* should be used.

When the French are discussing a point with others, they are not as gentle or reserved as Anglo-Saxons. They do not hesitate to disagree strongly, even with a member of the family or friends. In fact, it is not considered rude to disagree with another person, to "fight" for your opinion. The French worship intellectual ideas, they take a very serious philosophical approach to problems, and they are for this reason ready to "fight" for an idea, or a cause. It is not winning the discussion that is important to them; it is the challenge that counts. At first Americans may be shocked when exposed to this behavior, but since it is a current habit, they soon learn to adapt to it.

The French are perhaps more formal at times, but they are certainly not unfriendly, not antisocial or snobs, not all of them, in any case. But it is hard to be invited at home by the French if they don't know you well. They'll first meet you in a café or in a restaurant, and you must be better acquainted or a very special person to be asked for a meal at home right away. Why? I think that the reason is that the French want to treat people right; they want to receive you very well and, therefore, it takes them time to arrange for that very special occasion.

French children also behave somewhat differently from American children. American children on the whole are more boisterous in public, they sit for a few minutes, get up, talk, interrupt, in other words they are brought up feeling at ease, comfortable. French parents accept their children early in social occasions, in public and thus French children early learn the rules of behavior at the dining table or in the salon with their parents' friends. They sit quietly, talk if they are talked to, and politely ask to be excused when they get a nod from their parents. French children, depending on their family, also can be unruly, and the same good little boy or girl in front of their parents can be wild when away from authority. Someone has said that French children look like angels but behave at times like small devils. In fact, as the trend seems to go toward more leniency toward children, we are beginning to see the same behavior on both sides of the Atlantic. French children still dine frequently with their parents, but they also crash on couches, looking at TV and prefer pizza to their parents' meal.

The French are quite reserved about their finances. While in America practically every discussion is sprinkled with figures and dollar signs, the French are much more secretive, particularly about their own wealth. They consider that it is vulgar to flaunt one's wealth and so the rich in France live quietly behind walls that are often reinforced with broken glass, and behind these walls there might be dogs as announced on a plate on the entrance gate: *"Chien Méchant!" (Cave Canem!)*. If the French talk of finances to anybody, it is limited to their lawyer or *notaire*. In France money is a taboo subject, and if you don't know the person, you do not ask personal questions.

Some Trivia: The French and Lighting
Travelers from America may notice that the French are very parsimonious with their electricity. While Paris is the shining city of light, the French

in their houses and in hotels are frequently very "careful" with their electricity. While in America the 75 watts or 100 watts lightbulbs are the norm, in France the 40 watt bulb is much more common. This does not seem to bother the French, who can talk, read and work in what in America would be considered a very subdued light.

Dealing with Holidays and Short Vacations

About their holidays, the French have a strict rule: they are entitled to them. They not only have six weeks paid holidays, but a myriad of legal days off and when these days off happen in the middle of the week they don't hesitate to *"faire le pont"* (to make the bridge). If, for instance, the holiday *(jour férié)* is on a Tuesday, do not expect many Frenchmen to be at work on Friday. They'll "bridge" over till the following Monday. This is not officially allowed, but it is the current practice.

So, clearly, as we approach the Millennium, some French traditional habits persist, but many are changing and probably will even change faster when the current American influence will be compounded by the French becoming European.[46]

A French Society Far from France: France and Its Dom-Toms

Just like there is a French society in metropolitan France, far away, in the middle of oceans, there is still today a dynamic and important French society, with French police, French telephones, French mailboxes, restaurants, schools and cafés. This is because France has succeeded in keeping a good number of overseas possessions in spite of the increasing movements of independence of former lands owned by European colonial powers. Since 1946, French Guyane on the South American coast, the Guadeloupe and Martinique (in the Carribean), the Réunion in the Indian Ocean have been granted by France the statute of DOM or *Département d'Outre Mer*. Next to these lands, Nouvelle-Calédonie and Wallis and Futura as well as French Polynésie, the TAAF or *Terres australes et antartiques françaises*, that is to say, the islands of Amsterdam, Saint-Paul, Crozet, Kerguelen and Terre Adélie, have the statute of TOM or *Territoires d'Outre Mer*. Saint-Pierre-et-Miquelon in the north Atlantic, near Newfoundland, Mayotte in the Indian Ocean Comores, have a special hybrid statute of CT or *Collectivités Territoriales*.

Most of these lands are important to France because of their geographic and strategic position, and in some cases because of their economic value. They do not all ask for independence, but among them the demands of *Nouvelle-Calédonie* (New Caledonia) and of some lands of *Polynésie* (Polynesia) and the Carribean are strong and recognized by the French government. For instance, New Caledonia, off the coast of Australia, has reached an agreement with France on April 23, 1998, preparing for greater independence and a vote on total independence has been set set for 2013 or 2015. Then the 200,000 inhabitants of New Caledonia will determine if their land should gain more self-government. If the vote is yes, France will gradually transfer some executive powers to a new government run by Caledonians. The population is made up of 44.8% Kanaks (Malenesians) and 33.6% of people of European descent. Kanaks are represented by their FLNKS or Socialist Liberation Front party, and they are the most vocal in claiming independence from France. They teach their Kanak language in schools, changed the name of the country, created a new national anthem and printed a new currency representing the indegenous people's identity. The other group, the Loyalists, who want to retain ties with France, are represented by the RPCR party or rally for Caledonia and the Republic. In the meantime, France multiplies goodwill gestures toward the Kanaks. For instance, in May 1998 the French Prime Minister Lionel Jospin went to New Caledonia to inaugurate in Noumea, the capital, a cultural center dedicated to the artistic, linguistic and archaeological patrimony of the Kanaks.

Notes

1 The 58.7 million inhabitants constitutes an increase of 40% in 50 years, a spectacular increase if one considers that between 1901 and 1946 the increase was only 4%. It places France at the twenty-fourth rank worldwide, the whole population of the world being about 5.5 billion (figures for 1993). The increase in population is due to a decrease in deaths. In the 1930's there were 650,000 deaths a year, and at the end of the 1940's that figure had decreased below 550,000. Then there is the factor that after 1930 people began to live longer. Men's lives went from 54 years to 67 and women's lives rose from 59 to 74 years, and the lengthening of life continues. In the 1970's the figures were 68 for men and 76 for women, and in 1996 the figures had gone up with 74 for men and 82 for women.

2 A report from the INED (Institut National d'Etudes Démographiques) states that over 40% of the demographic increase since WWII is either directly or indirectly linked to immigration. Still, the French born from parents born in France represent three fourths of the population.

3 Since the laws passed by Jules Ferry in 1881–1882.

4 In 1998 there were 600,000 candidates for the Baccalauréat, and all those who passed were allowed access to a university. Understandably, most French universities are very crowded and short of space.

5 In order to put success on the side of their children, parents try to put them in the best *lycées* of the country, those who have a high rating of success with the Baccalauréat. In fact the Ministry of National Education publishes a list of the top lycées. For instance, in 1998 the Lycée Henri IV in Paris is at the top with 100% success at the Baccalauréat and the second best lycée with about 99% of success are the Lycées Condorcet, La Rochefoucault, Louis le Grand, Saint Louis de Gonzague, Charles Péguy and Alma in Paris. If our list includes Paris only, it does not mean that there are not excellent lycées in the regions, like in Strasbourg, Lille, Toulouse, etc., all continuing a tradition of educational excellence.

6 There is a reform proposal in the works, sponsored by the Prime Minister of Education, Allègre, which we discuss further on in this chapter.

7 Claude Allègre is disliked by French teachers these days, and their unions lose no occasion to call their members to manifest against the minister's proposed reforms. During the March 20–21 weekend, the *Syndicat national d'enseignement supérieur* had called a march in Paris against Allègre, announcing that 100,000 persons would be in the street. Only 20,000 to 25,000 showed up, showing that on the one hand Allègre is detested, but on the other hand that people are tired of stop gap measures. Matignon, i.e., Jospin, is careful in its reaction. It shows only some small signs of goodwill, promising to create new teaching positions and to increase the pay rate of additional hours of teaching. President Jacques Chirac, not forgetting the forthcoming presidential elections, preferred to make

an appearance to the *Salon de l'Etudiant* to show that he was aware and honestly preoccupied by the problems of students worried about their future. He particularly stressed that the important thing that he was seeking was that no one be prevented to pursue more advanced studies. He said: "La voie doit être ouverte" (The road must be open). Chirac continued, saying that one should be able to start with a simple CAP, but be able to go on and obtain an engineer's diploma later. Thus the President was offering a striking contrast with his hated minister of education. But in the long run Allègre may be right!

8   The following words of Claude Allègre represent quite accurately his vision of the new CNRS or, rather, what he thinks it should correct: "*Ce qui est en cause aujourd'hui, c'est l'idée qu'on peut être chercheur à vie*" (What concerns us today is the idea that someone may be a researcher for life).

9   The origin of the *Bibliothèque Nationale* actually goes back to Charles V.

10 The library, also known as BFM or TGB (très grande bibliothèque) was built at a cost of 8 billion francs and designed by French architect Dominique Perrault. The library has a web site for special events:. The cost of upkeep is high, about 10% of the Culture Ministry's budget, i.e., no less than 1.2 billion francs.

11 Out of 42 million French 18 years old or older, 32 million claim to be Catholic, and 13 million of those claim that they practice their faith. If the proportion of Frenchmen who declare practicing their religion is of 16%, up from 13% in 1987, it is thanks to those 60 years old and older. Twenty-five percent of the French declare not belonging to any religion.

12 France is divided into 34,000 parishes, but only 1/3 of them have a resident priest. Aging among the clergy is an increasing problem and, as an example, in 1997 only 166 priests were ordained while 750 left the priesthood.

13 In the middle of the nineteenth century, there were about 850,000 Protestants in metropolitan France, i.e., 2.36% of the population. Today they are a little more than 900,000, i.e., 1.7% of the population. Lutherans are 25,000 in France, Calvinists are about 600,000 and the others belong to smaller Churches like the Methodists, the Baptists and the Salvation Army *(L'Armée du Salut)*. Contrary to what has been said, Protestantism is not limited to the Lorraine and Cévennes regions. There are many Protestant communities in the Ile-de-France, Normandy, Loire, Béarn, Languedoc and Provence. For a good article on Protestants, see *L'Evènement du Jeudi*, No. 692, Fevrier 5–11, 1998, pp. 6–12.

14 The percentage of young people 20 years old and older, continuing their studies later has been increasing steadily since 1970 and has doubled since 1980. In addition, because of unemployment or difficulty to get a job, 60% of young men 20–25 years old and 38% of young women of the same age continue to live with their parents, while the respective percentages were only 47% and 25% in 1970. See "Une entrée de plus en plus tardive dans la vie adulte," O. Galland, *Economie et Statistique*, No. 283–284, 1995.

15 The French government recently discussed the recognition of a new type of marriage-like association, the *Pacs* or *pacte civil de solidarité*. This would, if passed

as law, grant to non-married couples, men or women, a certain number of rights and duties. This contract would be registered not in a Mairie, but in a préfecture and it could be annulled at any time by any of the two involved. Among the duties of the *pacs* are mutual and material assistance and repayment of debts contracted by either of the two. One of the advantage of the *pacs*, and its distinction from *concubinage* (heterosexual cohabitation), is that if one dies, the other is not considered as a total stranger like in the case of *concubinage* where simple donations are taxed 60%. With the *pacs* the surviving person will not be taxed as much and he or she will be able to keep the rental agreement of their common lodging. In addition if one of the two is not covered by Social Security, the other can extend coverage to him or her. Naturally this *pacs* proposal was initiated by the Left and is supported by Lionel Jospin. Many think that it is a natural consequence of the current social revolution of free unions. The fact is that living together is no longer considered a trial period, but it has become a choice for life, a lifestyle. The Assembly passed the bill on December 9, and sent it to the Senate for discussion. Now it must be said that outside the Left, many others, including Christine Boutin, leader of the *anti-pacs*, consider the *pacs* as an agression against society. In November 1998 100,000 persons marched in Paris shouting anti-pacs slogans.

On March 19, 1999, the TV station France 2 announced that the majority of the Senate had rejected the proposed *pacs* as irrealistic for several reasons, one being that it would create a sort of non-marriage-marriage. In fact, in June 1999 the Senate rejected the *pacs,* so it will be the turn of the National Assembly to vote a final time during the 1999–2000 session that will begin on October 1, 1999. The big question remains: will it be finally adopted as Elisabeth Guigou, *Garde des Sceaux,* and her supporters would like so much?

16   See an article of *L'Express*, no. 2477, December 12, 1998, pp. 32–40, "Les enfants rendent-ils heureux."

17   See F. Daguet,"Mariage, divorce et union libre," *INSEE Première*, No. 482, Août 1996; "Le mariage en déclin, la vie en couple aussi," C. Lefranc, *INSEE Première*, No 392, 1995. See a survey on the opinion of the French on divorce, in our Appendix 13.

18   See the article of Christian Saint-Etienne, "Ne tirez pas sur la République," in *L'Express*, no. 2477, December 24, 1998, p. 18.

19   While in France only 6% of women are deputies, in Germany they are 26.6%. Even the former Prime Minister Juppé who fired six women from his cabinet agreed that establishing a quota to assure more feminine voices in politics would be a good idea. President Chirac and his current Prime Minister Jospin are preparing a project of law on "la parité hommes-femmes" which would grant total equality between men and women in the French Constitution. If passed, this law would give women equal access to all functions and elective posts.

20   E. Badinter, "Ici, en droit, nous avons tout obtenu," *Le Nouvel Observateur*, 25 mai 1994, pp. 40–43.

21   Sheila Perry, *Aspects of Contemporary France,* Routledge, 1997.

22   See T. Blöss and A. Frickey, *La Femme dans la société française*, Paris: PUF, 1994, p. 121.

23   Social Security was introduced in France in 1945 after WWII. It is a general plan of health insurance for everyone with special plans for specific groups, such as farm workers, civil servants, the military, seamen, railroad employees, retailers, professionals. The biggest problem facing the Social Security system is its deficit and its funding because the number of people paying Social Security has declined owing to unemployment and the increase in living retired persons.

24   On the importance of Social Protection and Benefits in France, see our Appendix 15.

25   As an indication, the price of a visit by a generalist doctor in France was set in March 1998 at 115 francs or less than $25. The big expense of patients and, therefore for Social Security, is the prescriptions. And since in France most medicines come prepackaged, there is a great deal of costly waste.

26   For example, the French are reported to have consumed 85 million boxes of antidepressants, i.e., 8 times the amount used by the English. The French also took 67 million sleeping pills and other drugs against anxiety. The French government is worried, and as a first counter measure has decided not to reimburse the drug *Lysanxia* prescribed for deep anxieties.

27   In France today there are 16 million overweight individuals, i.e., 8.2% of the population. Obesity strikes mostly men 55 or older and the poor.

28   See the *Ann Arbor News, French regional disparities studied* (March 6, 1998).

29   Each year France produces over 20 million tons of household waste that end up in rubbish discharges. Some 30,000 tons of wastes are burned in incinerators, and in some the energy produced is recovered in the form of heat and electricity. Recycling has also been successful in France and illegal discharges of toxic material, still in existence, are being gradually eliminated.

30   Two out of three French people watch TV every day and 5,200,000 people have access to cable TV, 30% of households. French TV has four public channels and Canal+, a pay channel.

31   Nowadays the French buy fewer books and, according to publishers, print runs have fallen on the average from 1,500 copies to 900. It seems that our society is getting hyperspecialized and people tend to buy within their specialty, ignoring the wider intellectual concerns of life. If people buy fewer books, it is not only because books in France are expensive, it is because, mostly in schools and universities, students tend to photocopy the books they need, thus depriving publishers from sales. In France this is called "photopillage" (photorobbing).

32   The French travel more and more and further and further by plane, train and in their cars. They fill ski stations in winter and the West Indies are their favorite destination. In 1982 the French travelled about four times a year on the average, and now they travel six times or more. See "Les Français voyagent de plus en

plus," *Notes de synthèse* no 113, septembre 1997, DAE/SES, ministère de l'Equipement, des transports et du Logement. (*INSEE Première*, no. 565. Janvier 1998).

33   This *tourisme vert* is also called *agritourisme*. Urban guests are not taking part in the farm work, but they share their meals with the farmers and rediscover the serenity of nature absent in most towns.

34   For more information on French museums, see our Appendix 14.

35   *Le Nouvel Observateur* is a current affair newspaper-magazine founded in 1950 and very popular among intellectuals. It has a circulation of 475,000. *Le Figaro* is Paris' oldest newspaper, founded in 1826. It has a wide circulation of about 400,000. It appeals to the political Right. *Le Monde* is a serious daily newspaper founded in 1944. It tends to lean toward the Left politically. It appears in the afternoon and has a circulation of 500,000. *France Soir* was founded in 1941 and has a circulation of 187,000. *Libération* is a Left-wing newspaper founded in 1973 and has a circulation of 170,000.

36   About French casinos, it must be said that they are on the whole more aristocratic than the casinos in the USA, although the *machines à sous* (one arm bandits) are beginning to appear in France; however, they are often placed in a separate section of the casino.

37   After the doping scandal of the 1998 Tour de France, the French government is working on stricter preventive measures and punishments (up to two years in jail and up to 100,000 francs in fines).

38   A recent note in the magazine *L'Express* of December 24, 1998, p. 23, states that the French, according to a SOFRES poll, are buying fewer Christmas trees. If in 1997 they bought 6.7 million trees, in 1998 the number of trees bought would have been cut in half. Nobody knows exactly the reason for this disaffection, but some say that it is to prevent deforestation, others say that fewer people stay at home and many go away for the holidays.

39   A recent example of the contribution of the French government to culture is its 1999 budget. Even though the Senate decided to make some cuts as a contribution to the effort to control public expenses, the budget voted was of 15.5 billion francs, a clear testimony, in spite of the cuts, that culture is one of the main priorities of the State. In fact most of the senators made a plea that the funds allocated to culture first benefit the young who are, after all, the "relieving troops" of France as the country crosses the threshold of the Third Millennium.

40   André Malraux, President de Gaulle's Minister of Culture, wrote a remarkable book which incarnates the French vision of culture, *Les Voix du Silence* (the voices of silence) showing that museums and artworks are the memory of civilizations and that if war destroys them, civilizations are doomed. It is for the same reason that Malraux, when he was in power, encouraged the nation to preserve its cultural heritage and make it known to the largest number of people.

41 In order to encourage culture and making it more accessible, France offers many opportunities to its young, whether to study music, the fine arts, or poetry through a network of conservatories or workshops at a very small cost. In 1960, André Malraux, who was Minister of Culture, set up the *Maisons des jeunes et de la culture* (houses for the young and for culture) in view of opening culture to a larger group of the urban population. The initiative was welcomed in many large towns such as Montpellier, Grenoble, Toulon, Marseille, Pau, Lyon, Nancy and Tours. Following the example of the Center Pompidou in Paris, nearly 80 museums opened in the provinces since 1981. The French government always had a policy to encourage the French in French and foreign cultures and it has cultural representatives in most major cities of the world promoting French culture.

42 The decrease in the use of French is directly reflected by the decrease in enrollment in US French classes. Students who used to study French now tend to study Spanish.

43 Mr. Cerquiglini, director of the National Institute for the French Language, pointed to the symbolism of the Académie Française, saying that the académie was not only a club of learned people, but a creation of the French State, its protector.

44 *Franglais* is a bastardized mixture of French corrupted by the use of Anglo-Saxon terms or syntax.

45 An example of the French Académie's resistance to change can be found in a recent dispute concerning the feminization of job titles. There is the case of a lady Minister in the Jospin government who wanted to be called "Madame la Ministre", instead of the accepted traditional title of "Madame le Ministre." The French Académie immediately stated that "la" was an ungrammatical deviation in the French language. The lady's reply to them was that if certain words do not have a feminine variation in French, it is because no woman before occupied these functions. President Chirac seems to be in favor of "Madame la Ministre" and so, for the time being, "Madame la Ministre" is accepted. Many other women in high positions have followed suit, and Mr. Maurice Druon, Perpetual Secretary of the French Académie, has lost a battle and women feel that they won the war. It is interesting to note that one of the first reactions to the famous "la" came from the Minister of Culture of Québec, Louise Beaudoin. She pointed out that when in 1983 René Lévesque of Québec called her to his government to direct the Québec delegation to Paris, she assumed a title that reflected her womanhood as well as her function, adding that such feminized title was perceived as normal in Québec. Again, still according to Louise Beaudoin, the feminization of titles is a linguistic phenomenon that normally reflects the integration of women socially in functions that have long been held by men. It is Louise Beaudoin's opinion that if the French language wants to remain a living language, it must be free to adapt and to let usage make the final decision.

46 Since there are many excellent books dealing with the normal/strange behavior, mores, of the French, we decided not to enlarge the chapter, but to refer our readers to the following four books which will expand, sometimes with humor, on many more aspects of the French attitudes and customs: Ross Steele, *The French*

Way. Passport Books, 1995; Harriet Welty Rochefort, *French Toast.* Anglophone s.a. 1997; Polly Platt, *French or Foe?* Culture Crossings Ltd., 1994; Nick Yapp and Michel Syrett, *The Xenophobe's Guide to the French*, Ravette Publishing, 1993.

Chapter 5

Conclusion

France at the Eve of the Third Millennium
Its Assets, Pressing Problems and Challenges

Political, Social and Economic Problems That France Needs to Solve in the Third Millennium

The first major political problem for France was Jacques Chirac's *"surprise,"* the dissolution of the French Assembly in 1997 and a call for new elections. In fact it turned out to be more than a surprise, it was soon perceived as a major political blunder (*une gaffe stratégique*). What it did was to force Chirac's Right-wing government into another period of *Cohabitation* with a Socialist Prime Minister, Lionel Jospin. Chirac gambled and lost. By his move, the President was hoping to regain the confidence of his electorate and to take advantage of the apparent weakness of the Socialist Party (PS). He lost because the French no longer had confidence in Chirac's previous electoral promises and they were exasperated by some of the belt-tightening policies of the Prime Minister, Alain Juppé. Chirac lost by a wide margin and was forced to name the Socialist Jospin as Premier. Jospin immediately appointed three Communists in his government, a major blow to the Right. In voting against Juppé and Chirac, the French showed not only their anger, they showed that they were still able to rebel against those in power. They had already done that in December 1968 against de Gaulle. But why did the French vote Socialist this time aside from the reasons given above? When questioned, some observers said that there were six possible answers, but one will probably never know which one really made the scales tip: (1) They may have voted to help the 700,000 unemployed, or (2) To give back more voice to Parliament and to weaken the current executive, or (3) To bring much needed reforms to National Education, or (4) To bring in a government more favorable to the lot of foreign workers and immigrants, or (5) To create a social Europe rather than a capitalistic Europe, or (6) To counter the progress of the Front National (FN). Aside from these possibilities, Chirac may have lost simply because his government, with Juppé in particular, was too arrogant for most Frenchmen, and they were tired of the way they were governed, looking at it as a parody of Gaullism.[1]

France has been plagued by several serious problems, *financial frauds*, serious cases of public funds mismanagement and by terrible instances of waste of public finances.

Each year the French central accounting office, *La Cour des Comptes*, publishes a report that, unfortunately, almost always lists many abuses, cases of waste of public funds and various kinds of financial scandals. In 1997, the president of the *Cour des Comptes*, Pierre Joxe, found a lot of public money that was recklessly spent, and one of the major culprits was the State itself. He found, for instance, a project of conference center, commissioned by former President Mitterand in 1988, that never went beyond mere sketches by the architect Francis Soler. However, the cost of this aborted project was 382.6 million francs, for nothing. There are other examples of *"gabegie"* (muddled waste), such as some excessive subventions to Corsica. The accounting office discovered that seven out of ten Corsican farms received state subventions in an amount ten times that of the subventions granted French farms.[2] The French Post Office, *La Poste*, also lost 765 million francs in a first failed venture on the financial market. Another example of reckless management was the Eole project of the SNCF. It started building a RER line between the Gare de l'Est station in Paris and the Gare Saint Lazare station, but suddenly the cost soared from the 5 million estimated in 1991 to the new estimate of 12 billion francs in 1998. Many less major but still important cases of fraud occur, such as the disappearance from state-owned housing of furniture, of classified artworks and their reappearance at public auctions. There are other examples: There is the case of this bridge in the middle of a field connecting no roads and left standing after spending 3 million francs. We can also mention the unfinished tunnel in Toulon. First its cost was estimated at 900 million francs; however, the cost soon was revised at 1.43 billion francs for the first phase of the construction. But on March 15, 1996, the tunnel's structure collapsed and work was stopped. As Jean-Pierre Chanal wrote in *Le Point* (no. 1309, Oct. 18, 1997, p. 97): *"Restent deux trous: l'un sous la ville, l'autre dans les caisses"* (Two holes remain: one under the city and the other in the city's coffers).

Aside from state frauds or wreckless mismanaging of public funds, France also experiences white-collar crimes by individuals and public officials. For instance, there was the *Affaire Tibéri*. Tibéri, Paris' Mayor, alledgedly paid a substantial sum of money (200,000 francs) to his wife to write a brief (some say skimpy) report of 36 pages. There has been all over TV and the press the *Affaires Tapie*. Bernard Tapie, former Minister of the Cities, has been jailed for corruption and other important fraudulent financial dealings, particularly involving the *Crédit Lyonnais* bank. There was (and still is) also the *Affaire Roland Dumas-Christine Deviers-Joncour-Loïc Le Floch-Prigent*. Christine Deviers-Joncour was accused of receiving money in order to influence the political decisions of Roland Dumas, then Minister of Defense. All parties may not be totally guilty; however, this is an illustration of the types of white-collar crimes that plague France today.[3]

Another aspect of French political life that needs some correction is the vastly abused tradition among political officials of *holding several public functions*. For instance, the ex-Prime Minister Juppé was at the same time Prime Minister and Mayor of Bordeaux. France is the only country to allow such plurality of offices. There are rumors that the government is inclined to put an end to this practice, but so far nothing has been done.

Strikes have also plagued the Fifth Republic, disturbing traffic, blocking roads, and cutting gasoline supplies. For instance, in order to earn more pay and to obtain the right to retire at 55, the French truck drivers *(les Routiers)* paralyzed France during the fall of 1997 by blocking main roads, toll gates and accesses to gasoline supplies. This strike was in fact the first political test to Jospin.[4]

The *Front National,* judged by the vast majority of the French as a dangerous racist party, is also a serious problem France has to face.

Racism is one of the top topics of the time in France. On the one hand, the government wants to prohibit clandestine immigration that, in the long run, promotes racism, but on the other hand the government wants to respect France's long tradition of protection of foreigners legally settled in France and either integrated or willing to become French citizens. President Chirac has reaffirmed several times his opposition to all forms of racism and refuses to accept a France-mosaïc made up of juxtaposed (i.e., nonintegrated) communities. He wants a France open and generous, but uncompromising as far as its basic values. Like Chirac, most French people are not racist, but it is true that they are sometimes frustrated and speak *as if they were* racist. They are not only frustrated by the problems created by uncontrolled immigration, but they are also frustrated by those who claim that France is becoming racist. What this segment of the French fear is that they may no longer express themselves without being judged racists or anti-Semitic, or accused of xenophobia. They are frustrated by the double standard of those who pan them as racists, but at the same time accept the virulent racist speeches of several anti-French, anti-whites groups. These frustrations, this malaise are the fountain of youth of the Front National, they say.

Urban violence, anti-social behavior, boorishness, aggression, insults and vandalism are some of the plagues of France's urban centers and suburbs. Unfortunately, too many places in France are damaged, turned ugly and dangerous because of the lack of social respects of some uncivilized individuals. Those who attack bus drivers, spit at them, insult women, deface walls with graffiti, take a barbarian pleasure at destroying telephone booths, mailboxes, burn cars for their pleasure. Alas, younger and younger children, 10 years old and even younger are the authors of these acts. Practically every day the press reports cars demolished or persons assaulted, in town, in the subway, in buses. There is also an increase in juvenile delinquency in schools, some close to Paris, but in the provinces too. Students arrive in school with knives, tear gas or guns. The French government is eagerly trying to face the problem, but when one case is solved in one corner, trouble erupts elsewhere. No wonder that there is a growing feeling of insecurity particularly in large cities and in the poorest suburbs.[5] This is an area of French life that needs much improvement and in order to improve the situation the French must look at the very roots of the problem: low salaries, unemployment, insufficient housing and the need of more public responsibility.[6]

Cults are also a problem in France. They attract the young in particular. And when they join these cults they sometimes commit horrible crimes such as desecrating cemeteries in the name of Satan. For instance, there have been many regrettable incidents committed in the south of France against Jewish cemeteries, in Carpentras and Toulon.

Drugs are a plague everywhere, and France unfortunately does not escape it. Ectasy, an amphetamin derived drug prohibited in France since July 9, 1987, is attracting an increasing number of young persons, girls particularly. France is trying to do its share to fight drugs that increase delinquency,[7] crimes, thefts and deaths, but many adults too are taking cocaine, amphetamines or cannabis.

Unemployment, "Le Chômage," with several millions of unemployed and below the threshold of poverty, has been and continues to be in 1999 a plague for the French government and the nation. Even if during 1998 much progress has been achieved in the reduction of unemployment, it still remains an acute problem as it hovers just below the 12% mark. The *chômeurs* (unemployed) have showed that they are no longer willing to meekly accept their lot. They revolted in 1997 and 1998; they occupied official buildings and formed a movement to fight their cause, the MNCP *(Mouvement National des Chômeurs et Précaires)*. They did not get all the funds they demanded, but they demonstrated that they were no longer mere statistics, that they existed as human beings.[8] Jospin, although sincerely sympathetic to their plight, is not willing to give handouts each time the unemployed ask for them. He would like to see most of these unfortunate people reinserted in the active society.

A solution to reduce unemployment: The reduction of work time to 35 hours. In March 1998 the French government adopted a project reducing the weekly work time of French workers to 35 hours. The project was accepted, but many employers fear the consequences for the economy of their plants or businesses. They fear that the plan may not reduce unemployment enough, and that it may even push inflation upward because the plan does not include a decrease in salary. In fact the 35 hours may increase the cost of the hour of work that is already very high in France.[9] What is clear in June 1999, is that French business is still adamantly against Martine Aubry's 35 hours. (See, *Le Point*, No. 1397, June 25, 1999 "Martine Aubry: Le Fiasco des 35 Heures," pp. 54–62.)

Too many civil servants (fonctionnaires).[10] According to reports in the press, civil servants are too many, close to 5 million of them, representing 25% of the active population of France. This means that they take 25% of the State salaries and 40% of the budget, and they are not always used as efficiently as they should.

Another major problem for France is *the problem of immigration and illegal foreign workers.* According to a survey of the INSEE *(Institut National de la Statistique et des Etudes Economiques)*, 50,384 immigrants entered France in 1995, fewer than in 1994, however (64,100), fewer than in 1993 (94,152). They currently represent about 4.2 million individuals. These immigrants come from a great variety of countries seeking work. Half of them are males from Algeria, others from Portugal, Italy, Morocco, Tunisia and Spain. They constitute 60% of the foreign population of France. They live in large cities, one third of them in the suburbs of Paris, and they belong in general to the lower economic strata of French society. Most of them speak their native language; however, some try to speak French to promote their chances of employment. The children of these foreigners tend to be integrated faster because they attend French schools. Most foreign workers are manual laborers (70%), and because of their lack of qualifications, they are the first victims of unemployment. France is trying to integrate them, at least those who are legally in France, and when integrated, they indeed tend to contribute a great deal to the country's economy. Some of these people are occasionally the source of social problems and they are often used by the National Front to promote its racist policies.

France has always attracted a large number of foreigners, workers, but also foreign students, artists and intellectuals. France is a land dedicated to liberty and, in the name of its principles, it has welcomed many foreign political refugees. Since the beginning of the twentieth century France is the European country that has accepted the largest number of immigrants, a great gain to the country most of the time, even though it might be sometimes a problem.

It is true that there remains the acute problem of the "sans papiers" in France, those who entered the country illegally and stayed without residence or work permit. By the end of February 1998 there were 100,000 petitions of regularization by "sans papiers." So far 25,000 have had their petition refused, but the Jospin government wants to give a fair chance to all, even granting French nationality to those who show that they earnestly desire to be integrated in the nation. Still, this problem remains a serious political, economic, social and moral problem for France.

Another acute political and moral problem for France and its people is the haunting of the ghosts of the *Vichy years* during the German occupation. The recent trials of Paul Touvier and of Maurice Papon have reopened wounds in the collective memory of France. Even President Mitterand was alledgedly suspected of secret moments of collaboration with Vichy. With the latest traumatic trial of Maurice Papon, accused of having helped the deportation of 1,500 Jewish children when he was General Secretary of the Gironde Préfecture in Bordeaux, bad memories are revived. What Papon's trial revealed mostly was that it was not only Papon who was tried, but France and the French of the Vichy years. The trial, however, may have had a "purgative" effect, in the sense that the "abscess" was finally opened and the responsibilities that were repressed or denied were finally accepted, hard as it was.

France has many other problems, some that have been mentioned in past chapters, but the following ones need to be listed once more to complete this survey:

Corsica still remains a political problem for the French government as some minorities continue to push for independence.

Illiteracy of children and some adults also remains a problem in France. As respect for authority, for teachers waned, respect for the written text waned too. France recognizes that it must quickly remedy the situation. Some 9% of children still have trouble understanding what they read and even some adults (some say over 10%) also have trouble undertanding the meaning of a simple written text. Eradicating this cultural problem is one of the declared priorities of President Chirac.

Pollution, Asbestos, Radon are being fought with vigor in France, but unfortunately they remain dangerous problems particularly in poor housing complexes, in some older schools and public offices.

Suicides, AIDS (SIDA), Sexual Abuse still require much attention in France at the eve of the Third Millennium.

Terrorism seems to have somewhat abated in 1998–1999, but the French government is conscious that it is a problem that requires the continued vigilance of all since it may reappear at any moment.

The "Brain Drain" is not always a publicized problem in France these days; however, the fact is that many young and not so young persons leave France to work abroad. A number of French students, young workers and even employers are leaving France to go and work abroad, in London, Asia and the United States. When they leave, they generally claim that they are able to find greater opportunities outside of France and that taxes are generally lower. It is true that the new generation arrives on the job market with a world view and considers that its chances are no longer confined to the Hexagone. And those who leave France do not leave only for the money. They think that advancement is often too slow in France, that initiatives are often ignored, and that ambitions are too frequently stifled by a fossilized hierarchy. This has not reached the level of a crisis, fortunately, and perhaps the advent of the Euro and of Europe will take care of the problem.

What About the Glory of French Culture? Is It Dimming?

For hundreds of years, France has been recognized as the cultural hub of Europe and even the world. The French language was the diplomatic chosen language and the language of culture in many countries. The Courts of England and Russia proudly spoke French and French intellectuals and artists were revered abroad. Many foreign intellectuals, including Americans (Hemingway, Gertrude Stein, etc. . . .) chose Paris as their cultural haven.[11]

Lately, however, France's artistic and intellectual activity seems to be weakening and therefore France's place and role as a leader of culture has been perceived as declining, at least in wait for a renaissance. The *grandeur* of France in the past may be responsible for this perception. Because of its past influence and greatness, France is expected today to maintain its past image, but perhaps we should remember that France as it moves in history has new goals of greatness. True, if we look at literature and cinema, France has many fewer *stars* than in the nineteenth and early twentieth centuries, and those who exist, French philosophers, Michel Serres, Jean Baudrillard, Jacques Derrida, for instance, frequently do not live in France and many teach abroad. French intellectual thought, since Structuralism and Deconstruction, seems to be at a standstill. If we look at French TV, there are very few French cultural programs. Most of the shows and even the documentaries are imported from the United States and England. France needs to recover from this decline as it enters the Third Millennium.

What France and the French Should Do in Order to Have a Greater Chance of Success in the New Millennium

Perhaps the French should question the current practices of their state system. They ought to accept changes better and be less conservative. They should stop considering state social benefits as a birthright. If they started with these fundamental changes, perhaps France would be a better place for all the French in 2000 and later. But, without being cynical, we know how the French are attached to their state system and how fiercely they want to protect the privileges that their central government provides, schooling, health care, retirement, employee benefits and long vacations. In fact, if it is so hard for them to cast aside the old traditional state system, it is because it did so well and for so long for them. Yet, this might well be the significant reform that would change France for the better.[12]

The Great Assets of France

Surely, as we have seen, France has problems. It must recover its healthy ambition, regain its confidence in its cultural mission, in its mission and in its leaders. The problems France faces today may actually help in the recovery, forcing a rise in energies, in vitality and creativity and preventing the country from remaining self-satisfied, dormant.

The approaching Millennium is a crucial moment in history. It is the time for France and its people to prove once more that they are not decadent, and can overcome difficulties, that they are more than a nation, but a civilization very much alive.

France is a country still rich in open spaces, situated at the crossroads of Europe, with a population of over 61 million. France is a country that can easily feed its people, and its industry, commerce and economy are still dynamic. France is still a cultural power in spite of its problems and Paris is on the same footing of greatness as Tokyo, or New York. The French cultural patrimony is no doubt one of the richest of Europe, with its monuments, its art treasures and museums.

Some people have seriously asked if, with the New Millennium, with Europe, with the Euro, France was going to disappear, and Jean-Claude Barreau in his *La France va-t-elle disparaître?*[13] waved for a moment the metaphoric specter of sinking Venice in Italy[14] but in the long run remained (prudently) optimistic. He writes: "Si elle se réinventait un avenir, la France, notre cité pourrait redevenir l'école de l'Europe et du monde. En particulier parcequ'elle entretient avec la modernité des rapports plus humains que les Anglo-Saxons, sachant concilier la recherche et le plaisir de vivre; un fort patriotisme avec le métissage; une longue histoire pleine de drames et de gloires, avec un avenir qui ne dépend que de sa foi en elle-même."[15]

France's Future

At the end of this book and at the end of this Millennium, there is absolutely no doubt that, in spite of a myriad of problems, we can only be optimistic for France's future. First of all France is a beautiful country, with magnificent mountains, beaches, forests, rivers and rich fields. Its historic monuments, some dating back to the Romans and to prehistoric man, cathedrals, ancient and modern structures are the pride of France and admired by millions of visitors each year.

France, chiefly, has a certain special *quality of life*, a certain *"joie de vivre"* that cannot be found in many other places. France is a country where one eats very well and where the wines are the finest in the world. France is a country of culture, where children still receive an excellent education. France is also a country where the State watches over the health and happiness of its people during their active life, and after when they retire. France is a country where working people earn good salaries, enjoy many holidays and long paid vacations, and where it is all right to enjoy life fully. France is a country where the family has not fully deteriorated, and where the young and older people are still loved and cared for by close or even distant relatives.

France is the country of freedom, and it cares about human rights. It has no death penalty and refuses to surrender persons to countries who have the death penalty, and it is proud of it.

And, yes, France will remain France even while making Europe work. France's contribution to Europe is essential for political and economic reasons, but also for basic human reasons. The French are, deep down, still attached to true human values and have, throughout their long history, showed that, in their wisdom, they were capable of huge sacrifices that have always pulled them and their friends out the worst chasms.

So, as France is approaching the Third Millennium, there are excellent reasons to bet for "*l'avenir de la France*" (the future of France) within Europe and the world.

Notes

1   See the article of Georges-Marc Benamou in *L'Evènement du Jeudi*, May 29–June 4, 1997, p. 3.

2   Most of the farms in Corsica were receiving an average of 26,000 francs or about $43,000.

3   See *Le Point*, No. 1381, samedi 6 mars 1999, pp. 14–15.

4   But 1997 had in fact less days of strike (455,100) than in 1995.

5   For instance, in Strasbourg in 1997, there were 580 cars burned and at Christmas 1997, some 100 cars were torched again.

6   See *Le Point*, No. 1381, samedi 6 mars 1999, p. 16.

7   Edouard Balladur, in 1992, wrote in his *Dictionnaire de la Réforme* "Le problème des banlieues est un phénomène inquiétant qui menace la paix civile. Il concerne l'ensemble de la politique de tout gouvernement en matière économique, sociale et de sécurité" (The problem of suburbs is very serious because it is a menace against the peace of citizens. It is an economical, social concern for any government and it is also a matter of security).

8   In the weekly magazine *L'Evènement du Jeudi (EDJ)* of January 22–28, 1998, Jacqueline de Linares reports an interview with a *chômeur*, a former chemical technician. In a few words, his situation symbolizes the case of thousands of others when he says: "Toute ma vie, je me suis accroché pour réussir. J'ai travaillé depuis l'âge de 16 ans, payé plus de quarante ans de cotisations. Aujourd'hui, je n'ai droit à rien. Ni à ASSEDIC, ni RMI puisque ma femme travaille, ni retraite puisque je n'ai pas 60 ans. Je suis allé à l'Assemblée la semaine dernière. Les députés ne semblaient pas savoir que nous sommes 20.000 dans ce cas. Nous sommes des oubliés du système" (All my life I struggled to succeed. I was 16 when I started to work and I paid up over forty years of National Insurance Contribution. Today I am not entitled to anything, no ASS, no RMI since my wife is working, no retirement pension since I am not sixty years old. Last week I went to the National Assembly, but the deputies did not seem to be aware that there were 20,000 like me. We are the forgotten ones of the system). Jacqueline de Linares also interviewed Alain Touraine, a prominent French Sociologist. She asked him how he perceived the present situation of unemployment, and he answered that in France today the situation of unemployed was no longer an accident during a life of work, but it had become a permanent condition with few possibilities to get out of it. Touraine may be overly pessimistic, but his opinion reflects the current malaise of the French.

9   Since 1973 the cost of work has increased by 200%, the highest increase in Europe.

10   According to Charles Trueheart, in an article of the *Washington Post Weekly* (July 21–28, 1997 "Letting France Be France." "Its citizens don't want change— they've got the gall to say their country's better than most," one in every five working French people is a government functionary. Trueheart continues: "In a recent poll, nine out of ten French people said that they would be proud to see their children become public servants. . . . That's why 'touching the public service is considered a sacrilege, threatening to undermine the foundations of the state' according to Jacques Chevalier, author of a book *L'Etat de la France.*"

11   See Brian Morton. *Americans in Paris.* Ann Arbor: The Olivia and Hill Press, 1984.

12   See in *Le Point*, No. 1381, 6 mars 1999 the *Lettre de Catherine Pégard* in which she states that President Chirac is earnestly investigating the problems of France today. She writes: "Jacques Chirac s'est fait faire une compilation de tous les rapports qui, ces temps-ci, foisonnent, sur les fonctionnaires, la SNCF, les retraites, etc. Il espère convaincre la droite de réfléchir enfin sur cette France cassée par les privilèges." (Translation: Jacques Chirac has ordered a compilation of all the reports, and they are numerous lately, concerning civil servants, the SNCF, retirements. . . He hopes to convince the Right to finally reflect on this France broken by privileges . . .).

13   Jean-Claude Barreau. *La France va-t-elle disparaître?* Paris, Bernard Grasset, 1997.

14   Barreau, p. 181, writes: "En 1797, à cause de la démission de ses élites, Venise ne fut plus 'avec sa chevelure d'or, son front de marbre' qu'une reine déchue 'languissante au pied des Alpes du Tyrol.
      "En 1997, deux siècles plus tard exactement, la France 'européisée' avec sa chevelure de cathédrales, son front de Grand Louvre, deviendra-t-elle une reine déchue, languissante au pied de la Bundesbank?" In 1797, because of the renunciation of its elite, Venise, 'with its golden hair, with its facades of marble,' was no longer but a fallen queen, 'lying listless at the foot of the Tyrolian Alps.' In 1997, exactly two centuries later, will "Europeanized France," with its hair of cathedrals and its forehead of Great Louvre, become a fallen queen, languid at the foot of the Bundesbank?). Fortunately, even Barreau answers "NO" to his question and remains optimistic for France.

15   Barreau, p.194. Translation: France, if it reinvented its future, our *city* could become again the school for Europe and the world. Particularly because France has with modernity more modern relations than the Anglo-Saxons, because it knows how to conciliate research and the pleasures of life; a strong patriotism with crosscultures; a long history full of dramas and glories, with a future that only depends on its faith in itself.

Appendices

Appendix 1

The list of ministries and ministers is given below because it is indicative of the governing priorities of Prime Minister Lionel Jospin when he came to power in 1997.

The names of appointees, naturally, are given only for reference, as the names may change at any time:

Premier Ministre: Lionel Jospin
Ministre de l'Emploi et de la Solidarité: Mme Martine Aubry
Secrétaire d'Etat chargé de la Santé (health): Bernard Kouchner
Garde des Sceaux; Ministre de la Justice: Mme Elisabeth Guigou
Ministre de l'Intérieur: Jean-Pierre Chevènement
Secrétaire d'Etat for les territoires d'outre mer: Jean-Jack Queyranne
Ministre de l'Education Nationale, de la Recherche et de la Technologie: Claude Allègre
Ministre délégué chargé de l'enseignement dans les écoles: Mme Ségolène Royal
Ministre des Affaires Etrangères: Hubert Védrine
Ministre délégué pour les affaires européennes: Pierre Moscovici
Secrétaire d'Etat à la Coopération et à la Francophonie: Charles Josselin
Ministre de l'Economie, des Finances et de l'Industrie: Dominique Strauss-Kahn
Secrétaire d'Etat au Commerce extérieur: Jacques Dondoux
Secrétaire d'Etat chargé du Budget: Christian Sautter
Secrétaire d'Etat chargé des PME, du Commerce et de l'Artisanat: Mme Marylise Lebranchu
Secrétaire d'Etat chargé de l'Industrie: Christian Pierret

Secrétaire d'Etat pour les Anciens Combattants (veterans): Jean-Pierre
    Masseret
Ministre de la Défense: Alain Richard
Ministre de l'Equipement, des transports et du Logement: Jean-Claude
    Gayssot
Secrétaire d'Etat chargé du Tourisme: Mme Michelle Demessine
*Ministre de la Culture, de la Communication et Porte-parole (spokes-
    woman) du gouvernement*: Mme Catherine Trautmann
Ministre de l'Agriculture et de la pêche: Louis le Pensec
Ministre de l'Aménagement du territoire et de l'Environnement: Mme
    Dominique Voynet
Ministre des relations avec le Parlement: Daniel Vaillant
*Ministre de la fonction publique, de la réforme de l'Etat et de la
    décentralisation:* Emile Zuccarelli
Ministre de la Jeunesse et des Sports: Mme Marie-George Buffet

Appendix 2
The Symbols of the French Republic

The French Flag
The main symbol of any nation is its flag and France is no exception. The
French flag, used during all civil and military ceremonies and flying from
most official buildings, is the Blue-White and Red tricolor flag, the blue
being closest to the staff. It is an emblem of the Fifth Republic. In fact it
was instituted officially as the national flag in the constitutions of 1946
and 1958 (see Article 2). But it has a longer history. It originated during
the French Revolution, borrowing the color of the king (white) and the
blue and red colors of Paris. The law of February 15, 1794 (27 Pluviôse),
established the tricolor flag as the national flag of the Revolution. The
white royalist flag was briefly reintroduced during the post-Napoleon restoration, but Louis-Philippe reinstated the tricolor flag, adding the rooster
on top of the staff. Even the Royalists accepted the tricolor flag about
1914.

The Celebration of the French National Holiday: July 14
Next to the flag, the celebration of July 14, also called "Bastille Day" by
Anglo-Saxons, is another strong symbol of France. Foreigners who call
the French National Holiday "Bastille Day" are quite right because it first
commemorates in France the storming of the royal prison in Paris, the
Bastille, which took place during the Revolution on July 14, 1789.

Although historians have established recently that the storming of the Bastille was not much of an event because there were inside the prison only a handful of guards watching few prisoners, it somehow became a symbol of victory of the people against the monarchy, the Ancien Régime. After the Revolution, the celebration was forgotten until July 6, 1880, when Benjamin Raspail, a French député, proposed that July 14 be made a National Holiday. Parliament passed an act making July 14 France's National Holiday. Today July 14 is still an official and popular celebration in Paris and the provinces, with in Paris a parade down the Champs Elysées and a show of the French air force flying overhead. After the parade there are fireworks and public dances all over France.

The National Anthem: La Marseillaise
"Allons enfants de la patrie, le jour de gloire est arrivé. . . . " (Arise you children of our motherland, now our glorious day is here. . . .

Like for most nations, the French National Anthem is the incarnation of the values of the country and the patriotic pride of its people. In France the National Anthem was born during the Revolution as a hymn to freedom.

Why is it called "La Marseillaise"? Because the song was sung by the rebelling volunteer soldiers from Marseille as they attacked the Tuileries in Paris. The anthem was composed by a French officer, Rouget de Lisle, during the night of April 25–26, 1792, as a battle song of the army of the Rhine following the declaration of war of the Revolutionary forces against Austria. Rouget de Lisle was recognized later by having his ashes transported to the Invalides on July 14, 1915, under the Third Republic. The song was found symbolic and so strong that on July 14, 1795, it was adopted as France's national anthem. Under Napoleon's Empire and during the Restoration, the Marseillaise was banned, but it was reinstated during the 1830 Revolution with a musical orchestration by one of France's great musicians, Hector Berlioz. In 1887 a commission of professional musicians established an official version of the song, tune and harmony. The French Constitutions of 1946 and 1958 (Article 2) reaffirm the Marseillaise as the official French National Anthem.

The Nation's Motto: "Liberté, Egalité, Fraternité"
Not too surprisingly, the French motto "Liberté, Egalité, Fraternité" appeared during the French Revolution. Fallen into disuse during the Empire and the Restoration, it was adopted again as a symbol and principle of the Republic by the 1848 Constitution and again in the Constitutions

of 1946 and 1958. The motto is no longer painted on façades of buildings, but is used on coins and postage stamps. With the advent of the common monetary system (Euro), the motto will disappear from common currency coins.

The Bust of Marianne: Nickname and Embodiment of the French Republic

If the French flag is the main symbol of the French Republic, the female figure (bust) of Marianne embodies the republic in town halls (mairies) and on some postage stamps and coins. The bust of Marianne appeared during the Revolution, which explains why she is sometimes represented crowned with a Phrygian hat, the symbol of liberty worn by freed Greek and Roman slaves and adapted by the Revolution and worn by anti-monarchist fighters, the *sans-culottes* (name given by the aristocrats to the revolutionaries who had replaced the men's culottes or knee breeches by regular pantalons, or trousers). More recently Marianne was given the features of famous French actresses, Brigitte Bardot (which shows that its revolutionary origins are being forgotten). Recently the *mairie* of a small town adopted the bust of a black woman in order to celebrate France's social diversity.

The Coq Gaulois (Gallic Rooster): An Almost Forgotten Emblem of the French Nation

The rooster was never much in Favor after having been a symbol of Gaul and of the Gauls. It was resuscitated in 1830 when it adorned the buttons of the French National Guard, and during the Third Republic. The gates of the Elysées Palace (the presidential residence) are adorned with a rooster and some coins were struck with the rooster in the nineteenth century. It is represented also on shoulder and breast patches during sports events. But on the whole, the Gallic rooster has fallen into disuse, except for its presence on the Seal of State.

The Seal of State

Used today only rarely for signatures of Constitutions and amendments, the Seal of State is seldom used or seen. It dates back to the Second Republic and represents a seated woman, symbol of liberty, holding fasces in her right hand and her left hand resting upon a helm upon which stands a Gallic rooster whose claws rest on a globe. Next is represented an urn, symbol of the universal suffrage. At the foot of Liberty lie symbols of the fine arts and agriculture with the motto: "République Française démocratique une et indivisible" and, on the reverse side two other mottoes: "Au nom du peuple français" and above "Liberté, Egalité, Fraternité". The Seal of State is kept in the Ministry of Justice by the Garde des Sceaux (Keeper of Seals).

Vanishing Symbols: The Béret, the Gauloise, Cafés serving "Gros Rouge" or Café-Calvados, Bread, the Typical Frenchman in the Movies

The French black béret (Basque) has become more a fiction or a stereotype for the movies than a reality. This well-known cherished Gallic symbol exploited by publicity is practically extinct except in some isolated rural areas. Similarly the Frenchman dangling a Gauloise cigarette from his lips is more and more rare. In fact the manufacturers of Gauloises and Gitanes cigarettes admit that there is a marked decline in cigarette smoking as well as more popularity for other brands, American cigarettes in particular. Reduced sales are bringing SEITA to close some of its plants.

The cafés are closing fast too. In fact some people declare that the 150,000 cafés are "endangered species" because the French, while declaring that cafés are an essential part of French life, prefer to stay at home and watch television.

French bread is also somewhat menaced, and this is due to the current marked decline in bread consumption by French families. The consumption was of 500 grams per person in the mid-1930's, and in 1998 it is down to 60 grams.

Another fading breed is the traditional Frenchman as pictured in the movies, the Jean Gabin or Maurice Chevalier type. In other words, wearing a béret with a Gauloise dangling from your mouth, on a bicycle carrying a baguette, or kissing a girl like in Robert Doisneau's "kissing couple" are definitively old symbols of the past. These symbols are now hopelessly "passés" like the Breton hats and Provincial costumes (except when worn during festivals or folkloric events).

Appendix 3

French text of some articles of the French Constitution of the Fifth Republic concerning the President of the Republic.

Article 5:
Le Président de la République veille au respect de la Constitution.

Article 8:

Le Président de la République nomme le Premier Ministre. Il met fin à ses fonctions sur la présentation par celui-ci de la démission du Gouvernement.

Sur la proposition du Premier Ministre, il nomme les autres membres du Gouvernement et met fin à leurs fonctions.

Article 9:

Le Président de la République préside le Conseil des Ministres.

Article 12:

Le Président de la République peut, après consultation du Premier Ministre et des présidents des Assemblées, prononcer la dissolution de l'Assemblée Nationale.

Il ne peut être procédé à une nouvelle dissolution dans l'année qui suit les élections qui ont suivi la dissolution.

Article 17:

Le Président de la République a le droit de faire grâce.

Appendix 4

The 14 major ministerial agencies are:

1 *Ministère de l'Intérieur et de l'Aménagement du Territoire:* This agency is in charge of the national police and of maintaining public and national security.
2 *Ministère des Affaires Etrangères:* This agency deals with all foreign relations and problems.
3 *Ministère de l'Education Nationale et de l'Enseignement Supérieur et de la Recherche:* This agency deals with the formation of the young as well as with graduate studies and research.
4 *Ministère de la Défense Nationale:* This agency involves national security, defense of the French territories, involving all the branches of the army, the police to maintain or reestablish order.
5 *Ministère de l'Economie et des Finances:* This agency is in charge of national finances and taxes.
6 *Ministère de la Communication:* This agency is in charge of public information. It works closely with the ministries of Culture and Audivisual.
7 *Ministère de l'Agriculture, de la Pêche et de l'Alimentation:* This agency deals with all aspects of agriculture, including forests, fishing and food products.

8 *Ministère de la Justice*: This agency is under the juridiction of the Garde des Sceaux, whose role is to manage magistrates, justice professions and justice administration.

9 *Ministère de la Culture*: This agency is in charge of national culture; it deals with national archives, books, museums, theater, plays, music, dance, plastic arts, cinema, and the audiovisual.

10 *Ministère de l'Aménagement du Territoire, de la Ville et de l'Intégration*: This agency deals with all problems of immigration, foreign workers, persons without documents, etc. . . .

11 *Ministère de la Coopération*: This agency deals with developing countries, giving them financial and technical assistance.

12 *Ministère de l'Equipement, du Logement, des Transports et du Tourisme*: This agency tries to improve the environment of people through architecture. For instance, it looks for innovative modes of public transportation within cities and outside, and it also tries to improve the image of cities.

13 *Ministère de la Santé*: This agency deals generally with health, hospitals, and protection of food consumers.

14 *Ministère du Travail et des Affaires sociales*: This agency deals with work conditions, employment, salaries, etc. . . .

Appendix 5
List of French Departments, Including Their Code Numbers

01 Ain; 02 Aisne; 03 Allier; 04 Alpes-de-Haute Provence; 05 Hautes-Alpes; 06 Alpes Maritimes; 07 Ardèche; 08 Ardennes; 09 Ariège; 10 Aube; 11 Aude; 12 Aveyron; 13 Bouches-du-Rhône; 14 Calvados; 15 Canta; 16 Charente; 17 Charente-Maritime; 18 Cher; 19 Corrèze; 20 Haute-Corse; 21 Côte-d'Or; 22 Côte-du-Nord; 23 Creuse; 24 Dordogne; 25 Doubs; 26 Drôme; 27 Eure; 28 Eure-et-Loir; 29 Finistère; 30 Gard; 31 Haute-Garonne; 32 Gers; 33 Gironde; 34 Hérault; 35 Ile-et-Vilaine; 36 Indre; 37 Indre-et-Loire; 38 Isère; 39 Jura; 40 Landes; 41 Loir-et-Cher; 42 Loire; 43 Haute-Loire; 44 Loire-Atlantique; 45 Loiret; 46 Lot; 47 Lot-et-Garonne; 48 Lozère; 49 Maine-et-Loire; 50 Manche; 51 Marne; 52 Haute-Marne; 53 Mayenne; 54 Meurthe-et-Moselle; 55 Meuse; 56 Morbihan; 57 Moselle; 58 Nièvre; 59 Nord; 60 Oise; 61 Orne; 62 Pas-de-Calais; 63 Puy-de-Dôme; 64 Pyrénées Atlantiques; 65 Hautes-Pyrénées; 66 Pyrénées Orientales; 67 Bas Rhin; 68 Haut Rhin; 69 Rhône; 70 Haute-Saône; 71 Saône-et-Loire; 72 Sarthe; 73 Savoie; 74 Haute Savoie; 75 Paris; 76 Seine-Maritime; 77 Seine-et-Marne; 78 Yvelines; 79 Deux-Sèvres; 80 Somme; 81 Tarn; 82 Tarn-et-Garonne; 83 Var; 84

Vaucluse; 85 Vendée; 86 Vienne; 87 Haute-Vienne; 88 Vosges; 89 Yonne; 90 Territoire de Belfort; 91 Essonne; 92 Hauts-de-Seine; 93 Seine-St Denis; 94 Val-de-Marne; 95 Val d'Oise.

There are four overseas departments: Martinique, Guadeloupe, Réunion and French Guiana.

Appendix 6
France's Regions as Political Entities: Basic Facts and Statistics
(These facts may vary from one year to another, and are given here only as general average estimates)

1. Alsace:

Préfecture: Strasbourg. Two departments: Bas-Rhin (capital Strasbourg) and Haut-Rhin (capital Colmar).

Surface: 8,280 km2 (5,145 miles), 1.5% of Metropolitan France. Population (1994): 1,662,000 inhabitants, 2.9% of the population of Metropolitan France. Unemployment (1995): 7.1% compared to France, 11.7%. Alsace has been considered a fief of the Front National, but such allegiances tend to fluctuate in time.

2. Aquitaine:

Préfecture: Bordeaux. Four departments: Dordogne (capital Périgueux); Gironde (capital Bordeaux); Lot-et-Garonne (capital Agen); Pyrénées Atlantiques (capital Pau).

Surface: 41,308 km2 (25,668 square miles), 7.6% of Metropolitan France. Population (1994): 2,857,056 inhabitants, 4.9% of Metropolitan France. Unemployment (1995): 12.9%. Aquitaine was a fief of Alain Juppé, Chirac's former Prime Minister, elected Mayor of Bordeaux in 1995. The region although rich in wine, suffers from under-industrialization. It has a relatively low density of population with 68 inhabitants per km2.

3. Auvergne:

Préfecture: Clermont-Ferrand. Four departments: Allier (capital Moulins); Cantal (capital Aurillac); Haute-Loire (capital Le Puy–en-Velay); Puy-de-Dôme (capital Clermont-Ferrand).

Surface: 26,013 km2 (16,164 square miles), 4.7% of Metropolitan France. Population (1994): 1,314,260 inhabitants, 2.3% of Metropolitan France. Unemployment (1995): 10.6% or slightly higher. Auvergne suffers greatly of lack of industries and unemployment. The low figure of unemployment given does not take into account a large number of rural workers who can escape the census.

4. Bourgogne:

Préfecture: Dijon. Four departments: Côte d'Or (capital Dijon); Nièvre (capital Nevers); Saône-et-Loire (capital Mâcon); Yonne (capital Auxerre).

Surface: 31,582 km2 (19,625 square miles), 5.8% of Metropolitan France. Population (1994): 1,613,016 inhabitants, 2.8% of France. Unemployment (1995): 11.0%. Bourgogne (Burgundy) is a region rich in great wines and in tourism.

5. Bretagne:

Préfecture: Rennes. Four departments: Côtes-d'Armor (capital Saint-Brieuc); Finistère (capital Quimper); Ille-et-Villaine (capital Rennes); Morbihan (capital Vannes).

Surface: 27,208 km2 (16,906 miles), 2.5% of France. Population (1994): 2,835,374 inhabitants, 4.9% of France. Unemployment (1995): 10.5%. Brittany is suffering because of the decline in fishing activities and in naval constructions and military installations.

6. Centre:

Préfecture: Orléans. Six departments: Cher (capital Bourges); Eure-et-Loir (capital Chartres); Indre (capital Châteauroux); Indre-et-Loire (capital Tours); Loir-et-Cher (capital Blois), Loiret (capital Orléans).

Surface: 39,151 km2 (24,327 square miles), 7.2% of France. Population (1994): 2,411,905 inhabitants, 4.2% of France. Unemployment: 10.8%. The region wants to change its name to *Centre-Val-de-Loire*, but Parliament has yet to approve it.

7. Champagne-Ardennes:

Préfecture: Châlons-en-Champagne. Four departments: Ardennes (capital Charleville-Mézières); Aube (capital Troyes); Marne (capital Châlons-en-Champagne), Haute-Marne (capital Chaumont).

Surface: 25,606 km2 (15,911 square miles), 4.7% of France. Unemployment (1995): 12.3%.

8. Franche Comté-Territoire de Belfort:

Préfecture: Besançon. Four departments: Doubs (capital Besançon); Jura (capital Lons-le-Saulnier); Haute-Saône (capital Vesoul); Territoire de Belfort (capital Belfort).

Surface: 16,202 km2 (10,067 square miles), 3% of France. Population (1994): 1,110,122 inhabitants, 1.9% of France. Unemployment (1995): 9.0%.

9. Languedoc-Roussillon:

Préfecture: Montpellier. Five departments: Aude (capital Carcassonne); Gard (capital Nîmes); Hérault (capital Montpellier); Lozère (capital Mende), Pyrénées-Orientales (capital Perpignan).

Surface: 27,376 km2 (17,011 square miles), 5% of France. Population (1994): 2,203,270 inhabitants, 3.8% of France. Unemployment (1995): 16.1%.

10. Limousin:
Préfecture: Limoges. Three departments: Corrèze (capital Tulle); Creuse (capital Guéret); Haute-Vienne (capital Limoges).
Surface: 16,942 km2 (10,527 square miles), 3% of France. Population (1994): 718,860 inhabitants, 1.2% of France. Unemployment (1995): 9.3%. Depopulation is a serious problem in Limousin.

11. Lorraine:
Préfecture: Metz. Four departments: Meurthe-et-Moselle (capital Nancy); Meuse (capital Bar-le-Duc); Moselle (capital Metz); Vosges (capital Epinal).
Surface: 23,547 km2 (14,631 square miles), 4.3% of France. Population, (1994): 2,294,780 inhabitants, 4.0% of France. Unemployment (1995): 10.4%.

12. Midi-Pyrénées:
Préfecture: Toulouse. Eight departments: Ariège (capital Foix); Aveyron (capital Rodez); Haute-Garonne (capital Toulouse); Gers (capital Auch); Lot (capital Cahors); Hautes-Pyrénées (capital Tarbes); Tarn (capital Albi), Tarn-et-Garonne (capital Montauban).
Surface: 45,348 km2 (28,178 square miles), 8.3% of France; Unemployment (1995): 11.1%.

13. Nord-Pas-de-Calais:
Préfecture: Lille. Two departments: Nord (capital Lille), Pas-de-Calais (capital Arras).
Surface: 12,414 km2 (7,714 square miles), 2.3% of France. Population (1994): 3,988,569 inhabitants, 6.9% of France. Unemployment (1995): 15.4%.

14. Basse Normandie:
Préfecture: Caen. Three departments: Calvados (capital Caen); Manche (capital Saint Lô); Orne (capital Alençon).
Surface: 17,589 km2 (10,929 square miles), 3.2% of France. Population (1994): 1,408,925 inhabitants, 2.4% of France. Unemployment (1995): 11.5%.

15. Haute Normandie:
Préfecture: Rouen. Two departments: Eure (capital Evreux); Seine-Maritime (capital Rouen).

Surface: 12,317 km2 (7,653 square miles), 2.3% of France. Population (1994): 1,767,367 inhabitants, 3% of France. Unemployment (1995): 13.8%.

16. Pays de la Loire:
Préfecture: Nantes. Five departments: Loire-Atlantique (capital Nantes); Maine-et-Loire (capital Angers); Mayenne (capital Laval); Sarthe (capital Le Mans); Vendée (capital La Roche-sur-Yon).
Surface: 32,082 km2 (19,935 square miles), 5.9% of France. Population (1994): 3,132,433 inhabitants, 5.4% of France. Unemployment (1995): 11.7%.

17. Picardie:
Préfecture: Amiens. Three departments: Aisne (capital Laon); Oise (capital Beauvais); Somme (capital Amiens).
Surface: 19,399 km2 (1,054 square miles), 3.6% of France. Population (1994): 1,858,645 inhabitants, 3.2% of France. Unemployment (1995): 12.2%.

18. Poitou-Charentes:
Préfecture: Poitiers. Four departments: Charente (capital Angoulême); Charente-Maritime (capital La Rochelle); Deux-Sèvres (capital Niort); Vienne (capital Poitiers).
Surface: 25,810 km2 (16,038 square miles); 4.7% of France. Population (1994): 1,625,177 inhabitants, 2.8% of France. Unemployment (1995): 11.9%.

19. Provence-Alpes-Côte d'Azur:
Préfecture: Marseille. Six departments: Alpes-de-Haute Provence (capital Digne); Hautes-Alpes (capital Gap); Alpes-Maritimes (capital Nice); Bouches-du-Rhône (capital Marseille); Var (capital Toulon); Vaucluse (capital Avignon).
Surface: 31,400 km2 (19,511 square miles), 5.8% of France. Population (1994): 4,404,377 inhabitants, 7.6% of France. Unemployment (1995): 14.9%.

20. Rhône-Alpes:
Préfecture: Lyon. Eight departments: Ain (capital Bourg-en-Bresse); Ardèche (capital Privas); Drôme (capital Valence); Isère (capital Grenoble); Loire (capital Saint Etienne); Rhône (capital Lyon); Savoie (capital Chambéry); Haute-Savoie (capital Annecy).

Surface: 43,698 km2 (27,153 square miles), 8% of France. Population (1994): 5,521,219 inhabitants, 10% of France. Unemployment (1995): 10.8%.

21. Région Parisienne–Ile-de-France:
Préfecture: Paris. Eight departments: Paris (capital Paris); Seine-et-Marne (capital Melun); Yvelines (capital Versailles); Essonne (capital Evry); Hauts-de-Seine (capital Nanterre); Seine-Saint-Denis (capital Bobigny); Val-de-Marne (capital Créteil), Val d'Oise (capital Pontoise).
Surface: 12,012 km2 (7,464 square miles), 2.2% of France. Population (1994): 10,965,142 inhabitants, 19.0% of France. Unemployment (1995): 10.4%.

22. Corse:
Préfecture: Ajaccio. Two departments: Corse-du-Sud (capital Ajaccio), Haute-Corse (capital Bastia).
Surface: 8,680 km2 (5,394 square miles), 1.6% of France. Unemployment (1995): 11.8%.
Corsica has had many problems on account of the rising number of autonomist groups creating violence on the island. Recently (second part of 1998) the French government is trying to return order to the island.

Appendix 7
French Regions Are Not Only *Political Entities* (Appendix 6, They Are also *Cultural Entities*)

If the most extensive collection of art in Europe is to be found in Paris, and most of it is in Le Louvre Museum, art is certainly not absent from the various regions of France where many artists have lived and found their inspiration. Every province, towns and even some villages have their own museums with interesting art collections. In addition French culture in its different regional forms is found most everywhere, in architecture, in local folklore, native handicrafts and in the often rich history of the place.

North-North Western Regions
Normandy, N-NW of Paris, is the land of Duke William the Conqueror, who invaded England in 1066 in order to assert his claim to the English throne. The Medieval Dukes of Normandy encouraged the building of many Romanesque and Gothic religious buildings, many of which are still standing, attesting the rich history of the region. The ancient small town of Bayeux, north of Caen, not only possesses a large cathedral dating from the eleventh century, but also houses the famous *Tapisserie de la*

Reine Mathilde. It is in fact an embroidery representing scenes of the Conquest of Normandy by William and his victory over the English at Hastings in 1066. South of Bayeux, Caen is the capital of lower Normandy, where in the eleventh century William the Conqueror and his wife Mathilda lived. They are remembered there by the castle which they started to build overlooking the town, and by two major abbeys, the magnificent Romanesque *Abbaye aux Hommes* and *Abbayes aux Dames,* where each are respectively buried.

Closer to our times, the coastal towns of Trouville, Honfleur and Dieppe attract many tourists and have brought many artists because of the very special quality of the light of their area. Trouville is mostly associated with Courbet and his American friend Whistler, Manet, Valloton and Matisse. Dieppe became known thanks to Degas, who also brought there Whistler and the English painter Walter Sickert. Honfleur gave birth to the great landscape and seascape artist Eugène Boudin, who greatly influenced Monet.

Normandy is alas also famous for its *D-Day beaches* and extensive war cemeteries, reminding of World War II and the terrible fighting which took place there when the Allied landed to liberate France from the Germans.

Brittany is certainly one of the most individually distinct and picturesque areas of regional France with its very ancient prehistoric and Celtic past. Brittany has an incredible number of prehistoric monuments, standing stones or *Menhirs,* or flat, table-like stone monuments or *Dolmens.* Carnac, in the south of the region, has about 3,000 of these prehistoric aligned stones and tables dating from 2000 BC. Next, Brittany possesses a real jewel, one of Europe's greatest abbeys, the *Mont Saint Michel,* which is a monastery and Medieval fortress with imposingly high ramparts and frequently surrounded by the sea with huge tides. The building is dominated by the spire of the eleventh-century abbey church dedicated to the Archangel Saint Michael. It is a beautiful example of medieval architecture and an austere, inspiring place which attracts millions of tourists.

The Loire region, including Anjou, Berry and Orléanais, south of Brittany and of Normandy is famous for its wonderful châteaux dating from the fifteenth and sixteenth centuries. The royal courts at that time attracted many renowned artists from the Italian Renaissance and their influence may be seen and appreciated today in châteaux such as Blois, Chambord, Amboise, Azay-le-Rideau and Chenonceau along the Loire. It must be noted that King Francis I, an admirer of Italian Renaissance culture, was responsible for inviting the great Leonardo da Vinci to Amboise in 1516. Leonardo came to France and brought among many important paintings the famous *Joconde* (Mona Lisa) and settled at the foot of the château d'Amboise at the Clos-Lucé residence, where he died. Along the Loire, the town of Angers is famous with its twelfth–thirteenth centuries cathedral, but mostly because its medieval castle houses the magnificent tapestries of the Apocalypse (1373). East of Angers, along the Loire, the city of Tours still keeps vivid traces of its great medieval catherdral Saint Gatien, when the cult of Saint Martin was at its height. Tours has seen some great artists like the fifteenth-century painter Jean Fouquet and the great nineteenth-century novelist Honoré de Balzac, who included Tours at the core of one of his series of novels, *Le Curé de Tours*.

The Northeastern Regions of France:
Picardie, Vosges, Alsace, Lorraine and Champagne

These northeastern regions are very rich in history, for the better and sometimes for the worse. For the better they were very active economic and intellectual centers in the Middle Ages, with textile industries, fairs and great drama centers. For the worse, the regions have many memories of invasions and wars, with several episodes of German occupation. The towns of Strasbourg, Mulhouse, Colmar, and Metz have kept many German features, in their dialect and architecture. Strasbourg's rich history and cultural legacy is best represented by its museums and by its cathedral Notre Dame, one of the finest examples extant of Gothic architecture. In Champagne, the town of Reims deserves a special mention outside of its production of famous Champagne wines, because it was in Reims that a whole line of French kings were consecrated and crowned since Clovis, king of the Franks, was baptised a Christian by Bishop Saint Rémi.

The Regions of Eastern France:
Jura, Franche-Comté and Burgundy

Of all these regions, the most outstanding culturally is no doubt Burgundy with its famous vineyards dating from the Middle Ages and for its rich history dominated by the Dukes of Burgundy. Outstanding are the towns of Dijon and Beaune. Beaune, at the center of Côte d'Or has preserved from the Middle Ages the famous Hôtel Dieu, founded in 1443 as a charity hospital, and Dijon, which at its heyday was the ducal and cultural capital of the region, particularly under Philip the Bold. Dijon's cathedral, Saint Bénigne, is a beautiful fourteenth century Gothic structure, and the

Eglise St Michel is admired for its pure Renaissance-style façade. One cannot leave Burgundy without mentioning the hilltop village of Vézelay with its remarkable pilgrimage church and abbey, the Basilique Ste Madeleine, founded in the nineth century and with a superb tympanum, a masterpiece of the genre. Not far from Vézelay are two important religious centers, Autun and Cluny. Autun with its pilgrimage church in which the great Saint Bernard de Clairvaux preached to the pilgrims on their way to Santiago de Compostela in northwestern Spain, and Cluny, where one discovers the famous and impressive Benedictine abbey with its gigantic church and the memory of its 10,000 monks in the thirteenth century.

Supreme among the great artists of Franche Comté in the Jura area is Gustave Courbet, who loved the land of the Doubs river and was inspired by it, particularly by the town of Ornans, where his remains are buried.

The Western and Southwestern Regions (from La Rochelle to Bordeaux, to Bayonne and from Narbonne to Bayonne along the Pyrénées)

Most of the area around Bordeaux was part of the province of Aquitaine that fell to the hands of the English during the Middle Ages when Eleanor of Aquitaine married Henry II of England in 1152. This marriage brought about a lengthy conflict between France and England, the Hundred Years War. This area, particularly north of Bordeaux, knew great devastations during the sixteenth century's Wars of Religion. To the southeast of the region are two major towns, Albi and Toulouse. Albi's red medieval fortress-like cathedral overlooks a famous museum dedicated to the artist Henri de Toulouse-Lautrec situated in the Palais de la Berbie. Toulouse, once the capital of Languedoc, is a great city of culture and industry. Its Basilica Saint Sernin, dating from the eleventh century, is one of the finest examples of Romanesque architecture. Bordeaux on the Atlantic seaboard is the capital of Aquitaine. Its greatest period was the eighteenth century, as reflected in its architecture. In the eastern part of the region, one must mention the old medieval city of Carcassonne situated on a hill above the modern town and surrounded by imposing ramparts. The fortifications, it must be said, do not date from the Middle Ages as they would appear at first sight, but are the result of a restoration by the nineteenth-century architect Viollet-le-Duc. However, for a modern restoration, it is quite "authentic."

Perhaps the most striking cultural interest of the region is that it was in the Middle Ages, and to some extent it remains today, a corridor of pilgrim transit from the main Catholic shrines of Europe to the great cathedral of Santiago de Compostela in northwestern Spain. From Saint Denis and Paris, from Vézelay, Autun, Le Puy, Tours and Bordeaux, from Arles, Moissac, Conques, Toulouse, and from all over Europe, pilgrims passed and still pass today through Roncevaux in the Pyrénées down to Pamplona or Burgos and west to Santiago de Compostela.

The Region of Central France

The Central France region is limited at the north by the city of Bourges, by the towns of Moissac and Rodez in the south, by Brantôme and Saint Savin in the west and by Moulins and Le Puy in the east. Of all the areas of this region, the Dordogne is the richest culturally with its prehistoric caves, paintings and particularly with the famous sites of Lascaux and Les Eyzies dating back at least 25,000 years.

Southeastern and Southern France: From Lyon to the Mediterranean and from Carcassonne to Menton

This region is dominated in the east by the Alps, between France and Italy, and bordered in the south by the Mediterranean along the Côte d'Azur. In the north, several important towns must be mentioned on account of their rich cultural tradition: Lyon, on the two rivers Saône and Rhône, once the capital of Roman Gaul, and later a great silk production center. Today, Lyon is France's second largest city ahead of Marseille. Grenoble, in the Alps, is a renowned university town and a key scientific research center. In the south, in lovely, warm Provence, the town of Aix-en-Provence is an important university center and an important former Roman spa. Aix-en-Provence is also Cézanne's town on account of the many paintings he painted around Aix-en-Provence, particularly the Montagne Sainte Victoire. Avignon, northwest of Aix-en-Provence, on the Rhône, has a rich cultural heritage dating back to the years of residence of the Popes in the fourteenth century, with ramparts still standing around the city and overlooking the Rhône. It is in or close to Avignon that the poet Petrarca met the famous Beatrice.

The beauty of Provence has been appreciated by many artists like Van Gogh, who moved to Arles from Paris, Renoir, who painted Cagnes, Matisse in Nice, Picasso in Antibes and Vallauris, Chagall in Vence, Fernand Léger in Biot and of course Cézanne around Aix-en-Provence, to mention only the major ones.

Paris and the Ile de France

Paris, which cannot be told in a paragraph, is the driving center of France's politics, administration, art, culture, music and theater. It has been spared by wars and, although Hitler wanted to blow it up at the end of WWII, it came out intact thanks to the intelligence of some German generals who could not bring themselves to destroy this important and marvelous city. Paris is a monument to history and a model for the present and future. In the Middle Ages, Paris saw the construction of beautiful cathedrals and churches such as Notre Dame de Paris, a masterpiece of Gothic art dating from the twelfth and thirteenth centuries, and with a 270-foot tall central spire; La Sainte Chapelle, a glittering jewel of flamboyant Gothic art constructed in 1246 by king Saint Louis to hold the Crown of Thorns; and the Saint Germain-des-Prés church. Many artists have left their mark in Paris, such as Manet, Courbet, Gauguin, Matisse, and Picasso. Paris is also the seat of the most important university center of France, La Sorbonne, surrounded by a dozen of satellite campuses in the city and outside. The symbol of Paris is the Eiffel Tower, built in 1889 for the International Exhibition. Paris has at least 40 museums, the greatest of which is Le Louvre along the Seine.

The Ile de France region is famous for many Gothic buildings like the Cathedral of Chartres with its splendid thirteenth-century stained-glass windows, and it is well known too for its many royal residences like Versailles and Fontainebleau. The Ile de France has attracted many artists, Corot, Millet, Van Gogh and Monet, for instance.

Paris and the Ile de France are simply too rich to be described in a few lines, but to sacrifice to modern times, we must mention the recent arrival, 20 miles east of Paris, of Disneyland Paris, a popular tourist attraction with a strong US flavor, not to the taste of everyone in France.

Appendix 8

Brief Information on the Various Major French Trade Unions: CGT, FO, CFDT, CFTC, and FEN:

a. CGT.

The *Confédération générale du travail* was founded in 1895, a basically revolutionary socialist organization with a heavy communist representation (about 200,000–250,000). The current secretary-general of this powerful union is Louis Viannet.

b. FO or CGT-FO.

Force ouvrière was founded in 1947 and its membership is made up of mostly public employees, and although the secretary-general, Marc Blondel, is giving this traditionally moderate union a very militant attitude, he has been recently reelected.

c. CFDT.

The *Confédération française démocratique du travail* was created in 1964 by the members of the *Confédération française des travailleurs chrétiens* (dating from 1919) following the members' wish to drop the word "chrétien" from their organization. The CFDT is basically socialist, although not a part of the Socialist party. The well-liked, moderate but strong Nicole Notat was elected secretary-general in 1992 and reelected in March 1995.

d. CFTC.

The *Confédération française des travailleurs chrétiens* lost many of its members in 1964 when they joined the CFDT (above c.). It counts 190 000 members and its current president is Alain Deleu.

e. FEN.

The *Fédération de l'Education nationale* is composed of 33 unions. It is the largest organization in the State education system. Members do not join the FEN directly, but one of the 33 member unions. It was founded in 1928 and was under the hat of the CGT until 1948 when it became independent. The secretary-general of the FEN is currently Guy Le Néouannic.

Appendix 9

Sample of Some Average Monthly Salaries (as of October 1, 1997, According to the EDJ of October 23–29, 1997):
City policeman: 12,075 francs
Social worker: 12,279 francs
Schoolteacher: 15,175 francs
Police chief: 22,733 francs
Lycée professor: 24,621 francs
Lycée head: 28,282 francs
University professor: 31,200 francs to 41,000 francs
Nurse: 14,908 francs to 20,651 francs
Judge: 26,451 francs
Fireman: 8,500 francs

As a postscript we must mention that there is a difference between the private sector and the public sector. It has been said that the average salaries of the public sector, persons working for the state, are about 12% higher than in the private sector. This is particularly true for the 60% of persons employed by the public sector, 1.8 million of them, all being in the teaching profession. However, many others in the public sector such as hospital employees and nurses do not have higher wages than in the private sector.

Appendix 10

Households and Lodgings

According to a 1997 study of the INSEE, the number of main residences in 1996 was of 23.3 million, an increase of almost 300,000 units since 1992. This increase, according to the INSEE survey, is not only due to the increase in population, but it is also due to several factors, such as students who are now receiving a lodging allowance. Other factors are the number of split households due to divorce, the number of persons who delay taking a spouse, and there is also the fact that more older people (65 or older) are staying in their home. On the other hand it is getting more difficult for the young to own a house, and there are more tenants than landlords. See *"Les ménages et leur logement: analyse des enquêtes Logement de l'INSEE,"* Ministère de l'Equipement, des Transports et du Logement, Direction de l'Habitat et de la Construction, *Economica*, 1997, and "Les ménages et leurs logements au milieu des années quatre-vingt-dix," *Economie et Statistique* no. 288–289, 1995–8/9.

Lodging Conditions by the End of 1996

According to a survey of January 1998 by the INSEE, the new trends in lodging see less building of individual houses, but building of larger houses (105 m2) compared to apartments (66 m2) on the average.

The new buildings tend to be warmer and more soundproof. Today less than 4% of lodgings, most of them built before 1949, do not have the minimum comfort, i.e., inside bathrooms, a shower or a bathtub. The percentage keeps decreasing because many older lodgings are either being razed to make place for new constructions, or they are renovated. In apartments, unfortunately, there are still 10% to 20% of persons who do not enjoy the comfort of central heating and who must rely on portable gas or electric heaters. The noise coming from neighbors and chiefly coming from the street is a number one complaint of residents in urban centers, and particularly residents of HLMs, low-cost housing buildings. See the article *INSEE PREMIERE*, No. 563, Janvier 1998.

Appendix 11

History of Franco-American Relations, in Brief:

1:   French explorer Jacques Cartier leaves for America, travels along
the St. Lawrence river and claims territories for France.
The French set up fur trading posts in the New World (1534).

2:   Champlain becomes governor of New France in 1633.
Jean Nicolet, Father Jacques Marquette, Louis Jolliet, de La Salle
explore the Great Lakes, the Mississipi valley (1600's)

3:   La Salle takes possession of the Mississipi valley, Louisiana in the
name of the king of France (1682)

4:   Many French Huguenots settle in America (1685–1760)

5:   France signs the Treaty of Commerce and Friendship with America
and sends 44,000 French troops to serve during the American War
of Independence (1778–1781)

6:   France sells Louisiana to the United States for 80 million francs
(1803).

7:   France offers the Statue of Liberty to the United States (1886).

8:   The United States enters WWI (1917) and sends 2 million troops
to France. Fifty thousand US soldiers died in France by 1918.

9:   June 6, 1944: D-Day. American troops take part in the Normandy
landings. Over 2 million US soldiers fought in France to end WWII.

10: France joins the USA in the 1990–1991 Gulf war effort to liberate
Kuwait from Iraq.

Appendix 12

In the winter 1998–1999 edition of the magazine *France* (no. 9), there is
a very interesting article by Michel Faure under the heading "Rebel Rouser"
discussing his thoughts on the May 1968 student uprising almost half a
century later. Here is a sample of his article: "There are times when I feel
rather lonely. My erstwhile pals are now media stars, ad execs, politicians,
university professors, persons of influence. Some are in the business world,
others are flirting with power. Some are offering precarious jobs to young
people, others are making the kind of banal statements they once criticized their elders for. . . . I mention all this to put things in perspective. I
don't blame my friends for betraying their ideals. No, I blame them for
forgetting the spirit of their youth, their gusto for taking on the established order. . . ."

Appendix 13
Opinion Survey of the French on Divorce

Both French men and women think that divorce is too easy in France and that people divorce without thinking enough about the consequences. They agree in majority for the establishment of a time of reflection before divorce proceedings are begun. They further think in majority that when children are present, divorce ought to be made more difficult. A large number of persons polled seemed to agree that there perhaps should be a period of trial marriage, in the hope to reduce the number of divorces later on. Finally more than half of men and women polled answered that infidelity was not a sufficient ground for divorce. (This survey was made on August 22–23, 1997, with 601 persons responding).

The reluctance for divorce comes from the fact that most people in France think that couples live better than singles. They point out that they can save on housing, heating and other expenses. Estimates show that a couple needs only 1,5 the income of a single person to live at the same level.

Appendix 14
Major French Museums

A—Some Major Paris Museums:
1—The *Musée du Louvre* is the world's largest museum and growing still, housing the famous Venus de Milo, Leonardo da Vinci's La Joconde (Mona Lisa) and the Victoire de Samothrace (Samothrace victory). 2— The *Centre National d'Art et de Culture* Georges Pompidou, celebrates the artistic creativity of the twentieth century. 3—The *Musée d'Orsay* displays paintings, but also works of cinema and photography. 4—The *Musée Marmottan* houses some Impressionist paintings, including 100 works by Monet. 5—The *Musée Auguste Rodin*. 6—The *Musée Balzac*. 7—The *Musée National Eugène Delacroix*. 8—The *Musée National du Moyen-Age*, Thermes de Cluny, holds among Medieval treasures the "Lady and the Unicorn" tapestry. 9—The *Musée Picasso* with 200 paintings. 10—The *Institut du Monde Arabe* with a rich collection from the Islamic world.

B—Some Interesting or Curious Regional Museums:
1—Ile de France: *Musée National de la Céramique* in Sèvres; *Musée du Cheval de Course*, in Maisons-Laffitte. 2—Indre-et-Loire: *Manoir de Clos-Lucé*, in Amboise with models of Leonardo da Vinci's inventions.

3—Indre-et-Loire: *Musée du Cuir* in Château-Renault; *Maison Natale de Rabelais* in Chinon. 4—Calvados: *Musée de la tapisserie* in Bayeux. 5—Finistère: *Musée de la Pêche* in Concarneau. 6—Morbihan: Musée des Poupées in Josselin. 7—Orne: *Musée du Camembert* in Vimoutiers. 8—Nire: In Château-Chinon, the *Musée du Septennat*, an unusual museum showing the collection of gifts received by President Mitterand since 1981. 9—Haute-Saône: *Musée du Boomerang* in Lure. 10—Rhône: *Musée de la Marionette* in Lyon, featuring puppets from around the world. 11—Dordogne: *Musée du Tabac* in Bergerac. 12—Tarn: *Musée Toulouse Lautrec* in Albi.

Appendix 15

Social Protection and Benefits in France

France has one of the most comprehensive systems of social protection in the world, and since WWII it has been extended to the whole population. The Social protection and Benefits touch many areas of French life: the family, health, retirement, and problems of unemployment.

In health France has an excellent record. The State takes an active role in preventive medicine, in organizing awareness campaigns focused on smoking, alcoholism, cancer and AIDS. Health costs, naturally, have been rising faster than the rate of economic growth. This increase is mostly due to the attempt of covering the whole population and the aging of this population. Persons 70 or older account for a quarter of health expenditures, while they only represent 14% of the population.

This elderly population represents about 8.5 million persons 65 years old or older. In addition to the Social Security benefits, France tries to help these older persons to remain in their familiar surroundings and provides various services such as a network of home nursing care, and retirement homes with medical facilities.

France also takes care of the handicapped, 2.5 million of them. There are special training centers to help those of working age to enter the labor force. The civil service is a major recruiter of dependent handicapped persons.

France has also a comprehensive family policy, providing generous family allowances. There is a grant for the birth of the first child, an allowance for mothers remaining at home to take care of the children and fiscal advantages for large families. These allowances, which originally were to stimulate the birthrate, are now seen more as an aid for low-income families and single parents.

The French government is also trying hard to fight poverty, marginalization and conditions brought about by immigration and unemployment. In December 1988 the State instituted a new minimum allowance called RMI *(Revenu Minimum d'Insertion)*. It is aimed at individuals over the age of 25 whose resources fall below the poverty level that is 2000 francs a month. The goal of the RMI is to help and encourage these people to return to work.

Appendix 16
A Reconsideration of World War I in 1998

Lionel Jospin, current Prime Minister (1998) of the Fifth Republic, has just dared to reconsider the history of World War I and its horrors that have only in common the World War II's absolute horror of the Concentration Camps. Eighty years after World War I, Jospin as well as several historians tried to tell us what was never told about some repugnant aspects of WWI. It is true that, ever since its beginnning to its end, and up to our times, WWI has been represented as a war fought by France and its allies for saving humanity and Western civilization. In other words it was viewed as a sacred war of patriotic sacrifice and heroism to combat the ugly specter of "*les boches*," of Germany. World War I was looked at as the "*der des der*" (the last of the last) and fighting was done in the name of "*plus jamais ça!*" (nevermore that!). It is possible to say that WWI was conceived as a myth almost from the very start, a myth justifying war for soldiers who were also convinced (brainwashed?) that they had to fight to destroy the barbaric Germans who killed, maimed and murdered not only soldiers but women and babies. It must be understood today that it was this profound conviction which helped the French soldiers to stand the horrors of trench warfare and hand-to-hand combat. They found the strength to get up from their muddy trenches because they were told to do that by their officers, and in some way they convinced themselves that they were fighting to prepare a better world after eliminating the devil.

Today some historians and Lionel Jospin too feel that the history of WWI must be revised. They want us to understand today that the war was fought with equal barbaric violence on both sides and that, if the Germans were evil, the French were hardly less at times. They feel that what was covered up must be told now, for instance, that, if it is true that Germans killed prisoners in cold blood, the French did the same thing in the name of their deep-rooted hatred of Germany. They feel that the truth must be told today, and particularly that the heroism of the French *"poilus"* (a friendly nickname for the 1914–1918 French fighters) had a reverse side: exhausted, on the brink of insanity, some sodiers and officers refused to fight anymore, mutinied and were summarily shot to give an example to the others. Soldiers resorted to drinking *"gnole"* (acquavit/ *eau de vie*) in order to muster their strength and leap out of trenches while being almost sure to be mowed down by the enemy's machine guns or speared by bayonets. They took drugs and many indeed became crazy. What has not been told is that they underwent a treatment similar to some of the Nazis' tortures, electrotherapy, a "treatment" that was enough to scare the mentally ill soldiers to return and fight on the front. Modern historians want us to understand today that a part of the soldiers' heroism was the fear of being shot in the head by one of their officers if they hesitated to jump out of the miry trenches.

In the same way that we admired Chirac when he recently expressed France's apology to the Dreyfus family, we feel that it is fortunate that some historians and France's Prime Minister now dared to remove the mythical dust that covered up some somber realities of WWI on the French side.

Appendix 17
May 1968: Thirty Years After

The events of May 1968 have become a legend in the history of modern France. The kids of 1968 burned cars, tore up streets, built barricades in the middle of Paris and clashed with the police in an anti-bourgeoisie insurrection. They thought that they could change the world, and they did in many respects: Women were liberated, sex became less taboo and some aspects of the educational system were improved and to some degree the workplace became more humane. But 30 years later some of the *Soixante-huitards (former kids of 1968)* found themselves in positions of power. The 1968 moment of utopia was long past, and they now realized that aside from some gains, they lost the war to revolutionize France, to find an alternative to Capitalism, an alternative to a society which was ruled by "Papa knows best" and an aloof Gaullist government. The rebels of 1968 are now members of a not so different ruling class than the one they fought thirty years ago and they are, themselves, hardly less rigid in their thinking than their condescending predecessors. In 1968 they fought rigid ideas and now they impose with equal fervor their own brand of fixed ideas in order to avoid making hard choices in the 1990's.[1]

Note

1   The *Journal Français* of July 1998, p. 13, published an interesting article by their correspondant Guillaume Vial on the aftermath of 1968. Vial quotes the writer François Sureau, who said that the 1968 movement was for a major part the revolt of young people who were afraid to work (sic) and who rejected the patriarcal society of de Gaulle and of their fathers. According to Vial the situation of 1998 is very different and 1968 is even contested or rejected. So he sees the playing up of 1968 at the occasion of its anniversary as a media trick seeking sensationalism.

Bibliography

General

Ardagh, John. *France Today*. Penguin Books, 1988.

Bernstein, Richard. *Fragile Glory. A Portrait of France and the French*. A Plum Book, 1991.

Bersani, Jacques, Autrand, Michel, Lecarme, Jacques, and Vercier, Bruno. *La Littérature en France depuis 1945*. Paris-Montreal: Bordas, 1970.

Bouillon, J; Sorlin and Rudel, J. *Le Monde Contemporain. Histoire—Civilisation*. Collection d'Histoire dirigée par Louis Girard. Paris: Bordas, 1962.

Cole, Robert. *A Traveller's History of France*. New York: Interlink Books, 1995.

Corbett, James. *Through French Windows. An Introduction to France in the Nineties*. Ann Arbor: University of Michigan Press, 1994.

Curtius, Ernst Robert. *The Civilization of France. An Introduction*. New York: Vintage Book, V-67, 1962.

Faure, Michel. "Birds of Paradox," *France*, No 43, Fall 1997. *France*, A Quaterly Magazine, Maison Française, 4101 Reservoir Rd. NW, Washington, DC 20007–2182, USA.

Gramont, Sanche de. *The French. Portrait of a People*. New York: G.P. Putnam's Sons, 1969.

Jacobs, Michael and Stirton, Paul. *France. The Knopf Traveler's Guide to Art*. New York: Alfred A. Knopf, 1984.

L'Etat de la France, 97–98. Paris: La Découverte, 1997.

Maurin, Louis. *Les Français*. Les Essentiels Milan. Toulouse: Milan, 1995.

Perry, Sheila, ed. *Aspects of Contemporary France*. London and New York: Routledge, 1997.

Platt, Polly. *French or Foe?* Culture Crossings Ltd., 1994.

Price, Roger. *A Concise History of France*. Cambridge: Cambridge University Press, 1993.

Rochefort, Harriet Welty. *French Toast*. Anglophone s.a., 1997.

Taylor, Sally Adamson. *Culture Shock. A Guide to Customs and Etiquette*. Portland, Oregon: Graphic Arts Center Publishing Company, 1990. (reprinted 1996, 1997, 1998).

Weber, Eugen. *My France. Politics, Culture, Myth*. Cambridge, Mass. and London: The Belknap Press of Harvard University Press, 1991.

Wylie, Lawrence. *Village in the Vaucluse*. Cambridge, Mass., 1974.

Yapp, Nick and Syrett, Michael. *Xenophobe's Guide to the French*. Ravette Publishing, 1993.

Zeldin, Theodore. *The French*. Flamingo, 1983

History

Agulhon, Maurice. *The French Republic, 1879–1992*. Oxford: Blackwell, 1990.

Antommarchi, François. *Mémoires des derniers moments de Napoléon*, 2 vols. Paris: Barrois, 1825.

Ardagh, John. *France in the 1980s*. London, 1982.

Bainton, R.H. *The Reformation of the Sixteenth Century*. Boston: Beacon, 1952.

Bergin, Joseph. *Cardinal Richelieu. Power and the Pursuit of Wealth*. New Haven and London: Yale University Press, 1985.

Bloch, M. *Strange Defeat*. London: Oxford University Press, 1949.

Bogaert, J. and Passeron, J. *Moyen Age*. Les Lettres Françaises. Paris: Magnard, 1954.

Bony, Jean. *French Gothic Architecture of the 12ᵗʰ and 13ᵗʰ Centuries.* Berkeley: University of California Press, 1983.

Bordonove, Georges. *Les Rois qui ont fait la France. Clovis et les Mérovingiens, 456–511.* Paris: Pygmalion. (All titles of Bordonove below are in the same series.)
Charlemagne. Empereur et Roi, 742–814.
Hugues Capet, le Fondateur, 987–996.
Philippe Auguste le Conquérant, 1180–1223.
Saint Louis. Roi Eternel, 1226–1270.
Philippe le Bel, le Roi de Fer, 1285–1314.
Charles V le Sage, 1364–1380.
Charles VII le Victorieux, 1422–1461.
Louis XI le Diplomate, 1461–1483.
François Ier le Roi-Chevalier, 1515–1547.
Henri II Roi Gentilhomme, 1547–1559.
Henri III Roi de France et de Pologne, 1574–1589.
Henri IV le Grand, 1589–1610.
Louis XIII le Juste, 1610–1643.
Louis XIV le Roi Soleil, 1643–1715.
Louis XV le Bien-Aimé, 1715–1774.
Louis XVI le Roi Martyr, 1774–1793.
Louis XVIII le Désiré, 1814–1824.
Charles X Dernier Roi de France et de Navarre, 1824–1830.
Louis Philippe Roi des Français, 1830–1848.

Brinton, Crane, Christopher, John B. and Wolff, Robert L. *A History of Civilization.* Englewood Cliffs: Prentice-Hall, Inc., 2 vols, 1955.

Cobb, Richard. *French and Germans. Germans and French. A Personal Interpretation of France under Two Occupations, 1914–1918/1940–1944.* Hanover and London: Brandeis University Press/ University Press of New England, 1984.

Cohendet, M.-A. *La Cohabitation, leçons d'une expérience.* Paris: Presses Universitaires de France, 1993.

Cruttwell, C.R.M. *History of the Great War.* Oxford: The Clarendon Press, 1934.

Dansette, Adrien. *Mai 68.* Plon, 1971.

Debbasch, Charles. *La France de Pompidou.* Paris, 1974.

De Berthier de Sauvigny, G. and Pinkney, David H. *History of France.* Wheeling, Illinois: Forum Press, Inc., 1983.

De Carmoy, G. *Les politiques étrangères de la France, 1944–1966.* Paris: La Table Ronde, 1967.

Duby, G and Mandrou, R. *Histoire de la Civilisation Française. Vol. I: Moyen Age-XVIe Siècle. Vol. II: XVIIe–XXe Siècle.* Paris: Armand Colin, 1958.

Duby, G. *France in the Middle Ages, 987–1460.* 1991.

Duverger, M. *Bréviaire de la cohabitation.* Paris: Presses Universitaires de France, 1986.

Earle, E.M. *Modern France.* Princeton: Princeton University Press, 1951.

Elgey, Georgette. *Histoire de la IVe République.* Paris: Fayard, 1965; 1968; 1992.

Evans, J. *Life in Mediaeval France.* London: Oxford University Press, 1925.

Ewert, Alfred. *The French Language.* London, 1943.

Favier, Jean. *Philippe le Bel.* Paris: Fayard, 1978.

Favier, Jean. *La Guerre de Cent Ans.* Paris: Fayard, 1980.

Fay, S.B. *The Origins of the World War.* New York: Macmillan Company, 1932.

Focillon, Henri. *The Art of the West in the Middle Ages.* Oxford: Phaidon Press, 1963.

Fourastié, Jean. *Les Trente Glorieuses ou la Révolution invisible.* Paris: Fayard, 1979.

Fourastié, Jean et Fourastié, Jacqueline. *D'une France à une autre: Avant et après les Trente Glorieuses.* Paris: Fayard, 1987.

Fox, John. *A Literary History of France. The Middle Ages.* London and New York, 1974.

Frears, J.R. *France in the Giscard Presidency.* London, 1981.

Froissart, Jean. *The Chronicles.* New York: E.P. Dutton & Co., Inc., 1906.

Furet, François. *La Révolution. De Turgot à Jules Ferry. 1870–1880.* Paris: Hachette, 1988.

Ganshof, F.L. *Feudalism.* New York: Longmans, Green Company, 1952.

Gershoy, L. *The French Revolution and Napoleon.* New York: Appleton-Century-Crofts, 1933.

Gordon, P. *A Certain Idea of France.* Princeton: Princeton University Press, 1993.

Goubert, P. *Initiation à l'histoire de la France.* Paris: Fayard, 1994.

Goubert, Pierre. *The Course of French History.* London and New York: Routledge, 1991.

Grant, A.J. *The Huguenots.* London: T. Butterworth, Ltd., 1934.

Gregory of Tours. *History of the Franks*, O.M. Dalton, ed. Oxford: The Clarendon Press, 1936.

Guérard, Albert. *France. A Modern History.* Ann Arbor: University of Michigan Press, 1959.

Histoire de France. Préface de Jacques Le Goff. Paris: Seuil, 1992.

Huizinga, J. *The Waning of the Middle Ages.* New York: Anchor Books, 1954.

James, John. Medieval France. *A Guide to the Sacred Architecture of Medieval France.* New York: Alfred A. Knopf, 1986.

Joffrin, Laurent. *Mai 68. Histoire des événements.* Paris: Seuil, 1988.

Keller, Barbara G. *The Middle Ages Reconsidered.* New York: Peter Lang Publishing, Inc., Studies in the Humanities, No 11, 1994.

Kukenheim, L. and Roussel, H. *Guide de la littérature française du Moyen Age.* Leiden: Universitaire pers Leiden, 1959.

La Libération de la France (Coll. Actes du Colloque de 1974), ed. CNRS, 1976.

Lefebvre, G. *The Coming of the French Revolution.* Princeton: Princeton University Press, 1947.

Lefranc, Georges. *Histoire du Front Populaire.* Paris: Payot, 1963.

Liebling, A.J. *The Republic of Silence.* New York: Harcourt, Brace & Co., 1947.

Lot, L. *The End of the Ancient World and the Beginnings of the Middle Ages.* New York: Alfred A. Knopf, Inc., 1931.

Loyn, H.R. and Percival, John. *The Reign of Charlemagne. Documents on Carolingian Government and Administration.* New York: St. Martin's Press, 1975.

Mâle, Emile. *The Gothic Image: Religious Art in France of the Thirteenth Century.* New York: Harper and Row, 1972.

McKay, D.C. *The United States and France.* Cambridge, Mass.: Harvard University Press, 1951.

McMillan, James. *Dreyfus to De Gaulle.* London, 1985.

Mermier, Guy R. *Le Bestiaire de Pierre de Beauvais.* Paris: Nizet, 1977.

Mermier, Guy. *Béroul: Tristran and Yseut.* New York: Peter Lang Publishing, Inc., 1987.

Mermier, Guy. *Adam d'Arras. The Play of Madness.* New York: Peter Lang Studies in the Humanities, No 22, 1997.

Mermier, Guy. *A Medieval Book of Beasts. Pierre de Beauvais' Bestiary.* Lewiston, N.Y.: The E. Mellen Press, 1992.

Mermier, Guy, *The romance of Jehan de Paris.* Lewiston: The E. Mellen Press, Studies in French Literature, No 15, 1993.

Mollat, Michel. *Genèse médiévale de la France moderne, XIVe–Xve siècle.* Arthaud, 1977.

Noguères, Henri. *Histoire de la Résistance en France*, 5 vols. Laffont, 1967.

Painter, Sydney. *French Chivalry.* Baltimore: Johns Hopkins University Press, 1940.

Painter, Sydney. *Mediaeval Society.* Ithaca: Cornell University Press, 1951.

Perroy, E. *The Hundred Years War.* New York: Oxford University Press, 1951.

Price, R. *A Concise History of France.* Cambridge, Mass.: Cambridge University Press, 1993.

Quermonne, J.-L. *Le Gouvernement de la France sous la Ve République.* Paris: Dalloz, 1980.

Rashdall, H. *The Universities of Europe in the Middle Ages*, 3 vols. Oxford: The Clarendon Press, 1936.

Renouvin, P. *The Immediate Origins of the War.* New Haven: Yale University Press, 1928.

Rioux, Jean-Pierre. *The Fourth Republic, 1944–1958.* Cambridge: Cambridge University Press, 1987.

Rioux, Jean-Pierre. *La Guerre d'Algérie et les français.* Paris: Fayard, 1990.

Runciman, Steven. A *History of the Crusades.* Philadelphia: University of Pennsylvania Press, 1971.

Schapiro, Meyer. "The Romanesque Sculpture of Moissac," *Art Bulletin* 13 (1931): 464ff.

Schom, Alan. *Napoléon Bonaparte.* New York: Harper Perennial, 1997.

Sinclair, Anne. *Deux ou trois choses que je sais d'eux.* Paris: Grasset, 1997.

Stevens, A. *The Government and Politics of France.* Basingstoke and London: Macmillan, 1992.

Taylor, H.O. *The Mediaeval Mind.* Cambridge, Mass.: Harvard University Press, 1949.

Thomson, D. *Democracy in France: Third and Fourth Republics.* London: Oxford University Press, 1952.

Thompson, J.M. *Louis Napoleon and the Second Empire.* Oxford: Basil Blackwell, 1954.

Thompson, J.W. *The Wars of Religion in France, 1559–1576.* Chicago: University of Chicago Press, 1909.

Torrey, N.L. *The Spirit of Voltaire.* The New York: Columbia University Press, 1938.

Ysmal, C. *Les Partis politiques sous la Ve République.* Paris: Montchrestien, 1989.

Zarka, J.-C. *Le Président de la Ve République.* Paris: Ellipses, 1994.

Ziegler, Philip. *The Black Death*. New York: Harper & Row, 1971.

Politics

Adereth, M. *The French Communist Party*. Manchester, 1984.

Barreau, Jean-Claude. *La France va-t-elle disparaître?* Paris: Grasset, 1997.

Bell, D.S. and Criddle, Byron. *The French Socialist Party. The Emergence of a Party of Government*. Oxford: The Clarendon Press, 1988.

Cole, Alistair. *François Mitterand. A Study in Political Leadership*. London and New York: Routledge, 1989.

Duhamel, Alain. *Une Ambition Française*. Paris: Plon, 1999.

Dupin, Eric. *L'Après Mitterand. Le Parti Socialiste à la dérive*. Paris: Calmann-Lévy, 1991.

Girling, John. *France. Political and Social Change*. London and New York: Routledge, 1998.

Hazareesingh, Sudir. Political Traditions in Modern France. Oxford and New York: Oxford University Press, 1994.

Hunter, Mark. *Un Américain au front: Enquête au sein du FN*. Paris: Stock.

Mamère, Noël. *Ma République*. Paris: Seuil, 1999.

Mény, Yves. *La Corruption dans la République*. Paris: Fayard, 1992.

Meyer, Nonna and Perrineau, Pascal. "Why Do They Vote for Le Pen?" *European Journal of Political Research*, 22, 1992, 123–141.

Mouriaux, R. *Le Syndicalisme en France*. Que Sais-Je, PUF, 1992.

Prendiville, Brendan. *L'Ecologie. La politique autrement?* Paris: L'Harmattan, 1993.

Economy

Annuaire Statistique de la France. Edition 1998. 101e volume. Nelle série No 43. Résultats de 1996. Ministère de l'Economie, des Finances et de l'Industrie.

Belassa, B. "L'Economie française sous la cinquième République 1958–1978," *Revue économique* 30, 1979.

Dufour, A. "Les Français et l'environnement: de l'intention à l'action," *Economie et statistique* No. 258–9: 19–26.

Eymard-Duvernay, "Combien d'actifs d'ici l'an 2000," *Economie et statistique* 115, Oct. 1979.

Fourçans, A. "L'impact du SMIC sur le chômage: les leçons de l'expérience," *Revue d'économie politique* 6, 1980: 881–893.

Fourçans, André. *L'économie expliquée à ma fille*. Paris: Seuil, 1998.

Galland, O. "Une entrée de plus en plus tardive dans la vie adulte," *Economie et Statistique* No. 283–284, 1995.

Gordon, Colin. *The Business Culture in France*. Oxford: Butterworth-Heinemann, 1996.

Hampshire, D. *Living and Working in France*. Survival Books, 1993.

Izraelewicz. *Ce monde qui nous attend. Les peurs françaises et l'économie*. Paris: Grasset.

Mendras, Henri. *The Vanishing Peasant. Innovation and Change in French Agriculture*. Cambridge, Mass.: MIT Press, 1970.

Mermet, Gérard. *Francoscopie, 1997*. Larousse, 1996.

Spivey, W. Allen. *Economic Policies in France, 1976–1981. The Barre Program in a West European Perspective*. Ann Arbor: University of Michigan Business Studies, No 18.

Todd, Emmanuel. *La Nouvelle France*. Paris: Seuil, 1988.

Society

Aubin, C and Gisserot, H. *Les Femmes en France, 1985–1995*. Paris: La Documentation Française, 1994.

Bédarida, C. *SOS Université*. Paris: Seuil, 1994.

Bernard, P. "L'Affaire du foulard, La circulaire Bayrou," *Problèmes politiques et sociaux* 746: 30–2.

Index

Studies in Modern European History

The monographs in this series focus upon aspects of the political, social, economic, cultural, and religious history of Europe from the Renaissance to the present. Emphasis is placed on the states of Western Europe, especially Great Britain, France, Italy, and Germany. While some of the volumes treat internal developments, others deal with movements such as liberalism, socialism, and industrialization, which transcend a particular country.

The series editor is:

Frank J. Coppa
Director, Doctor of Arts Program
in Modern World History
Department of History
St. John's University
Jamaica, New York 11439

To order other books in this series, please contact our Customer Service Department:

(800) 770-LANG (within the U.S.)
(212) 647-7706 (outside the U.S.)
(212) 647-7707 FAX

or browse online by series at:
WWW.PETERLANG.COM